Lecture Notes in Computer Science

Edited by G. Goos and J. Hartmanis

433

W. Schröder-Preikschat
W. Zimmer (Eds.)

Progress in Distributed Operating Systems and Distributed Systems Management

European Workshop, Berlin, FRG, April 18/19, 1989
Proceedings

Springer-Verlag
Berlin Heidelberg New York London Paris Tokyo Hong Kong

Editorial Board
D. Barstow W. Brauer P. Brinch Hansen D. Gries D. Luckham
C. Moler A. Pnueli G. Seegmüller J. Stoer N. Wirth

Editors
Wolfgang Schröder-Preikschat
Wolfgang Zimmer
GMD Research Center for Innovative Computer Systems
and Technology at the Technical University of Berlin
GMD-FIRST
Hardenbergplatz 2, D-1000 Berlin 12, FRG

CR Subject Classification (1987): D.4, C.2

ISBN 3-540-52609-9 Springer-Verlag Berlin Heidelberg New York
ISBN 0-387-52609-9 Springer-Verlag New York Berlin Heidelberg

This work is subject to copyright. All rights are reserved, whether the whole or part of the material is concerned, specifically the rights of translation, reprinting, re-use of illustrations, recitation, broadcasting, reproduction on microfilms or in other ways, and storage in data banks. Duplication of this publication or parts thereof is only permitted under the provisions of the German Copyright Law of September 9, 1965, in its version of June 24, 1985, and a copyright fee must always be paid. Violations fall under the prosecution act of the German Copyright Law.

© Springer-Verlag Berlin Heidelberg 1990
Printed in Germany

Printing and binding: Druckhaus Beltz, Hemsbach/Bergstr.
2145/3140-543210 – Printed on acid-free paper

Preface

This volume constitutes the proceedings of the first European workshop on *Progress in Distributed Operating Systems and Distributed Systems Management*. The purpose of the workshop was to provide a general forum for distributed systems researchers. Contributions by well-known European research groups, completed by J.H. Saltzer from MIT's Athena project, were presented and thoroughly discussed during two days.

As the workshop title indicates, special emphasis was placed on research activities in distributed operating systems and management of distributed systems, whereby the first workshop day was dedicated to operating system research and the second day dealt with management aspects of distributed systems.

It was not planned to provide a forum where only concepts, without any relation to technical project work, could be presented or 'business talks' could be given. The fifteen presentations focussed on the illustration of existing concepts and solutions in distributed systems research and development, exemplified by a case study analysis of various projects. Each day closed with a panel discussion on the key research directions, recent progress and future developments in these areas. The panels were composed of the presenters of the same day and chaired by J.H. Saltzer and A.J. Herbert.

The order of papers included in this volume reflects the order of presentations given. All papers have been carefully reviewed by the programme committee and the best ones have been selected for publication. The volume annex contains the position papers as prepared by the authors for the panel discussions.

We would like to thank all the people of GMD FIRST and FOKUS who have helped to organize the workshop and especially the authors of the presented papers, without whom this workshop would not have been such a success. Special thanks are dedicated to Rolf Speth of the CEC and to Alwyn Langsford, the project coordinator of the MANDIS project, for the financial support of the workshop. Finally we would like to thank the GMD for their generous support.

In the meantime, we have received a very positive echo concerning the quality of the Berlin workshop. Especially the wide spread of topics handled at the workshop was generally appreciated. This encourages us to look forward to the second workshop of this kind.

Berlin, March 1990
                              Wolfgang Schröder-Preikschat
                              Wolfgang Zimmer

European Workshop on

PROGRESS IN DISTRIBUTED OPERATING SYSTEMS AND DISTRIBUTED SYSTEMS MANAGEMENT

Supported by the CEC Cost 11 ter Action

Organized and hosted by GMD FIRST and GMD FOKUS Berlin

FIRST - Research Center for Innovative Computer Systems and Technology
FOKUS - Research Center for Open Communication Systems
GMD - German National Research Center for Computer Science

Programme Committee

W. K. Giloi, GMD FIRST (Chair)
B. Butscher, GMD FOKUS
J. Hall, GMD FOKUS
W. Schröder-Preikschat, GMD FIRST
W. Zimmer, GMD FIRST

Organizing Committee

D. Emons, C. Freytag, Yee-Mei Guo, R. Kallerhoff, D. Koop,
W. Schröder-Preikschat, C. Schulze, G. Tysper, W. Zimmer

GMD FIRST

Table of Contents

Technical Papers

The Evolution of a Distributed Operating System 1
R. van Renesse, A. S. Tanenbaum - Vrije Universiteit Amsterdam,
S. J. Mullender - CWI Amsterdam

AIL - a Class-oriented RPC Stub Generator for Amoeba 13
G. van Rossum - CWI Amsterdam

PEACE - A Distributed Operating System for High-Performance Multicomputer Systems 22
W. Schröder-Preikschat - GMD FIRST Berlin

Virtual Memory Management in Chorus 45
V. Abrossimov, M. Rozier, M. Gien - Chorus Systèmes Paris

Is Object Orientation a Good Thing for Distributed Systems ? 60
C. Horn - Trinity College Dublin

Experiences with a Portable Network Operating System 75
K. Geihs, H. Schmutz - IBM ENC Heidelberg

On the Implementation of Abstract Data Types in BirliX 87
W. Lux, H. Härtig, W. Kühnhauser - GMD Birlinghoven

Monitoring and Management-Support of Distributed Systems 110
D. Haban - ICSI Berkeley, D. Wybranietz - Universität Kaiserslautern,
A. Barak - ICSI Berkeley

DAPHNE - Support for Distributed Computing in Heterogeneous Environments 138
K.-P. Löhr, L. Nentwig - Freie Universität Berlin,
J. Müller - Universität Bremen

Distributed Computing with a Processor Bank 147
J. M. Bacon, I. M. Leslie, R. M. Needham - University of Cambridge

MANDIS: Management of Distributed Systems 162
D. Holden, A. Langsford - UKAEA Harwell Laboratory

OAI - Concepts for Open Systems Cooperation 174
V. Tschammer, K.-P. Eckert, J. Hall, G. Schürmann, L. Strick - GMD FOKUS Berlin

Annex: Position Papers for the Panel Discussions

R. van Renesse - Vrije Universiteit Amsterdam *193*

S. J. Mullender, G. van Rossum - CWI Amsterdam *195*

W. Schröder-Preikschat - GMD FIRST Berlin *196*

T. King - Perihelion Software Limited *197*

C. Horn - Trinity College Dublin *198*

H. Schmutz - IBM ENC Heidelberg *199*

H. Härtig - GMD Birlinghoven *200*

J. Nehmer - Universität Kaiserslautern *201*

J. H. Saltzer - MIT Cambridge *202*

J. M. Bacon - University of Cambridge *203*

A. Langsford - UKAEA Harwell Laboratory..*204*

V. Tschammer - GMD FOKUS Berlin *206*

The Evolution of a Distributed Operating System

Robbert van Renesse
Andrew S. Tanenbaum

Dept. of Mathematics and Computer Science
Vrije Universiteit
Amsterdam

Sape J. Mullender

Centre for Mathematics and Computer Science
Amsterdam

AMOEBA is a research project to build a true distributed operating system using the object model. Under the COST11-ter MANDIS project this work was extended to cover wide-area networks. Besides describing the system, this paper discusses the successive versions in the implementation of its model, and why the changes were made. Its purpose is to prevent ourselves and others from making the same mistakes again, and to illustrate how a distributed operating system grows in sophistication and size.

1. Why This Paper

"Those who learn nothing from history are doomed to repeat it" — Santayana

For about eight years now, we have been doing research on distributed operating systems, not only behind our desks, but also behind our terminals. The distributed system we are developing is called AMOEBA[1], and it is constantly evolving. It is being developed at the Vrije Universiteit and the Centre for Mathematics and Computer Science (CWI), both in Amsterdam. AMOEBA currently runs on Motorola 68020, National Semiconductor 32032, and MicroVax II processors. Both Ethernet and the Pronet token ring are supported by AMOEBA, and can be connected by a bridge.

COST11-ter MANDIS is an international project investigating the management requirements for large international networks of computers. It has adopted the object-model as a framework within which to discuss the management of wide-area distributed systems. To experiment with this, the MANDIS project adopted the Amoeba distributed operating system, extended with a gateway for wide-area communication. Amoeba systems in Holland (Vrije Universiteit, CWI), the U.K. (Harwell Laboratories, Hatfield Polytechnic), in Berlin (GMD/FOKUS) and in Norway (University of Tromsø) have been connected into a single, transparent distributed system.

This research was supported in part by the Netherlands Organization for Scientific Research (N.W.O.) under grant 125-30-10.

In any system, mistakes can appear in the design: features that are missing, features that are obsolete, and features that are too hard to handle. Sometimes the solution needs a considerable redesign of the system, and a new version is born. One has to be prepared to redo systems [2-4]. When designing a system, it is important not to make mistakes twice, be they your own, or anyone else's. Therefore it is necessary to read about other comparable projects, and to document your own.

2. The AMOEBA Architecture

Bradley's Bromide: "If computers get too powerful, we can organize them into a committee—that will do them in"

The AMOEBA architecture consists of four principal components, as shown in Fig. 1. First are the workstations, one per user, which run window management software, and on which users can carry out editing and other tasks that require fast interactive response [5]. Second are the pool processors, a group of CPUs that can be dynamically allocated as needed, used, and then returned to the pool. For example, the "make" command might need to do six compilations, so six processors could be taken out of the pool for the time necessary to do the compilation and then returned. Alternatively, with a five-pass compiler, $5 \times 6 = 30$ processors could be allocated for the six compilations, gaining even more speedup [6].

Third are the specialized servers, such as directory [7], file servers [8], and various other servers with specialized functions. Fourth are the wide-area network gateways, which are used to link AMOEBA systems at different sites in possibly different countries into a single, uniform system, such as investigated in the MANDIS work [9-13].

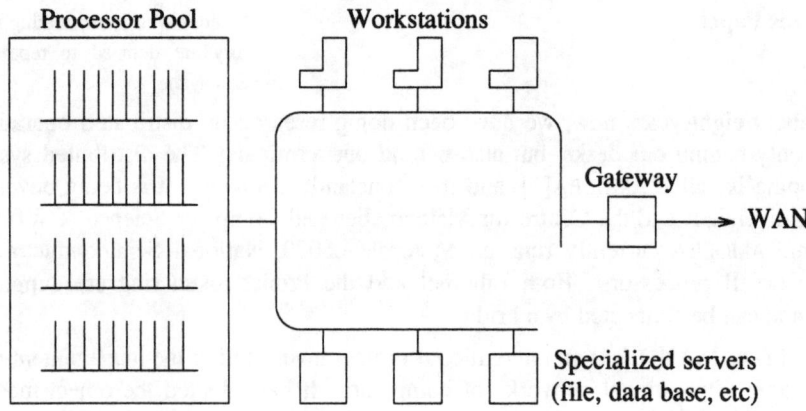

Fig. 1. The AMOEBA architecture.

All the AMOEBA machines run the same kernel, which primarily provides communication services and little else. The basic idea behind the kernel was to keep it small, not only to enhance its reliability, but also to allow as much of the operating system as possible to run as user processes, providing for flexibility and experimentation.

2.1. Transactions

AMOEBA is an object-oriented distributed operating system. Objects are abstract data types such as files, directories, processes, and are managed by server processes. A client process carries out operations on an object by sending a request message to the server process that manages the object. While the client blocks, the server performs the requested operation on the object. Afterwards the server sends a reply message back to the client, which unblocks the client. We have named this request/reply exchange a *transaction* (not to be confused with data base transactions) [14, 15]. AMOEBA guarantees *at-most-once* execution of transactions. Remote procedure calls [16, 17] are implemented by collecting a code identifying the procedure to be executed and the arguments in a request message, and performing a transaction with the appropriate server. The result of the procedure is retrieved from the reply message.

After starting a transaction, a client process blocks to await the reply. A server process blocks when it is awaiting a request. To handle multiple transactions going on at the same time a process can be subdivided into lightweight subprocesses called threads. By having a thread for each request, a server process can handle multiple requests simultaneously. A client process can perform several transactions at the same time by having a thread per transaction. To avoid race conditions and simplify programming the threads are only rescheduled when the currently running thread blocks, that is, threads are not pre-empted.

2.2. Capabilities

All objects in AMOEBA are named and protected by *capabilities* [18, 19]. Capabilities, combined with transactions, provide a uniform interface to all objects in the AMOEBA system. A capability has 128 bits, and is composed of four fields:

1) The *server port*: a 48 bit sparse address identifying the server process that manages the object. A server can choose its own port.
2) The *object number*: an internal 24-bit identifier that the server uses to tell which of its objects this is. The server port and the object number together uniquely identify an object.
3) The *rights field*: 8 bits telling which operations on the object are permitted by the holder of this capability.
4) The *check field*: a 48-bit number that protects the capability against forging and tampering.

When a server is asked to create an object, it picks an available slot in its internal tables, puts the information about the object in there as well as a 48-bit random number. The index into the table is used as the object number in the capability. The rights in the capability are protected by encrypting them together with the random number, and storing the result in the check field. A capability can be checked by performing the encryption operation again, and comparing the result with the check field in the capability.

Capabilities can be stored in directories that are managed by the *directory service*. A directory is effectively a set of <ASCII string, capability> pairs, and is itself just another object in the AMOEBA system. Directory entries may, of course, contain capabilities for other directories, and thus an arbitrary naming graph can be built. The most common directory operation is to present an ASCII string and ask for the corresponding capability. Other operations are entering and deleting directory entries, and listing a directory [7].

3. AMOEBA Incarnations

"Experience is that marvelous thing that enables you to recognize a mistake when you make it again" — F.P. Jones

To get experience with distributed operating systems, and with the object model in particular, we have built an implementation of the AMOEBA system. This implementation consists of a small, highly portable, and efficient kernel, capable of providing local and remote communication, driving peripherals, and running processes; all other services are provided by user processes. In the following we only discuss the kernel.

Working with the first version of AMOEBA, we became aware of some of the deficiencies in its design. After a while we threw it away and built a new version. As this version did not solve all the problems, we designed and implemented the third, and current, version. We are currently designing the fourth version. Each of these versions are discussed more or less independently in the next sections. In section 4 we will compare them and describe why the changes were made.

3.1. AMOEBA 1.0

The AMOEBA 1.0 kernel [20] is a simple multiprogramming kernel, with intra-machine communication based on software interrupts. It has three layers. The bottom layer catches all hardware interrupts. Each interrupt causes a message to be put into a *task queue*. Messages may contain parameters, such as the value of a character just received on a communication line. Mostly these are the values of some of the devices that generated the interrupt. Furthermore, the layer schedules the kernel *tasks*, that constitute the middle layer of the kernel, and the user processes in the highest layer.

A task takes care of a particular device, for example, a disk or a clock. It is called whenever there is a message for it on the task queue. A user process is scheduled when there are no tasks left to run, or if the current running process has eaten up its time slice. Both tasks and processes are able to put something in the task queue, thus scheduling a task.

Tasks run to completion. When an interrupt occurs, a message is put on the task queue, and the task is resumed. This means that there are no race conditions in interrupt handling, and only one run-time stack is needed for all tasks. Tasks can be programmed entirely in a high-level language.

The two most important tasks are the clock task and the network task. The clock task simulates multiple timers: it has functions to set and cancel timers. The network task provides a network interface that does not guarantee delivery. A user process needs both services to implement a reliable network interface.

A user process can suspend itself, enable or disable certain messages from specific sources, and send or cancel messages. It invokes a task by sending a message to it by placing an entry in the task queue. The message contains four parameters, such as the specific function that must be executed by the task. As in the kernel, these messages are queued when arriving inconveniently. When a process is properly enabled, it is informed that a message is pending by an interrupt.

This way a process can call the three functions performed by the network task: *get(header, buffer)*, *put(header, buffer)*, and *unget(header)*. The header (see Fig. 2) is a 40

length
destination port
reply port
signature port
out-of-band data

Fig. 2. Header format.

byte structure containing the total length of header and buffer, the destination *port*, the reply *port*, the *signature port*, and 20 byte out of band data. A port is a network independent address, chosen from a sparse 48 bit address space, and protected by a cryptographic one-way function. The signature port can be used for sender authentication.

Get enables receiving, while *put* sends a packet. Neither are 100% reliable in that packets may get lost. An interrupt is generated on completion. *Unget* disables receiving. The data buffer has a maximum size of 2 Kbytes, enough to contain about two thirds of the files in an average file system.

A user library of procedures uses these primitives, together with timers, to implement the transaction interface. A client invokes a service by calling *trans(hdr1, buf1, hdr2, buf2)*. The request is put into *hdr1* and *buf1*; the reply will be put into *hdr2* and *buf2*. The server calls *getreq(header, buffer)* to enable receiving of a request, and *putrep(header, buffer)* to send a reply back. In each of the three calls, an interrupt is generated on completion.

The protocol used is simple, yet makes efficient use of the network bandwidth. Normally the reply acknowledges the request, and the reply is acknowledged by the next request. Separate acknowledgements are generated only when the reply or the next request is taking too long. It is possible to have multiple outstanding *getreq*'s, to handle more than one client, or to have multiple *trans*'s going on, thus enabling parallel programming.

3.2. AMOEBA 2.0

Intra-machine communication in AMOEBA 2.0 is through 26-byte typed messages, called *mini-messages*. When a hardware interrupts occurs, the real-time information is put into a mini-message and sent to the appropriate task. The user interface to the tasks is also through these messages. This kernel has formed the base for the MINIX operating system [21].

The calls to send and receive messages are:

send(destination, message);
recv(source, message);
sendrec(destination, message).

Send sends the message to the specified destination: tasks are identified by negative numbers, processes by positive numbers. When the destination is not ready to receive, the message is queued. *Recv* is called when a task or process wants to await a message from the specified source, which may be ANY. *Sendrec* is provided for efficiency: it sends the message to the destination and awaits a reply message.

A process may be interrupted by a task or another process with a special interrupt message. Interrupts go at most one level deep, to simplify interrupt handling. Other messages that arrive during interrupt handling are queued as usual.

The services provided by the kernel are the same as in AMOEBA 1.0., including the clock task and the network task. The transaction mechanism interface to the user processes is almost identical, so existing user services for AMOEBA 1.0 are easily ported. Later the transaction interface of AMOEBA 3.0, the currently used incarnation of AMOEBA, has been implemented for MINIX.

3.3. AMOEBA 3.0

In AMOEBA 3.0, all communication, both intra-machine and inter-machine, is through transactions. The interface is slightly modified and extended:

>   *getreq(header, buffer, length);*
>   *putrep(header, buffer, length);*
>   *trans(hdr1, buf1, len1, hdr2, buf2, len2);*
>   *new_thread(procedure);*
>   *thread_exit();*
>   *sleep(event);*
>   *wakeup(event).*

The server, either a kernel task or a user process, calls *getreq* to await a request message, and *putrep* to send a reply back. A client process calls *trans* to send the request in *hdr1* and *buf1*, and to await the reply, which will be put into *hdr2* and *buf2*. The header contains the capability identifying the service and object, and 20 bytes of out of band data containing the command to the server and its parameters. The buffer, with a specified *length* of maximally 30 Kbytes, contains the data associated with the request or the reply.

Note that these calls are blocking, and prevent parallel computing. To allow concurrent programming, we introduce *threads*, a light-weight sub-process. Within a process, only one thread can run at a time; another one may be scheduled when the current running thread does a blocking call. While some threads are awaiting a request or a reply, another thread may run. A server that wants to be able to service multiple clients will have several identical threads, created with *new_thread*, capable of executing requests.

The kernel is just another process, having threads (tasks) to drive the peripherals. The bottom layer in the kernel schedules the threads of all processes, executes the transactions, copies local messages, and runs the network protocol. Device interrupts are still queued, but not transformed into messages. Instead, interrupt routines are invoked at "save" times, that is, in between thread switches. The network protocol sends separate acknowledgements for request and reply fragments, and network DMA is done simultaneously with the other side as much as possible. No separate timers are maintained, but a simple, once in a while "sweep" procedure restarts stopped protocols. All this results in simple and efficient message passing [14, 15].

The physical location of ports, and thus of servers and objects, is maintained in a cache per site. When the location of a port is unknown or out-of-date, it is located with a special broadcast *locate message*, and the cache is updated.

Threads within a process can synchronize using *sleep* and *wakeup*. A thread that wants to await an event invokes *sleep*; a thread that wants to resume other threads waiting for a certain event calls *wakeup*. Since threads run to the next blocking system call, there is no danger of race conditions.

Under the COST11-ter project AMOEBA 3.0 was extended to wide-area networks using a special gateway [11, 12]. The gateway manages the wide-area communication without affecting the local networks. This management includes naming and protection of objects, accounting, and fault management of communication. The gateway is high-level: it intercepts complete messages, and if access is granted, establishes a virtual circuit to the intended destination to forward the message across. The gateway at the destination site repeats the transaction, and forwards the reply over the same virtual circuit back to the source The gateway registers all remote servers and their locations to know which messages to forward and which not. site.

3.4. AMOEBA 4.0

In AMOEBA 4.0 [22] processes are subdivided into light-weight threads, but now we no longer guarantee that threads run unpreempted to the next blocking system call. Moreover, we allow threads to await requests for multiple ports, and to specify message buffers of up to one Gigabyte. This has affected the user interface as follows:

>   *getreq(port-list, header, buffer, length);*
>   *putrep(header, buffer, length);*
>   *trans(hdr1, buf1, len1, hdr2, buf2, len2);*
>   *new_thread(procedure);*
>   *thread_exit();*
>   *mu_lock(mutex);*
>   *mu_trylock(mutex, timeout);*
>   *mu_unlock(mutex).*

Note that *sleep* and *wakeup* cannot be used as synchronization primitives anymore, since they would be fraught with race conditions because of the preemptive scheduling of tasks. *mu_lock* and *mu_unlock* respectively acquire and release a mutex variable. *mu_trylock* tries to acquire the lock within *timeout* milliseconds, and returns an error if this fails.

An important change in this new incarnation of AMOEBA is the format of the capability, which, as we will see, also influences the semantics of *trans*. The new format is shown in Fig. 3. The sizes of the different fields have been increased. Moreover, there is an extra field designating the creation site. In AMOEBA 4.0 it is assumed that objects hardly ever migrate away from the site of their creation. This obsoletes the necessity to register all remote services at the gateways, thus decreasing the amount of management necessary considerably.

64	64	32	32	64	# bits
Service Port	Creation Site	Object	Rights	Check	

Fig. 3. An AMOEBA 4.0 capability.

4. Comparison

> "I have made mistakes but I have never made the mistake of claiming that I never made one" — James Gordon Bennett

Having discussed each of the implementations of the object model more or less independently, it is now time to look what changed and why. The differences concern efficiency and programmability; these goals are often conflicting. Both metamorphoses are discussed in the following sections.

4.1. AMOEBA 1.0 → AMOEBA 2.0

Our first objection against AMOEBA 1.0 was the difficulty in programming with it. All communication with the outside world was through asynchronous messages. Although flexible, it puts us back some decades when programmers had to work at a very low level. The processes were pelted with interrupts. Each process had to do its own job scheduling.

Furthermore, the interrupts carried too little information—often additional information had to be transported by a special copying task. In addition to the complexity involved, it was inefficient, and it had protection problems. When data had to be copied between two processes, one had to do this, and thus had full access to the address space of the other process.

Furthermore, debugging was difficult, because it was hard to trace a process that can be interrupted at any moment, and each time somewhere else. Moreover, interrupts might arrive in another order when the process was executed again, and debug statements in the code changed the behaviour. Thus AMOEBA 1.0 processes were nondeterministic, and a failure might occur only once in a month, making it hard to find the error.

We abolished these problems in AMOEBA 2.0 by abolishing needless interrupts. All ordinary communication was through typed mini-messages, and although small, they were large enough for an average command with parameters or a reply. Messages only arrived when called for, which made both programming and debugging considerably easier, because a program could be written in the usual structured way.

4.2. AMOEBA 2.0 → AMOEBA 3.0

Although happier, we were not completely satisfied with our basis for a distributed operating system. To begin with, too little concurrency was left in with the new intra-machine communication mechanism. The receive call was blocking, and it was not possible to check if there was something in the message queue. Moreover, it was not possible to give a set of sources from which to receive a message, so the messages had to be handled in the order they arrived.

Also annoying were the different intra-machine and inter-machine communication mechanisms. This problem also existed in AMOEBA 1.0, but in AMOEBA 2.0 the mechanisms are much more alike. Furthermore, to start a transaction, a mini-message had to be sent to the network task, another to enable receipt of the acknowledgement, and a third to the clock task to set a timer. When the acknowledgement arrived, the timer had to be canceled, which cost another mini-message. All this made inter-machine communication inefficient.

These problems were solved in AMOEBA 3.0 by making the transaction the only communication primitive. Moreover, the messages are much larger, so a special task to copy data became obsolete. At the same time, the protection problem with copying disappeared. Communication became transparent, having obvious advantages.

Like the mini-message calls, transaction calls were blocking now. Concurrent programming was made possible through threads: each thread can handle one client and one server. This way we have the profit of concurrent programming combined with the ease of simple, every-day programming.

4.3. AMOEBA 3.0 → AMOEBA 4.0

AMOEBA 3.0 is the first incarnation that is heavily used for distributed applications [23-25], and has led to several suggestions for improvements. Also, the hardware technology has improved considerably, making multi-processors more and more interesting. In the first three incarnations we envisioned only loosely-coupled hardware, but now we also have to deal with processors sharing memory over a shared bus. Yet another factor that makes a new implementation necessary is the advance of wide-area networks, making large distributed operating systems interesting.

There are two reasons for preemptive scheduling of threads. The first reason is one of software engineering. Due to the high level of transparency, the programmer cannot be expected to know if the standard library routine for printing makes calls to a remote printer or not. It was bad programming practice to rely on procedures being local, and thus trusting that no scheduling would occur. Therefore the advantages of non-preemptive scheduling largely disappeared. The other reason for preemptive scheduling of threads is that the performance of a multi-threaded process can be increased by running the different threads on different processors in a multi-processor.

The other important change in AMOEBA 4.0 is the Creation Site field in capabilities. This has to do with scaling. It was found unfeasible to have a purely flat name space that would cover the world [26, 27]. Using the old capability, it was impossible to transparently locate the server for the object in a world-wide AMOEBA system. Now, with the new capability lay-out, requests for operations on an object can be sent to the site that created the object immediately, where the server can then be located using the old broadcast-oriented mechanisms. In the rare event that an object migrates between AMOEBA sites, a *forwarding server* has to be left behind at the site that created the object to forward the request to the site where the object actually lives.

5. What We Have Learned

> "The only thing we learn from history is that we learn nothing from history" — Hegel

The versions we have implemented, and the reasons for making them, have now been discussed. It is time to look why we went wrong in the design and to learn our lessons, to prove Hegel was wrong.

In the design of AMOEBA 1.0 we aimed at a simple and efficient kernel, and forgot the user interface. We did not appreciate the importance of the simplicity and the functionality of the user interface enough, which is an error in any system. Furthermore, in implementing the inter-machine interface, we forgot that its efficiency was likewise important.

In the design of AMOEBA 2.0 we were determined not to make the same mistakes again, so we concentrated too much on have a clean user interface, and did not worry about efficiency. The interface was not flexible enough, and too much intra-machine communication was necessary to send a simple message, because the decomposition into layers and modules was too finely grained.

In AMOEBA 3.0 the networking primitives were made an integral part of the operating system instead of a separate attached task. This made all communication transparent and resulted in a high performance [14, 15]. Under the COST11-ter MANDIS work a gateway was added that made international communication transparent.

The last incarnation, AMOEBA 4.0, was developed mainly to deal with new technologies of multi-processors and wide-area networks. Using the experience gained with AMOEBA 3.0, several small changes where made to the system.

We feel that we are converging to a good distributed operating system. This paper shows the importance of implementing prototype systems for the development of a large distributed operating system. Prototype systems produce the flaws in the design of the system and give the necessary experience for developing the next version. It is necessary to document the mistakes to avoid making them again.

6. References

[1] Mullender, S. J. and Tanenbaum, A. S., "The Design of a Capability-Based Distributed Operating System," *The Computer Journal*, Vol. 29, No. 4, pp. 289-300 (March 1986).

[2] Lampson, B. W., "Hints for Computer System Design," *Proc. of the 9th ACM Symp. on Operating Systems Principles*, New York (October 1983).

[3] Tanenbaum, A. S. and Renesse, R. van, "Making Distributed Systems Palatable," *Proc. of 2nd SIGOPS Workshop Making Distr. Systems Work*, Amsterdam (September 1986).

[4] Mullender, S. J., "Making Amoeba Work," *Proc. of 2nd SIGOPS Workshop Making Distr. Systems Work*, Amsterdam (September 1986).

[5] Renesse, R. van, Tanenbaum, A. S., and Sharp, G. J., "The Workstation: Computing Resource or Just a Terminal?," *Proc. of the Workshop on Workstation Operating Systems*, Cambridge, MA (November 1987).

[6] Baalbergen, E. H., "Design and Implementation of Parallel Make," *Computing Systems*, Vol. 1, No. 2, pp. 135-158 (Spring 1988).

[7] Renesse, R. van and Tanenbaum, A. S., "A Directory Service supporting Availability and Consistency," *internal report* (1989).

[8] Renesse, R. van, Tanenbaum, A. S., and Wilschut, A., "The Design of a High-Performance File Server," *Proc. of the 9th Int. Conf. on Distr. Computing Systems*, Newport Beach, CA (June 1989).

[9] Langsford, A. E. and others, "Distributed Systems in Wide-Area Networks," pp. 96-104, in *Proc. European Telematics Conf.*, Elsevier Science Pub., Amsterdam (October 1983).

[10] Hall, J., Renesse, R. van, and Staveren, J. M. van, "Gateways and Management in an Internet Environment," *Proc. of the IFIP TC6 WG6.4A Int. Workshop on LAN Management*, Hahn-Meitner-Institute, Berlin (West) (July 1987).

[11] Renesse, R. van, Tanenbaum, A. S., Staveren, J. M. van, and Hall, J., "Connecting RPC-Based Distributed Systems Using Wide-Area Networks," *Proc. of the 7th Int. Conf. on Distr. Computing Systems*, pp. 28-34, Berlin (West) (September 1987).

[12] Renesse, R. van, Staveren, J. M. van, Hall, J., Turnbull, M., Janssen, A. A., Jansen, A. J., Mullender, S. J., Holden, D. B., Bastable, A., Fallmyr, T., Johansen, D., Mullender, K. S., and Zimmer, W., "MANDIS/Amoeba: A Widely Dispersed Object-Oriented Operating System," *Proc. of the EUTECO 88 Conf.*, pp. 823-831, ed. R. Speth, North-Holland, Vienna, Austria (April 1988).

[13] Bacon, J. M., Horn, C., Langsford, A., Mullender, S. J., and Zimmer, W., "MANDIS: Architectural Basis for Management," *Proc. of the EUTECO 88 Conf.*, pp. 795-809, ed. R. Speth, North-Holland, Vienna, Austria (April 1988).

[14] Renesse, R. van, Staveren, J. M. van, and Tanenbaum, A. S., "The Performance of the World's Fastest Distributed Operating System," *ACM Operating Systems Review*, Vol. 22, No. 4, pp. 25-34 (October 1988).

[15] Renesse, R. van, Staveren, J. M. van, and Tanenbaum, A. S., "The Performance of the Amoeba Distributed Operating System," *Software—Practice and Experience*, Vol. 19, No. 3, pp. 223-234 (March 1989).

[16] Birrell, A. D. and Nelson, B. J., "Implementing Remote Procedure Calls," *ACM Trans. Comp. Syst.*, Vol. 2, No. 1, pp. 39-59 (February 1984).

[17] Spector, A. Z., "Performing Remote Operations Efficiently on a Local Computer Network," *Comm. ACM*, Vol. 25, No. 4, pp. 246-260 (April 1982).

[18] Mullender, S. J. and Tanenbaum, A. S., "Protection and Resource Control in Distributed Operating Systems," *Computer Networks*, Vol. 8, No. 5-6, pp. 421-432 (October 1984).

[19] Tanenbaum, A. S., Mullender, S. J., and Renesse, R. van, "Using Sparse Capabilities in a Distributed Operating System," *Proc. of the 6th Int. Conf. on Distr. Computing Systems*, pp. 558-563, Cambridge, MA (May 1986).

[20] Tanenbaum, A. S. and Mullender, S. J., "A Simple, Efficient Multiprogramming Kernel," Dept. of Mathematics and Computer Science, Vrije Universiteit, Amsterdam (1982).

[21] Tanenbaum, A. S., "Operating Systems—Design and Implementation," Prentice-Hall, Englewood Cliffs, NJ (1987).

[22] Mullender, S. J., Jansen, A. J., and Rossum, G. van, "Amoeba Kernel Interface Specification," Centre for Mathematics and Computer Science, Amsterdam (March 1988).

[23] Bal, H. E., Renesse, R. van, and Tanenbaum, A. S., "Implementing Distributed Algorithms Using Remote Procedure Calls," *Proc. of the 1987 National Computer Conf.*, pp. 499-506, Chicago, Ill (June 1987).

[24] Bal, H. E. and Renesse, R. van, "A Summary of Parallel Alpha-Beta Search Results," *ICCA Journal*, Vol. 9, pp. 146-149 (September 1986).

[25] Johansen, D. and Anshus, O. J., "A Distributed Diary Application," *Proc. of the IFIP TC 6 First Iberian Conf. on Data Communications*, ed. A. Cerveira., North-Holland, Lisbon, Portugal (May 1987).

[26] Mullender, S. J. and Vitányi, P. M. B., "Distributed Match-Making for Processes in Computer Networks," *Proc. of the 4th ACM Conf. on Principles of Distr. Computing*, Minaki, Canada (August 1985).

[27] Mullender, S. J. and Vitányi, P. M. B., "Distributed Match-Making," *Algorithmica, 2nd special issue on distributed algorithms* (1988).

AIL - a Class-Oriented RPC Stub Generator for Amoeba

Guido van Rossum

CWI, Center for Mathematics and Computer Science
P.O. Box 4079, 1009 AB Amsterdam, The Netherlands
E-mail: guido@cwi.nl or mcvax!guido

ABSTRACT

AIL – an acronym for Amoeba Interface Language – is a class-oriented RPC stub generator, used with Amoeba's RPC primitives. Together with Amoeba's facilities for manipulating capabilities (bit patterns that are unforgeable references to objects maintained by servers anywhere on a network), AIL provides a completely object-oriented view of a distributed operating system.

Input to AIL consists of class and type definitions and generator directives; output are several files containing function definitions to be compiled and linked with clients and servers. Class definitions consist mainly of function headers (specifying parameter types, etc.). Classes can inherit multiple other classes. AIL can (in principle) generate stubs for different programming languages, so clients and servers need not be written in the same language.

Introduction

Modern distributed operating systems use Remote Procedure Call (RPC) as their primary communication paradigm. The principle of RPC is as follows: A client program calls a *stub routine* which marshals its parameters into a buffer, ships the buffer over the network to a server, and waits for a reply. The server that receives the buffer unmarshals the parameters and calls the implementation procedure with these parameters. When the implementation procedure returns, the server marshals its output parameters into a buffer and ships it back to the client. The client stub awakes once it receives the reply buffer, unmarshals the output parameters, and returns to its caller.

The attractive value of the RPC paradigm lies in its resemblance with ordinary, local procedure calls: the client just calls a procedure to execute a remote operation, and the operation is done when the procedure returns. Since ordinary compilers do not generate code to call remote procedures, a tool is needed to generate the stub routines and the corresponding server code (like unmarshaling the parameters). Such a tool is called a *stub compiler* or stub generator. Stub compilers are used for several reasons: to simplify the interface to the underlying communication primitives, to cope with heterogeneity in the environment (like byte order problems), and to support interface abstraction.

This paper describes AIL, a stub compiler for Amoeba,[1] a capability-based distributed operating system. Besides doing the jobs that stub compilers normally do, AIL provides a powerful mechanism to define common subsets of interfaces in the form of class inheritance.

Amoeba RPC

Amoeba provides a highly efficient RPC mechanism. A client process sends a request to a server by calling

```
trans(&reqhdr, reqbuf, reqbufsize,
      &replhdr, replbuf, replbufsize).
```

A server process waits for a request by calling

```
getreq(&header, buffer, buffersize)
```

and sends a reply with the call

```
putrep(&header, buffer, buffersize)
```

(not necessarily using the same parameter values). A header is a data structure defined in a standard definitions file containing space for a capability (which includes a 64-bit service port number identifying the service), a few numeric parameters to the request, and some extra information that can be used for access rights checking. A buffer is an array of memory bytes and is transferred uninterpreted. Amoeba's RPC layer locates the server based on a match (involving a one-way function to prevent forgery) between the ports specified by client and server in their request headers, and ensures that at most one server gets the request and that the reply is sent back to the correct client.

In common usage a server, say a file server or a time server, recognizes a number of request types: e.g., a file server would support the requests create-file, write-file, read-file, and delete-file, and a time server would support the requests get-time and set-time. All requests to one server are normally directed at the same port; the server differentiates between request types by inspecting a command code in the request header.

To provide a nice interface to the service for client programmers, stub routines for a service are normally provided in a library. Generally, a stub routine copies its input parameters into a request header and/or buffer, sets the request code in the header, does the transaction with the server, and returns relevant fields from the reply header and/or buffer to its caller through output parameters or the function result.

Why A Stub Generator

There are at least two reasons why it is desirable to automate the generation of client stubs and request decoding code for servers.

First, such code almost always follows a standard pattern, so it is boring to write (and hence mistakes such as unchecked error conditions slip in easily).

Second, a stub generator can more easily ensure that servers support exactly the same interface where this is required: for instance, multiple file server implementations should show the same face to their clients, so clients needn't know on which server their files reside.

There are other desirable properties of good client-server interfaces that can benefit from mechanical assistance: when client and server reside on machines with different architectures, transformation of data between client and server representations may be necessary. Amoeba automatically translates the integers in the request and reply headers when necessary, but data in the buffer is copied as-is. Hence, sending an array of integers from a little-endian machine such as a VAX to a big-endian machine like a 68000 requires swapping the bytes in each integer. Transfer of floating point values between machines poses even bigger problems. Inclusion of proper data conversion code is better done mechanically, especially since its absence often isn't spotted in tests.

Design Goals
The AIL stub generator was designed with the following goals in mind:
- Generate client stubs and server main loops for the majority of server interfaces envisioned for Amoeba.
- Support easy incorporation of predefined standard interfaces into specific interfaces.
- Support multiple implementations of the same server interface.
- Support clients and servers written in different programming languages.
- Support clients and servers running on different machine architectures.
- No changes to the Amoeba kernel.
- As efficient as equivalent handwritten code.

AIL does not attempt to solve the following issues:
- Name binding: the basic binding of clients to servers is done by Amoeba's 'locate' mechanism (on a per-request basis); an additional level of naming is available through the directory service.
- Transparency between local and remote calls: because of the inherently different semantics, we find it a bad idea to try and make remote calls look exactly like as local calls.
- Backward compatibility with existing server interfaces in Amoeba: most were such a mess that they weren't worth saving anyway.

There are some beneficial side effects from using AIL as well:
- AIL helps to enforce uniform error handling.
- AIL can output the data packing and unpacking code (together called marshaling code) by itself, providing a simple way for applications to save their data structures to disk in a portable yet binary (and hence efficient) format.

Input Language
Initially, the idea was to put special markers in C source and preprocess this. This soon proved impractical, especially in the light of the multi-language goal, so we decided to design a language specialized to the specification of RPC interfaces. Although we made up the combination, most language building blocks were borrowed from other languages:
- the lexical elements, source preprocessing mechanism and type system was borrowed from C (perhaps not the ideal choice but with the advantage of compatibility with existing software in the Amoeba project);
- the class concept (although extensively modified) and the function prototype notation were borrowed from C++;[2]
- the notion of separate in and out parameters was borrowed from Ada and Modula-2+.[3]

There are good reasons for borrowing language elements when designing a special-purpose language like this one:
- the advantages and disadvantages of concepts and notations are well understood;
- users need little time to learn the new language (if they know the language borrowed from);
- because we chose C's preprocessor, lexical elements and type system, we can actually

include C definition files to import types that are needed by AIL interfaces.

Classes

The class concept in AIL differs quite a bit from that in C++. A class in AIL can contain only constant and type definitions and function prototypes; there are no data members. AIL classes specify only public information; there are no private definitions as in C++.

Functions And Parameters

Interface stub functions generated by AIL always return an error code as their function result and have a capability as their first parameter. Thus, AIL function prototypes do not specify a return type, and the first parameter is represented by a single '*'. Each following parameter must be completely specified by listing its transfer direction, type and name.

- The transfer direction can be 'in' (which is the default), 'out', or 'in out'; it indicates whether the parameter is input to the server, output from the server, or both. There is a fourth transfer direction, 'var in', which means (in C) a parameter that is input to the server but passed to the stub by reference instead of by value. In other languages this may be the same as 'in'.
- The type of a parameter determines the type of expressions or variables acceptable as actual parameters, including properties like array size.
- The name is used only for documentary purposes.

Since the client stubs are intended to be called by programs written in C or Pascal (for example), the class member call notation from C++ cannot be used to call client stubs generated by AIL. Instead of writing

```
object->member_function(argument1, argument2, ...)
```

the user must write

```
member_function(object, argument1, argument2, ...)
```

To make this work, the client stubs must have global scope (unless the language supports modules, like Modula-2). A consequence of this restriction is that there may be no overloading of function names used in different interfaces. A simple convention to prevent name clashes in practice is to prefix all function names with an abbreviation of their class name, followed by an underscore.

Class Inheritance

The power of the class mechanism lies in the possibility to extend existing classes by creating *derived classes*. A derived class has all the properties of its *base class(es)*, plus any properties added by its own definition. In C++, a derived class must be derived from exactly one base class; in AIL, a class can be derived from multiple base classes. This property is called *multiple inheritance*.

As an example of an application of multiple inheritance, consider two interfaces: a class 'tty' implementing the operations write-to-tty and read-from-tty, and a class 'window' implementing create-window and move-window (and probably others). If we now want to implement a terminal emulator in a window, the interface to a terminal emulator window should support both the tty and the window interface. This is easily accomplished by creating a class 'tty-emulator-window' inheriting the classes tty and window.

Suppose that the tty and window classes both inherit the class 'standard'; this is now also inherited by the new class.

AIL does not need the concept of 'virtual functions' present in C++. The 'virtual' predicate in C++ means that a derived class can override the implementation of that function, and since AIL functions are implemented in servers, this is true for all AIL functions.

Variable Length Arrays

AIL's type system, mostly borrowed from C, has an extension to specify arrays of variable length. Variable length arrays are needed to provide reply buffers for stubs that can return a variable amount of data: the client has to specify a buffer containing space for the maximum amount expected, but the reply must indicate the actual amount returned.

By specifying two expressions for the size of an array, separated by a colon, an actual and a maximum size can be set. This construct may occur only in function prototypes (where both expressions may refer to other parameters) and in structure definitions (where the maximum must be constant but the actual size may refer to other members of the structure).

Overriding Marshalers

For data types containing pointers, C's type notation isn't powerful enough to derive adequate marshaling code: a pointer may point to exactly one object of the given type, or to an array containing a variable number of objects, whose length can in general only be determined by inspecting the data. For this purpose, amongst others, the user may provide the names of routines to do the actual marshaling for a particular type. The most trivial example is the C string data type: the library defines a marshaler to marshal characters up to the terminating zero. For other languages than C (assuming these support variable-length strings), marshalers must be provided that support the same network format. The syntax used to specify marshalers (an option tacked onto the typedef syntax) isn't wonderful, but additional marshalers are rarely needed in practice.

Examples

Here are some examples of AIL class definitions. These classes do not necessarily correspond to actual classes used in Amoeba. The numeric ranges in square brackets after the class name are used to generate request codes; for various reasons AIL cannot be trusted to choose request codes itself.

```
#include <amoeba.h>        /* Defines capability, etc. */

class standard [1000..1999] {
    std_info(*, out char info_buffer[buflen:100],
              in int buflen);
    std_restrict(*, int rights_mask,
                out capability restricted_cap);
    std_destroy(*);
};

class tty [2000..2099] {
    inherit standard;
    const TTY_MAXBUF = 1000;
    tty_write(*, char buffer[size:TTY_MAXBUF],
              int size);
    tty_read(*, out char buffer[size:TTY_MAXBUF],
             out int size);
};

class window [2100..2199] {
    inherit standard;
    win_create(*, int x, int y, int w, int h,
               out capability win_cap);
    win_move_resize(*, int x, int y, int w, int h);
};

class tty_emulator_window [2200..2299] {
    inherit tty, window;
    /* No additional features */
};
```

The Stub Generator

AIL works in three phases.
- Phase one reads and checks all class definitions in the input.
- Phase two determines, for each function of each class, the request and reply message formats.
- Finally, phase three, instructed by generator directives in the input, writes source files in the desired language containing interface definitions, client stubs and/or server code.

The request and reply message formats determined in the second phase are a function only of the class definitions found in the input, not of the generator directives: if the stub generator used a different message format when directed to generate stubs for Pascal than when directed to generate C stubs, communication between clients and servers written in different languages would fail.

Server Structure

Amoeba servers generally create a number of threads, each executing the same server main loop (get request, process it, put reply). The details of thread creation are server-specific and not handled by AIL; it only generates the server main loop itself. For each function in the class that the server is to implement (including those in base classes), when a request for that specific function arrives, the server main loop calls a function 'impl_*function-name*' with the same parameters as the corresponding client stub, except that the first parameter (a capability in the client stub) points to the request header, to save copying a few bytes.

The server writer must provide implementation functions even for standard functions: although their meaning is standardized, their implementation is not. Every implementation function must return a status code indicating whether it succeeded or failed, which will become the return value of the client stub. Marshaling of return values is only done if the implementation function succeeds.

Possible Extensions

The AIL stub generator is designed to support extensions: it is easy to add generator modules to support new languages, different stub types, or different RPC mechanisms. Some possible extensions are:
- Certain interfaces would like to have some objects maintained by a library inside the client program. Rather than starting a server thread in the client (possible, but expensive since the data will be copied at least three times), we could have AIL generate a test in the client stubs for a particular port, and call a local implementation routine instead of engaging in an RPC call.
- For C++ and other class-based languages (Modula-3?), it should be possible to generate client stubs adhering to the language's standard method-calling syntax.
- The input syntax could be augmented to tell more about the semantics of the remote functions, like idempotency, so a failed operation can be retried instead of returning an error immediately.

Performance

For many simple interfaces, AIL generates almost the same code as we would by hand. AIL-generated code never calls external functions besides user-specified marshalers and the RPC primitives, so there is no extra function call overhead.

However, there are a few tricks unknown to AIL when determining the optimal packing of parameters into header and buffer (e.g., to pack a long int in two shorts in the header), it does rather conservative error checking, and its server code always contains byte swapping code in case a request comes from a client on an 'other-endian' machine.

But the byte swapping code is never executed unnecessary: clients send and receive data in their native byte order, so the server needs to swap bytes only if their native byte order is different. All byte swapping is done in the server, to minimize the code size of the client stubs.

Comparison To Other Stub Generators

None of the RPC stub generators mentioned below support classes: each interface stands completely on its own.

- Sun RPC.[4] This is a stub generator for Sun RPC, which runs on SunOS (and other derivatives of 4.2 BSD Unix), and implements RPC on top of UDP/IP (unreliable datagrams). Like AIL, Sun RPC uses a special-purpose language derived mostly from C to specify server interfaces. The language is less powerful than ours, but directly supports the marshaling of discriminated unions. The input is not run through the C preprocessor. Rpcgen only generates C as output language.
- Flume.[5] This is an RPC stub generator for Modula-2+ (a derivative of Modula-2) under the Topaz operating system.[6] Flume reads Modula-2+ interface definition modules, but imposes some restrictions; because the modules must still be understandable by the Modula-2+ compiler, extra syntax for Flume's benefit could not be added, so certain options must be specified by embedding reserved strings in identifiers (a similar trick to lint's use of /*NOSTRICT*/ etc.). Flume tries to hide the difference between local and remote calls to the extreme: it even marshals recursive data structures. Since the same function name is used for the client stubs as for the implementation function in the server, a server cannot use its own client stubs to interface to another server (this would be useful in a 'gateway' service, for instance). Flume is completely bound to Modula-2+, and since (in practice) it is the only way to use Topaz RPC, programs writting in other languages cannot use RPC.

Conclusions

Here are a few points we have learned from our experience in building and using AIL:
- It is worthwhile to spend some time to design and implement a special-purpose language that is just right for your needs.
- Class-based interface definitions with multiple inheritance simplify the creation of new interfaces with a rich functionality.
- Automatically generated stubs can be as fast as handwritten ones.

This leads to:
- Every self-respecting distributed system should have an RPC stub generator.

And even:
- Every RPC stub generator should be class-based and support multiple inheritance.

Acknowledgements

I would like to thank first and foremost Siebren van der Zee, who has written the stub generator almost completely on his own, starting with a rather vague and incomplete description, and contributed quite a bit to the design in the process. Many discussions with Jack Jansen, Sape Mullender and Irvin Shizgal also contributed to the design. Robbert van Renesse's enthusiasm for the idea of a class-based stub compiler when I first proposed it gave me the little push that was needed to go forward with the project.

References

1. S. J. Mullender and A. S. Tanenbaum, "The Design of a Capability-Based Distributed Operating System," *The Computer Journal* **29**(4), pp. 289-300 (1986).
2. Bjarne Stroustrup, *The C++ Programming Language,* Addison-Wesley (1986).
3. Paul Rovner, "Extending Modula-2 to Build Large, Integrated Systems," *IEEE*

Software 3(6), pp. 46-57 (November 1986).
4. *rpcgen – an RPC protocol compiler*, Sun man page.
5. Andrew Birrell, Ed Lazowska, and Ted Wobber, *flume – remote procedure call (RPC) stub generator for Modula-2+*, Topaz manpage.
6. Paul R. McJones and Garret F. Swart, *Evolving the UNIX System Interface to Support Multithreaded Programs,* DEC SRC, Palo Alto, CA (1987).

PEACE – A Distributed Operating System for High-Performance Multicomputer Systems[*]

Wolfgang Schröder-Preikschat

GMD FIRST

Hardenbergplatz 2, 1000 Berlin 12, FRG

ABSTRACT

The next generation of supercomputers will be largely parallel MIMD architectures consisting of several hundreds to thousands of processing nodes. These architectures will be realized as multicomputer systems with distributed control and are based on distributed memory, rather than shared memory. Consequently, distributed operating systems for global control of system resources are required and communication is to be based on message-passing. Major aspects of these operating systems will be a very high degree of distribution (i.e., actual modularization) as well as an extremely fast implementation of message-passing services. The paper deals with the organization of a distributed operating system, PEACE, which has been designed for a largely parallel MIMD supercomputer, SUPRENUM. It discusses the implementation of the message-passing kernel.

1. Introduction

The next generation of supercomputers will be largely parallel MIMD architectures consisting of several hundreds to thousands of processing nodes. These architectures will be realized as multicomputer systems with *distributed control* and are based on *distributed memory*, i.e., its nodes are autonomous, cooperating computers that communicate through message passing. Consequently, each node has its own operating system controlling local resources; whereas global functions of the multi-node system are performed jointly by the collective of operating systems. This necessitates *function replication* as well as *data replication* among the nodes, leading to a global *distributed operating system*. Inter-node cooperation takes the form of a multitude of client-server relationships among system processes residing on different nodes. For this reason the communication model will be based on *inter-process communication*, rather than inter-node communication.

Above all, distributed numerical applications for these MIMD machines merely require a problem-oriented processing environment which has to provide system-wide

---

[*] This work was supported by the Ministry of Research and Technology (BMFT) of the German Federal Government under grant no. ITR 8502 A 2.

and very high-performance message-passing services, low-level process management as well as naming facilities. Traditional operating system services (i.e., file handling, resource control, job management, etc.) are assumed of being provided elsewhere, maybe on a front-end host machine. The key requirement is to have all the computing power of the MIMD machine available for application programs, rather for the execution of system programs. Primarily, this is a requirement which addresses the actual system structure of the operating system, i.e., the degree of modularization and the way how the various modules are mapped onto the machine. A monolithic and rigid system organization must be avoided such that the system user is able to configure the MIMD machine with respect to his own application-oriented demands.

It is the original idea of PEACE® [Schroeder 1988] to provide such a process execution and communication environment. In this sense, PEACE differs from presently available distributed operating systems, such as MACH [Young et al. 1987] and CHORUS [Rozier et al. 1988], in that it was primarily designed to support the execution of distributed MIMD programs on largely parallel computer systems. The guideline was to make these programs work, rather than to implement another distributed operating system.

With respect to largely parallel MIMD machines, the architectural framework for PEACE is SUPRENUM [Giloi 1988], a supercomputer based on distributed memory. Besides this hardware environment, design and development of PEACE was, and is, consequently based on a software engineering principle [Parnas 1975] which makes the construction of a *family of operating systems* feasible [Habermann et al. 1976]. Strongly influenced by the MOOSE project [Schroeder 1986], PEACE is *process-structured* and *message-based*. Extending fundamental MOOSE ideas, it is *distributed* and supports the implementation of *networked system services* provided by a large set of arbitrarily distributed system processes.

The paper explains fundamental PEACE concepts for the construction of distributed application programs. Of major interest will be the functionality of the message-passing kernel. A general description of the overall PEACE system structure can be found in [Schroeder 1988]. Before considering basic design decisions, a short discussion on PEACE hardware environments, performance requirements and general design aspects takes place.

1.1. Basic SUPRENUM System Architecture

There are two major classes of nodes a SUPRENUM operating system has to deal with, *processing nodes* (PNs) and *service nodes* (SNs). Several PNs and SNs constitute a *cluster*, and a configurable number of clusters represent the SUPRENUM *core system*. It is the core system which is to be managed by PEACE.

Each PN is supplied with a high performance vector floating-point unit and primarily used for numerical processing. In addition to these user-dedicated nodes,

---
® PEACE is a registered symbol of GMD.

SNs are used for cluster interconnection as well as for attaching peripherals directly or indirectly, via *hosts*, to the core systems. Interconnection of nodes/clusters is achieved by a high-speed, two-stage network system. Figure 1 depicts the global system organization in terms of hardware building blocks.

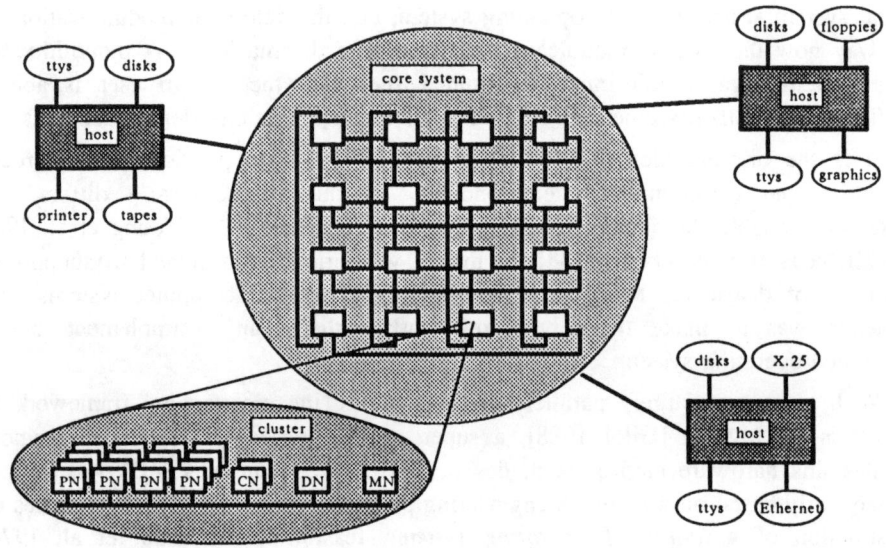

Figure 1: Global Hardware System Organization

The SUPRENUM host machine is controlled by UNIX™ and provides access to global mass storage devices (disks, tapes, etc.), hardcopy devices (printer, plotter, etc.) terminals, workstations as well as local-area and/or long-haul networks. Dependent on the services required, several hosts may be attached to the core system. The basic idea is to distinguish between general program development, graphic tools and system maintenance. As illustrated in the figure, this leads to 3 host machines.

Besides the PNs, several types of SNs must be managed by PEACE. The *disk node* (DN) interfaces two disks to a cluster, each disk providing more than 1 Gbytes of mass storage. Establishing connections between clusters as well as interfacing the core system to host machines is the domain of the *communication node* (CN). Each cluster is equipped with two CNs, one for row coupling and another one for column coupling. For this purpose a single CN has two physical interconnection links with a per-link data transfer rate of up to 125 Mbit/sec. In contrast to that, intra-cluster communication between nodes is on the basis of two 64 bit parallel cluster busses, each one offering a data transfer rate of up to 160 Mbytes/sec. Dedicated

---

™ UNIX is a registered trademark of AT&T Bell Laboratories.

communication hardware automatically routes messages between different nodes of different clusters via the proper CN, i.e., selects the row or column link for the message transfer. A *maintenance node* (MN) is used for cluster diagnosis purposes.

The actual configuration of the SUPRENUM machine will consist of 16 clusters, whereby each cluster contains 16 PNs and 4 SNs. Thus, a total of 256 PNs and 64 SNs, i.e., 320 nodes, must be managed by PEACE. The nodes itself are based on the 20 MHz MC 68020 supported by the paged memory management unit MC 68851. In addition to the vector processing unit with 64 Kbytes vector memory, each PN is supplied with the scalar floating-point unit MC 68882. Excepted the CN, which has only 256 Kbytes local memory, each node has 8 Mbytes local (on-board) memory.

1.2. The Real Challenge

Because the SUPRENUM core system is based on a *distributed memory* organization, each node has only access to its local on-board memory. Communication between the nodes, i.e., between processes executed by different nodes, is exclusively based on *message-passing*. In order to achieve utmost high efficiency, one of the most important requirements is to guarantee an extreme low message startup time[1].

As pointed out in [Kolp, Mierendorff 1987] and considering the final SUPRENUM configuration, the ideal startup time will be 50 μsec; whereas a 600 μsec startup time is acceptable only in case of a specific class of SUPRENUM applications. Besides a very carefully designed communication protocol architecture and a well tuned implementation, the only chance to meet this requirement is to support software-based message-passing activities by dedicated communication hardware units; more precisely, to migrate specific software functions down to the hardware. Therefore, each SUPRENUM node is equipped with a *communication co-processor* (CP) that handles low-level inter-node communication.

Nevertheless, there is the necessity of a software package that interfaces higher-level application programs to the CP, for the CP functionality is not powerful enough to perform basic inter-process communication which implies process scheduling and de-scheduling activities, for example. This software package will be represented by the PEACE message-passing kernel. The performance requirement is to ensure a delay of less than 600 μsec for network-wide message startup between user-level processes, assuming a multi-processing mode of operation of the single SUPRENUM nodes. Basically, this message startup means to execute a low-level *send-receive-reply* sequence between processes without exchanging any user data, i.e., to perform network-wide synchronization.

---

[1] The message startup time is determined by system activities performed by the sender and receiver site to start the transfer of user-level data objects. This includes hardware as well as software activities such as performing context switches and process dispatching, handling of interrupts, setting up message descriptors as well as the exchanging and the processing of communication protocol header information. It is the time during which the node is not able to further process the application program.

1.3. Towards a Family of Operating Systems

The motivation to build a family of operating systems primarily grows out of the necessity to manage hundreds of PNs and a large number of SNs. Although the nodes are based on the same processor unit, PEACE is faced with the management of a heterogeneous computer system, for the variety of functionally dedicated SUPRENUM nodes. Consequently, different local operating systems are required and, most importantly, the PNs must not be overloaded with operating system functions. Without a common design philosophy there will be a set of heterogeneous operating systems and, because having designed artificial boundaries, loss of system performance will be the agenda.

Not only the SUPRENUM hardware organization calls for a variety of dedicated system services, different (numerical) application programs require different operating system support, too. Being only based on a single, monolithic, operating system will have several disadvantages for user programs because, in this case, the nodes are always equipped with a superset of system services. Besides the potential of overall poor performance, one obvious fact is that a large operating system for a single node will require a large memory space, which is to the debit of user programs. The concept of virtual memory generally solves this resource problem, however, because of paging overhead, this solution implies loss of performance for memory-bounded user programs. Typical representatives of these application programs can be found within the numerical programming area, the major application field of the SUPRENUM machine.

Another important fact is that computer system development in general is an evolutionary course of hardware/software design and implementation. *Flexibility* is the keyword in order to meet future user requirements and to optimally support forthcoming hardware architectures. This especially is of significant importance for the design of operating systems, whose task is, besides other functions, to bring user programs onto the actual hardware. Therefore, an operating system has to be open with respect to both aspects, user requirement and hardware architecture.

2. Program Distribution Support by PEACE

There are three basic PEACE concepts by which distributed programs are constructed. The *entity* is the unit of structuring a program into distributable parts. A *process* is the unit of sequential execution within the entity and a *message* is the unit of communication between processes, i.e., between entities. These concepts are implemented by low-level kernel facilities, supported by higher-level server functions. The following subsections will discuss the most important implementational details of these concepts.

2.1. The PEACE Entity

Basically, a program is organized as a *PEACE entity*. This generally holds for user programs as well as for system programs, both in the following referred to as application program. A distributed application program will be organized as a couple of entities interconnected by some communication system. Figure 2 gives a rough outline of the PEACE entity structure.

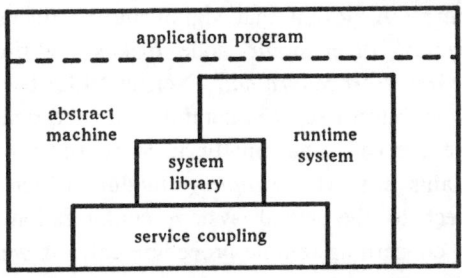

Figure 2: Structure of a PEACE Entity

A single entity consists of five major building blocks. As was already pointed out above, a PEACE *application program* is assumed to be either a user program or a system program. At least for user programs, the need for transparency with respect to the actual system organization (hardware as well as software) is one of the major aspects. Therefore, some means of abstraction from low-level system organization is required.

In order to provide system transparency, an *abstract machine* interface is specified. Typically, user programs are written in terms of primitives provided by the abstract machine. In case of SUPRENUM, these primitives are directly derived from traditional FORTRAN constructs and from fundamental message-passing operations for distributed computing. Communication semantics at this level will be a *no-wait send* [Liskov 1979]. In addition to that, a dynamical process model is provided and communication between processes is based on typed data objects, such as scalars and vectors, exchanged via messages. It is assumed that the abstract machine is completely implemented by a compiler and, thus, defines a programming language for distributed computing.

The *runtime system* is closely related to the programming language or the compiler being used. Typical services are formated i/o and local memory management (e.g., *scanf/printf* and *malloc/free* in C). In terms of programming support for MIMD programs, dedicated mailbox services are provided. This, for example, includes the implementation of abstract machine primitives for inter-process communication.

Interface to PEACE system functions is by the means of a *system library*. Part of this interface are functions found in most UNIX installations, namely the *UNIX system calls*. These system calls are provided on a compatibility library basis and the UNIX interface is extended by functions which are closely related to the PEACE distributed operating system. By this way, *lightweight processes* are provided just as *naming* and *checkpointing*, to give some examples.

The building blocks discussed so far all together provide services which only can be efficiently implemented if the corresponding modules share the same address space with the original application program. However, the bulk of operating system services may be located elsewhere. A design that significantly reduces system overhead in terms of memory utilization of a single node makes traditional operating system services available on a *remote procedure call* [Nelson 1982] basis. Moreover, in case of largely parallel MIMD architectures, it is natural to invoke operating system services in terms of remote procedure calls and, finally, in terms of message-passing. For this purpose the entity contains a *service coupling* module which implements topology transparency with respect to the actual system configuration. This module hides implementational details concerning remote procedure calls as well as naming.

The broken line in the figure indicates that the boundary between abstract machine and real machine (i.e. *runtime system*, *system library* and *service coupling*) is not fixed. The precise position of the boundary depends on the semantics of high-level abstract machine primitives and on the functionality of low-level system services in order to implement the abstract machine. There is always a *semantical gap* between these two levels and the optimal solution for programs being based on the abstract machine definition will be if this gap is only of conceptual nature. That is to say, in order to avoid performance limiting mapping overhead at runtime, a functional specification of the abstract machine always has to reflect technical facts of the underlying system architecture[2].

2.2. Lightweight Processes, Teams and Leagues

The PEACE process model is based on *teams* and *lightweight processes* [Cheriton 1979]. A team defines a common framework for a couple of lightweight processes mapped into the same address space, which then can be physically isolated from other team address spaces by means of a memory management unit. In this sense, a team is the unit of isolation as well as distribution and not a single process. The basic idea of lightweight processes is to encapsulate and uniquely represent separate threads of control within a single address space. A single team encapsulates one or more PEACE entities, whereby each of which may be controlled by a couple of lightweight processes.

In order to execute a team at least one process is needed at the application program level. If necessary, a PEACE entity additionally uses lightweight processes at the runtime system level, system library level and/or service coupling level. Typical examples are to provide support for system-wide (i.e., network-wide) exception handling, checkpointing, asynchronous communication and multi-threaded server.

Technically, a distributed PEACE application program is constituted by a group of teams. Such a group of related teams is called a *league*, which defines an application-related communication environment. The most important aspect associated

---

[2] With respect to forthcoming MIMD hardware architectures, there is a natural *loss of transparency* [Parnas, Siewiorek 1972] because the ideal SUPRENUM abstract machine is SUPRENUM hardware dependent.

with leagues is that they provide a *communication firewall* between different applications. Thus, to support a multi-user mode of operation at least a two-level security mechanism is implemented in PEACE; for different jobs will be mapped onto different leagues and teams constituting a league will be isolated from each other by means of a memory management unit.

2.3. Message Passing

Different PEACE entities are coupled by a communication system that is based on message-passing and implemented by a collective of small message-passing kernels. Each node will be equipped with one message-passing kernel. Active elements within the entity are lightweight processes. Consequently, message-passing takes the form of *inter-process communication* rather than inter-node communication.

The message-passing kernel implements synchronous communication, providing the following basic communication services:

- *remote invocation send* of fixed-size messages for efficient implementation of *remote procedure calls*, i.e., system service requests
- *high-volume data transfer* of arbitrarily sized data segments, i.e., non-buffered network-wide data exchange between peer address spaces
- *synchronization send* of non-buffered and arbitrarily sized messages for efficient implementation of user-level communication

Asynchronous communication then is provided by lightweight processes, maybe on a library basis, and is performed by the entity itself.

2.3.1. Port-Based Addressing Scheme

For performance reasons, PEACE message-passing is non-buffered – therefore synchronous – and directly performed between processes addressed via ports. Each process is associated with a *gate*, which will act as a port-based communication endpoint without buffering capabilities, but rather routing capabilities. A communication endpoint will be represented by a *system-wide unique identifier*. This identifier contains a hint on which node the corresponding process (i.e., gate) is located. They will be normally associated in one-to-one correspondence with processes, i.e., the creation of a process also results in the creation of a process gate. The effect is that both the process object and the gate object are bound to the same unique identifier.

Gates can also be associated dynamically with processes, thus allowing dynamic reconfiguration in case of team migration as a result of load balancing. Moreover, there might be several gates associated with the same process, thus having more gates available than processes. Even after team migration, the kernel will automatically route an incoming message to the new destination process. In this sense, the gate takes the form of a *forwarding identifier* associated with a specific process.

2.3.2. Symbolic Addressing Scheme

The actual checking whether a message is to be forwarded, i.e., routed, introduces no loss of communication performance. However, in case of incoming messages, performance loss will be caused by the handling of interrupts and context switches, for the message-passing kernel is to be activated to perform the checks. In order to keep kernel complexity small and to achieve high-speed inter-process communication, dynamic reconfiguration will not be exclusively supported by the kernel, but rather in co-operation with global symbolic naming functions provided by dedicated system processes.

Unlike team migration, maintaining network-transparency in case of a node crash is more complex. Because gates that have been managed by the kernel of a crashed node can no longer be used to address associated processes and because a system-wide unique gate identifier will have to contain a hint on which node the gate object is located, the communication endpoint identifier for a process changes if the process gate is migrated from the crashed node onto a running node[3]. Local caching of gates (i.e., communication endpoint identifiers) associated with remote processes will help to maintain transparency – at least if the cache store does not exhaust –, however only to the expense of communication performance. In this case, hashing strategies must be implemented and, most importantly, executed along with each message-passing activity. This organization would make it impossible to keep the message startup time (i.e., the time needed to perform a remote rendezvous by a *send-receive-reply* sequence) significantly below the 600 µsec boundary, because all these activities must be executed by a node under the control of the sender/receiver process. For all these reasons, the kernel will not cache communication endpoint identifiers, i.e., gates, which have been managed by remote kernels of crashed nodes.

The solution to overcome the crash problem, while maintaining high-performance inter-process communication, only can be to propagate a system exception to application processes. Note, communication endpoints already must be known by the processes in order to address their peers, thus, these processes necessarily will have to cache corresponding communication endpoint identifiers. As a result of exception propagation, the processes itself are directed to get knowledge of the new endpoint identifier in case of a node crash. As part of exception handling, the processes itself will invoke PEACE naming services. These services are provided by system processes (e.g. name server) instead of being implemented by the kernel. Consequently, a PEACE entity itself is responsible to recover from a node crash, at least with respect to requesting the resolution of communication endpoint identifiers.

In this approach, node crash transparency for the application program will be maintained by the runtime system, the system library or the service coupling module. In a similar way, team migration exceptions are propagated, thus giving application processes the opportunity for rebinding. The effect will be that system overhead caused by the forwarding of messages is avoided.

---

[3] Of course, this may also imply process migration, for the normal situation will be that both gate and process are located on the same node.

2.3.3. A Message-Passing Kernel Family

A PEACE entity will be directly interfaced to the message-passing kernel which enables system-wide communication between different entities. Depending on the mode of operation, i.e., whether single-processing or multi-processing is to be supported on a single node, different kernel representations are provided. With respect to message-passing primitives, common to these different representations is the same interface, only the implementation changes.

The extreme situation will be that, in case of a single-processing implementation, the message-passing primitives are directly linked to the entity and, thus, take the form of a *communication library*. Consequently, application programs are directly interfaced to the network, leading to a minimum of system overhead during communication. The consequence is also that scaling problems may arise, namely in cases where the number of entities exceeds the number of presently available nodes. Note, single-processing support requires a one-to-one correspondence between entities and nodes.

In order to overcome possible scaling limitations, multi-processing on a node is supported. In this situation, basic communication services are provided on a trap handling basis, i.e., as traditional system calls. The effect, however, is the potential of a significant loss of communication performance, when compared with the single-processing variant [4]. Dependent on the number of available nodes, a mixed mode of operation is possible for the distributed application. For the same application, some entities may share a node, requiring multi-processing support, while others are exclusively allocated to their own nodes, requiring single-processing support only.

3. Structuring Principles

As was outlined in the previous section, distributed user/system programs are assumed of being organized as a couple of PEACE entities. Interconnection between the entities is by means of the message-passing kernel. In this section, it is illustrated how these entities are used to construct distributed applications. Furthermore, the basic organization of the message-passing kernel is explained. Figure 3 gives a brief overview of major building blocks.

From bottom up, the various building blocks deal with communication, kernel extensions, kernel interfacing and user as well as system extensions. In the following subsections, the functionality of these building blocks is discussed in more detail.

---

[4] A preliminary performance analysis of a PEACE remote invocation send shows a total system overhead of approximately 60% of the overall rendezvous timing. Thus, from the 1.2 ms network-wide *send-receive-reply* sequence nearly 720 μsec where wasted by interrupt handling, context switching, process dispatching, message buffering and address space isolation; which all is necessary to support multi-processing, but causes performance limiting overhead in case of single-processing [Behr et al. 1988].

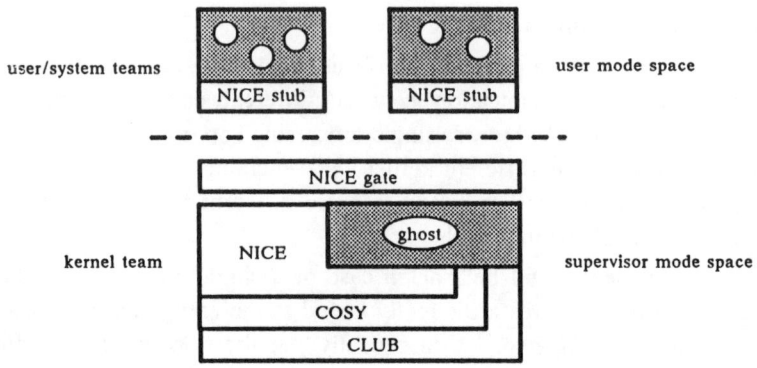

Figure 3: PEACE Building Blocks

3.1. Welcome to the NICE COSY CLUB

At least three layers of low-level communication are distinguished in PEACE. The physical network-interface is represented by the *CLUB* module [5], which hides network device specific details. It merely provides low-level network device driver functionalities such as performing device control, setting up message DMA descriptors, handling of interrupts, etc.

Communication between different nodes is enabled by COSY, the <u>co</u>mmunication <u>sy</u>stem. This module represents the most fundamental *abstract machine* on top of which inter-process communication will be implemented. It enables network-wide data transfer and, dependent on network interface capabilities, performs segmenting and blocking of large message segments. A problem-oriented *data transfer protocol* is implemented. In case of SUPRENUM, it supports non-buffered data transfer between sender and receiver address spaces. Consequently, COSY is functionally dependent on the network interface as well as the memory management unit (if there is any one).

Above COSY, the <u>n</u>etwork <u>i</u>ndependent <u>c</u>ommunication <u>e</u>xecutive, NICE, is layered. The purpose of this module is to provide network-wide inter-process communication. Basically, it implements a management protocol, rather than a communication protocol. This protocol deals with system-wide process synchronization and dispatching, and hence is called *dispatching protocol*.

The difference between a single-processing and a multi-processing variant of message-passing primitives is realized by different NICE implementations. Neither CLUB nor COSY do have any knowledge about processes.

---

[5] CLUB stands for <u>cl</u>uster <u>b</u>us. It is derived from SUPRENUM, in which the cluster bus represents the basic interconnection media within a cluster.

3.2. About the Ghost, Couriers and Deputies

Kernel extensions are provided by lightweight *kernel processes* on a remote procedure call basis. A standard representative of these kernel processes is the *ghost*, which provides node-bounded system services related to the message-passing system, such as routing and monitoring, as well as to the naming facility, such as the association between a team and its corresponding name server[6]. On the other hand, there always is the need for at least one process on a node if either a user program or a system program is to be executed. The ghost represents this process and – "joining the NICE COSY CLUB" – builds up the *kernel team*. For example, a single-processing mode of operation may imply that the ghost is responsible for the execution of an application program, i.e., that the ghost is the application process.

Dependent on the kernel software configuration, lightweight processes may be added to the original kernel team. These processes are called *couriers*. They introduce kernel services such as allocation/deallocation of gate, process and team objects, association of processes with teams and teams with leagues, execution control of processes and teams, the logical coupling of different nodes in a shared-memory environment, etc. Courier services all are concerned with the management of data structures used to implement kernel abstractions for the representation of low-level process names, communication endpoints as well as to execute application programs.

Couriers deal with logical objects, management of physical objects is the domain of *deputies*. They are used to implement a coupling between higher-level processes (i.e., teams) and devices attached to the node, thus acting as a *device deputy*. By means of this process representation, device control is made feasible on a message-passing basis; more specifically, on the basis of remote procedure calls. Consequently, deputies need direct access to low-level device driver routines and, hence, are device dependent. For example, a cluster bus deputy directly interfaces to the CLUB module. Integration of a new device means the creation of the corresponding device deputy.

Kernel processes control a PEACE kernel entity (highlighted by the shaded box). These processes always are encapsulated by the same team, which is always executed in supervisor mode. Excepted the kernel team, any other team is executed in user mode and may be arbitrarily distributed. Note, only fundamental system services are provided to dynamically manage node-bounded system objects, network-wide. Strategies are implemented by higher-level system teams, thus consequently following the ideas for the construction of program families [Parnas 1975] and extending these ideas into a distributed computing environment.

---

[6] In PEACE, naming is application-oriented, i.e., each team may be associated with an own name server which implements a team-related name space excerpt. In case of distributed applications, a group of teams will be bound to the same name server, sharing the same name space excerpt. The corresponding name server binding is realized by the kernel and not the naming itself. Naming will be performed by the service coupling module of a PEACE entity in co-operation with a set of name server.

3.3. The NICE Interface

Each PEACE process has to use NICE primitives in order to interact with its outside world. However, the way of accessing these primitives is different, depending on the team relationship of the processes. In case of supervisor mode processes, i.e., lightweight processes constituting the kernel team, NICE takes the form of a communication library, for a common address space is defined.

In case of user mode processes, NICE primitives are invoked indirectly, via the *NICE gate* module. This module implements a system call interface in the traditional sense, namely it handles *system call traps* and passes arguments as well as results between user and supervisor space. The issuing of these system calls is made hidden by means of the *NICE stub* module which is a traditional system call library. Either user processes or system processes will have to use the NICE stub to switch from user to supervisor mode, i.e., to invoke the message-passing kernel.

3.4. Node-Independent PEACE Entities

On top of the message-passing kernel user and system teams are layered. However, there is no need to place on each node both types of teams. The mapping depends on the actual choice of system configuration. It is one of the most important requirements for the implementation of PEACE system teams to ensure absolute node independence. A single system team (e.g. a name server) is required to be capable of handling system objects which are actually located anywhere within the system. Consequently, the migration of such a team has no impact on its management capabilities.

There are a couple of system teams, making PEACE a real distributed operating system. These teams implement application-oriented services concerned with naming, team, memory and trap management, signal propagation, clock and i/o management, file handling and loading, synchronization, checkpointing and recovery, etc. All these services may be distributed arbitrarily. Only performance requirements will limit the freedom of distribution, and not the system design.

4. Inter-Process Communication

The message-passing kernel, i.e., NICE, implements three fundamental communication principles: *remote invocation send*, *high-volume data transfer* and *synchronization send*. All these principles work system-wide and they are based on unique process gate identifiers in order to address processes.

Design and implementation of PEACE message-passing protocols was strongly influenced by three major aspects, namely:

- avoidance of redundant low-level protocol functions, for higher levels often will have to implement them any way [Saltzer et al. 1984]
- loss of communication performance is not only a problem of transmission errors, but also because of packet lost caused by operating system buffer management problems [Lantz et al. 1985]

- transmission errors within the SUPRENUM network occur with the same probability as in case of local memory-to-memory copies [Behr et al. 1986]

For all these aspects, the guideline for the implementation of inter-process communication was to *keep things as simple as possible* [Lampson 1983]. Kernel simplicity is the consequence of not distributing process state information over the network and, therefore, being forced to manage replicated data at the kernel level.

4.1. The Dispatching Protocol

The major aspect of the PEACE inter-kernel communication protocol is trying to reduce the message buffering problem, rather than providing secure communication in order to deal with unsecure data transmission links. Considering todays network capabilities, it is not the latter which causes loss of communication performance. Management of remote kernel buffer resources is the main task of the PEACE *dispatching protocol*, executed by NICE. This protocol is based on the fact that buffer pool utilization strongly depends on the communication semantics as well as on the runtime behaviour of the communicating processes, especially server processes. The design decision was to have only one clearly identified communication service, the *remote invocation send*, which is associated with resource management problems (e.g. buffering, synchronization, dispatching, etc.) on a kernel level.

In case of a remote invocation send, the kernel of the server site does not implement long-term buffering of client state information which reflects the blocked-on situation between client and server. Thus, there are no alien descriptors as found in V [Cheriton 1984], i.e., descriptors used to implement virtual processes. Maxim is to keep the PEACE kernel as stateless as possible, which especially is of major importance if software fault-tolerance is to be supported. State information will be always managed by the kernel (i.e., courier) which implements the process object.

In order to reduce buffering problems within the kernel, incoming messages produced by a remote invocation send are not queued until the reply message is sent back. If the server receives the message, the corresponding message buffer is immediately reclaimed by the kernel. Consequently, duplicate suppression protocols used to implement remote procedure calls are not performed by the kernel, rather they are performed by PEACE entities, i.e., the service coupling module. Merely the message-passing and synchronization aspect of a remote procedure call is implemented by the kernel, recovery strategies are handled by higher levels, related to the application context.

Buffering of incoming messages only is performed at the network interface driver level, nevertheless it is strongly server dependent. If the buffer pool at the server site exhausted, this is considered as a *service collision* and a retry message is passed back to the client site. The retry indication carries a server-relative collision counter, which is incremented if the message cannot be delivered to the server and decremented when the server is ready to receive a message. Note, an empty buffer pool is a consequence that the server is not able to immediately consume an incoming message, for the server is not synchronized (i.e., blocked) on the incoming message. The collision counter, passed back in the retry message, is used at the client site to determine the client-relative delay before the same message is sent again. By this way, client starvation is made more improbable, for different retries are issued at different times.

A solution of the starvation problem is to maintain server-relative buffer pools. Consider the situation in which for each client a lightweight process is used in the server team to execute the service request, i.e., completes the remote invocation send. In this case, client starvation is no longer present, for the one-to-one correspondence between client and server. Thus, the client buffer is implemented by a lightweight process of the server team. The PEACE remote procedure call protocol, performed between client and server entities, follows this approach by the implementation of a *server pool* of problem-oriented size.

4.2. Remote Invocation Send

As outlined above, implementation of PEACE remote procedure calls is strongly supported by a *remote invocation send* principle which corresponds to a *synchronous request-response model* of communication between a *client* and a *server*. Between both types of processes, 64 byte fixed-size messages are exchanged on a *send-receive-reply* basis.

Upon request to send, a message is stored in the per-process message buffer maintained by NICE, making it impossible for processes sharing the client team to overwrite the original message contents. Moreover, replying the response message to the client causes no problems in case of out-core team memory areas (i.e., in case of paging or swapping). A kernel message buffer acts as a *protocol data unit* (PDU) template. The user-level 64 byte message is considered as the *service data unit* (SDU) which will be copied into the *user data field* of the PDU upon sending or replying.

The NICE PDU is allocated at the time the corresponding process is created. Some initialization is already done at creation time such as setting the unique identification of the sending process (i.e., gate), the message type as well as the type of protocol[7]. In addition to that, a DMA descriptor for this PDU is allocated and initiated accordingly. Consequently, sending the PDU merely causes to copy the SDU, to store the unique identification of the receiver process (i.e., gate), to setup the packet type and to pass the DMA descriptor to COSY[8]. In figure 4 the network-wide rendezvous protocol between client and server is illustrated.

The figure shows basic activities to be performed by the NICE *dispatching protocol*. It is the fundamental protocol to achieve synchronization between a sender

---

[7] There may be different protocols defined on a per-process basis. For example, one process may demand a full acknowledgement protocol while others require only very simple datagram services, because they use their own, application-oriented, acknowledgment protocol.

[8] Sending a message implies the blocking of the client process, leading to a very specific process state in order to unblock the process. This state contains a blocked-on value, which is the receiver identification, and the execution state, which is the packet type. Thus, setting up the corresponding PDU fields is already done along with NICE de-scheduling activities.

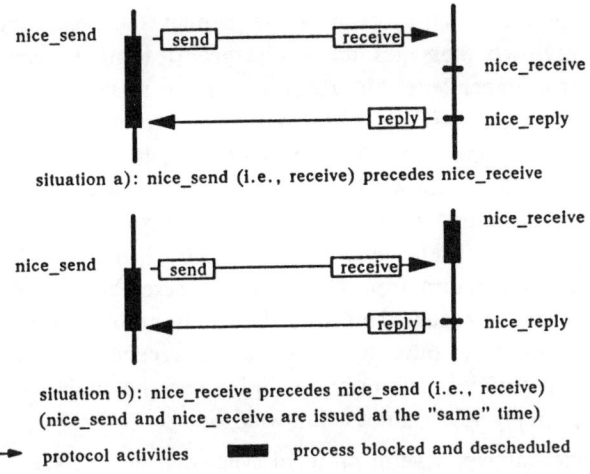

Figure 4: Remote Invocation Send

and receiver process. Upon issuing a *nice_send(server, request, response)*, the client requests the transmission (*send*) of a NICE PDU and blocks until it receives a reply message, i.e., the response. Arrived at the server site, this PDU will be queued (*receive*) and the possible blocked server will be unblocked (i.e., scheduled).

If the server is ready to establish a rendezvous, it issues *nice_receive(request)*. Rendezvous are established, i.e., messages are delivered, in the order of having been accepted by the receiving NICE module. If a message is pending at the server site, the server will directly proceed and consume the message. Otherwise, the server is blocked; it is unblocked upon the acceptance of the first message, i.e., PDU. As a result of *nice_receive* the process gate identification of the client is delivered. This identification will be used for replying the client.

In order to resume execution of the client, a *nice_reply(client, response)* is issued by the server team. Note, once a server has received a message from a client, the entire server team is allowed to reply the response message. Thus, a reply access right is given to the entire server team. Effect of replying will be the transmission (*reply*) of a corresponding PDU to the client site, without blocking the issuing process. The SDU carried this way is directly copied into the per-client message buffer, without any queuing overhead[9]. Finally, the client is reactivated.

---

[9] There is no need to enqueue the response message into a sender list as it will be necessary in case of request messages. Note, in case of the remote invocation send there always is only one server which will be able to send the response message. Caused by the handling of interrupts, queuing may be necessary at the low level network driver interface, i.e., either CLUB or COSY.

The default protocol is to acknowledge neither the send nor the reply PDU. Consequently, only two messages are exchanged, leading to one interrupt at each receiving site. At a higher level, the request message is acknowledged by the receive of the response message, which is of end-to-end semantics between client and server. Thus, if necessary, only the reply PDU must be explicitly acknowledged by the client site. The need for this acknowledgement depends on the service provided by the lower-level communication system, i.e., COSY. For example, the SUPRENUM interconnection network itself uses a synchronous protocol for data exchange. Consequently, upon the return from COSY, one is sure that the reply PDU has been passed to the peer site. Because there is no buffering problem at the client site, for the client is still blocked at the time the reply PDU is received, one is also sure that the SDU having been passed was successfully copied into the client's message buffer. For all these reasons, a reply PDU is not acknowledged.

As was outlined above, several protocol types can be selected on a per-process as well as per-PDU basis. If a process requires low-level acknowledgement, the NICE PDU is qualified accordingly (e.g. in case of a reply message only). The need for an acknowledgement is application dependent as well as dependent on low-level network interface capabilities. This is reflected by the functionality of NICE communication protocols.

4.3. High-Volume Data Transfer

Remote invocation send semantics is used to primarily achieve synchronization between client and server team. Transfer of arbitrarily sized data streams then is made feasible during the synchronization phase and, hence, is provided by a separate set of NICE primitives. This transfer functionality is called *high-volume data transfer*, because it means the transfer of memory segments between peer team address spaces without intermediate buffering. Figure 5 depicts the principle protocol steps.

As with the reply access right, once the server has synchronized on the client team the entire server team receives the authorization to read from/write into the address space of the client team. Reading will be requested by the issuing of a *nice_movefrom (client, from, to, size)*, whereby *from* denotes a client team memory segment of *size* units [10] and *to* refers to a server team memory segment of equal size. On the other hand, writing is requested by a *nice_moveto (client, from, to, size)*, and in this case *from* addresses a server segment and *to* addresses a client segment of maximal *size* units.

Because client state information is not available at the server site, the protocol for reading from a remote team address space is simpler than writing. The effect of both protocols, however, will be the same, namely to setup the DMAs at the client and the server site in order to "blast" the memory segment directly from source to destination. In case of reading, the DMA at the server site is initialized and then a request for

---

[10] Based on SUPRENUM, a DMA data transfer unit is a 64-bit memory word. For performance reasons, DMA source and destination addresses are assumed of being 64-bit aligned.

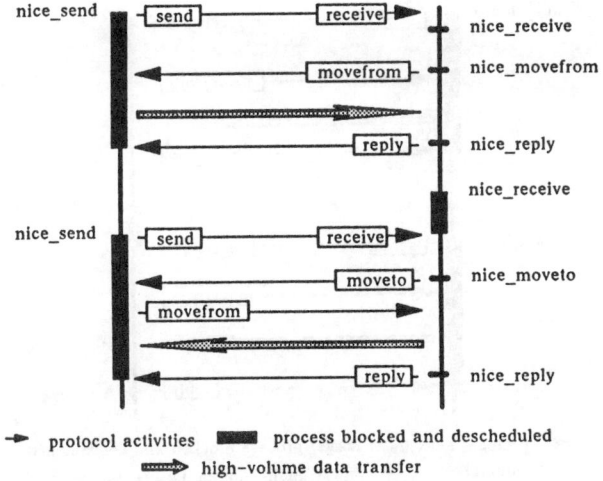

Figure 5: High-Volume Data Transfer

DMA setup is passed to the client site (*movefrom*). In case of writing, first a request for DMA is passed to the client site (*moveto*) which must be acknowledged (*movefrom*) before the DMA at the server site can be initialized. As illustrated in the figure, the implementation of *nice_moveto* issued by the server site is mapped onto a *nice_movefrom* issued by the client site.

A request for DMA setup is coded as a NICE PDU which basically carries two informations (i.e., a 8 byte SDU), base address as well as size. The PDU header is used at the client site to verify the client-server inter-relationship. Thus, high-volume data transfer is only granted if the client is still blocked on the server team. If in case of reading the transfer is not granted, an abort is sent back to the server site, which then clears the DMA. Therefore the need for an explicit client state verification if writing is requested. Before the server site is allowed to initialize its DMAs (and to transfer data) it must be known if the client is still blocked on the server team.

4.4. Synchronization Send

Communication between processes constituting a distributed user application does not necessarily follow the client-server model. This is especially the case for distributed SUPRENUM programs. The more application-oriented way often is to use a *synchronization send* communication mechanism which supports the exchange of arbitrarily sized messages. Basically, a *send-receive-movefrom-reply* sequence exactly implements this mechanism. For performance reasons, it is migrated down to the message-passing kernel. In figure 6 the resulting communication protocol is shown.

As illustrated in the picture, downward migration implies no significant implementation overhead, because already present functionalities (remote invocation

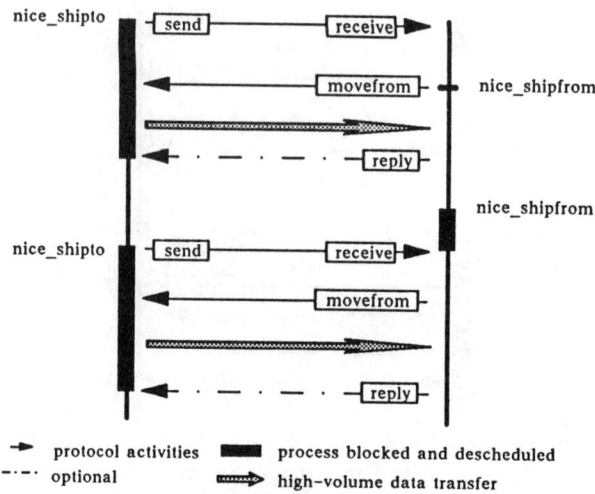

Figure 6: Synchronization Send

send and high-volume data transfer) are used. As a consequence, several sources of communication overhead are avoided. First of all, there are only two NICE calls instead of four. The two calls are *nice_shipto (receiver, data, size)*, in order to transfer a message, and *nice_shipfrom (sender, data, size)*, in order to accept a message; whereby *data* refers to a message buffer of *size* units. Most importantly, however, it is not necessarily the server team which needs to be active in order to read in data segments. That is to say, scheduling of high-volume data transfers will be possible without the intervention (i.e., re-scheduling) of the server team and may be performed immediately as part of handling the interrupt caused by the receive of a data transfer request (*receive*). This requires that the receiver is already blocked, i.e., is ready for a high-volume data transfer.

With *nice_shipfrom* two receive strategies are available, *specific* and *non-specific*. In the former case, the calling process is blocked until from process *sender* a message will be received, i.e., the receiver directs NICE to perform selective message acceptance. In the latter case (*sender* set to *NOPID*), messages passed by any sender are accepted and delivered to the calling process in first-come-first-serve order.

Either a single data segment or a *data vector* can be transferred to the receiver. This is achieved by using the fixed-size message buffer in order to pass transfer information to the server site (*send*). In the present implementation, up to 8 segment descriptors, consisting of the pair {*data, size*}, can be passed this way by *nice_shipto*. At the peer site, the receiver is expected to pass a descriptor packet to the kernel, too, by issuing a *nice_shipfrom*. If both packets have been made available, the receiver kernel automatically will read in data segments (*movefrom*) from the client site. Dependent on the protocol type encoded as part of the transfer information (*send*), a *nice_shipto* may be explicitly acknowledged by a reply message sent by the receiver kernel (*reply*). Note, both sender and receiver are responsible for the content of the descriptor packages with respect to the number of segment descriptors as well as segment sizes.

The primitives *nice_shipfrom* and *nice_shipto* can also be used by server processes to transfer structured data from/into the client team address space. For this purpose, the client (i.e., either the system library or the service coupling module of a PEACE entity) has to apply *nice_send* with a properly defined fixed-size request and response message buffer. In this situation the server is not blocked on executing these two primitives, merely the vectored data transfer capabilities of *nice_shipfrom* and *nice_shipto* are considered by the kernel. Following the pattern of V, large memory segments can be directly transferred by a single client-server interaction. This approach is generalized in PEACE and realized if the server applies *nice_shipfrom* instead of *nice_receive* and *nice_shipto* instead of *nice_reply* to accept and complete a service request.

5. Concluding Remarks

So far, experiences drawn from running the first message-passing kernel implementation [Schroeder 1987] confirm the overall PEACE design philosophy, i.e., the construction of a family of operating systems. The most important aspects covered by the actual implementation are very high-performance inter-process communication as well as good modularization and flexibility.

A prototype implementation for 10 Mbit/sec ETHERNET based configurations delivered a performance between 1 ms and 1.2 ms for a network-wide *send-receive-reply* sequence, depending on whether interrupt handling has been disabled (former case) or enabled (latter case). On the actual SUPRENUM prototype using the 20 MHz MC 68020, the same sequence is performed within 1 ms, based on a software emulation of the CP interface which will be downward migrated into firmware/hardware. In case of local communication, this type of client-server interaction takes about 200 μsec. Interrupt propagation as a message-passing activity to a synchronized device deputy is performed within 100 μsec. Switching between lightweight processes takes 50 μsec for a user-level configuration and 25 μsec for a kernel team configuration.

Considering the 64 byte message interchange between client and server, PEACE performs faster than AMOEBA [van Renesse et al. 1988]. A significant improvement of these performance figures is possible if different kernel implementations for single-processing and multi-processing mode of operation are used. If one will not sacrifice on multi-processing, functionally dedicated communication hardware support is absolutely necessary in order to reach utmost high efficiency [Giloi, Schroeder 1989].

Presently, a verification of design decisions of the first PEACE version takes place and fine grain tuning for the final SUPRENUM release is in work. The near future of PEACE activities will focus on mechanisms for dynamical configuration and re-structuring of distributed applications. This includes a user-friendly bootstrap procedure for largely parallel MIMD machines as well as a generalization of the PEACE configuration and interface language. In addition to that, based on MOOSE experiences a UNIX emulation will be started this year. That is to say, the development of PEACE is an evolutionary course of software design and implementation and, therefore, is still in progress. In this sense, the best way to conclude the paper is to quote John Lennon, namely

> "... *give PEACE a chance* ...".

Acknowledgments

Besides the very productive work of a lot of PEACE project members, the author especially wishes to express his gratitude to Jörg Nolte and Lutz Eichler. Both are the major implementors of the most crucial PEACE message-passing kernel components dealing with network-wide message-passing. Without their meticulousness in making PEACE message-passing work, writing this paper would have been impossible at that time.

References

[Behr et al. 1986]
 P. M. Behr, W. K. Giloi, H. Mühlenbein: **Rationale and Concepts for the SUPRENUM Supercomputer Architecture**, Gesellschaft für Mathematik und Datenverarbeitung (GMD), 1986

[Behr et al. 1988]
 P. M. Behr, F. Schön, W. Schröder: **The PEACE Message-Passing Kernel Family**, Technical Note, GMD FIRST, 1988

[Cheriton 1979]
 D. R. Cheriton: **Multi-Process Structuring and the Thoth Operating System**, Dissertation, University of Waterloo, UBC Technical Report 79-5, 1979

[Cheriton 1984]
 D. R. Cheriton: **The V Kernel: A Software Base for Distributed Systems**, IEEE Software 1, 2, 19-43, 1984

[Giloi 1988]
 W. K. Giloi: **The SUPRENUM Architecture**, CONPAR 88, Manchester, UK., 12th-16th September, 1988

[Giloi, Schroeder 1989]
 W. K. Giloi, W. Schröder-Preikschat: **Very High-Speed Communication in Large MIMD Supercomputers**, ICS '89, Crete, Greece, June 5–9, 1989

[Habermann et al. 1976]
 A. N. Habermann, P. Feiler, L. Flon, L. Guarino, L. Cooprider, B. Schwanke: **Modularization and Hierarchy in a Family of Operating Systems**, Carnegie-Mellon University, 1976

[Kolp, Mierendorff 1987]
O. Kolp, H. Mierendorff: **Performance estimations for SUPRENUM systems**, Parallel Computing 7 (1988), 357-366, North-Holland, Proceedings of the 2nd International SUPRENUM Colloquium, Bonn, Germany, Sept. 30 to Oct. 2, 1987

[Lampson 1983]
B. W. Lampson: **Hints for Computer System Design**, ACM Operating Systems Review, 17, 5, Proceedings of the Ninth ACM Symposium on Operating Systems Principles, Bretton Woods, New Hampshire, 10-13 October, 1983

[Lantz et al. 1985]
K. A. Lantz, W. I. Nowicki, M. M. Theimer: **An Empirical Study of Distributed Application Performance**, Technical Report STAN-CS-86-1117 (also available as CSL-85-287), Department of Computer Science, Stanford University, 1985

[Liskov 1979]
B. H. Liskov: **Primitives for Distributed Computing**, Proceedings of the Seventh ACM Symposium on Operating Systems Principles, 33-42, 1979

[Nelson 1982]
B. J. Nelson: **Remote Procedure Call**, Carnegie-Mellon University, Report CMU-CS-81-119, 1982

[Parnas 1975]
D. L. Parnas: **On the Design and Development of Program Families**, Forschungsbericht BS I 75/2, TH Darmstadt, 1975

[Parnas, Siewiorek 1972]
D. L. Parnas, D. P. Siewiorek: **Use of the Concept of Transparency in the Design of Hierarchically Structured Systems**, Department of Computer Science, Carnegie-Mellon University, Pittsburgh, PA. 15213, 1972

[Rozier et al. 1988]
M. Rozier, V. Abrossimov, F. Armand, I. Boule, M. Gien, M. Guillemont, F. Herrman, C. Kaiser, S. Langlois, P. Leonard, W. Neuhauser: **CHORUS Distributed Operating Systems**, Computing Systems Journal, Vol. 1, No. 4, University of California Press & Usenix Association, also as Technical Report CS/TR-88-7.9, Chorus systemes, Paris, 1988

[Saltzer et al. 1984]
J.H. Saltzer, D.P. Reed, D.D. Clark: **End-To-End Arguments in System Design**, ACM Transactions on Computer Systems, Vol. 2, No. 4 (November), 277-288, 1984

[Schroeder 1986]
W. Schröder: **A Family of UNIX-like Operating Systems – Use of Processes and the Message-Passing Concept in Structured Operating System Design**, thesis, in German: "Eine Familie von UNIX-ähnlichen Betriebssystemen – Anwendung von Prozessen und des Nachrichtenübermittlungskonzeptes beim strukturierten Betriebssystementwurf", Department of Computer Science, Technical University of Berlin, 1986

[Schroeder 1987]
W. Schröder: **A Distributed Process Execution and Communication Environment for High-Performance Application Systems**, Lecture Notes in Computer Science, Vol. 309 (1988), 162-188, Springer-Verlag, Proceedings of the International Workshop on "Experiences with Distributed Systems", Kaiserslautern (West Germany), Sept. 28 - 30, 1987

[Schroeder 1988]
W. Schröder: **PEACE: A Distributed Operating System for an MIMD Message-Passing Architecture**, Third International Conference on Supercomputing, Boston, MA, May 15-20, 1988

[Young et al. 1987]
M. Young, A. Tevanian, R. Rashid, D. Golub, J. Eppinger, J. Chew, W. Bolosky, D. Black, R. Baron: **The Duality of Memory and Communication in the Implementation of a Multiprocessor Operating System**, ACM Operating Systems Review, 21, 5, Proceedings of the Eleventh ACM Symposium on Operating Systems Principles, Austin, Texas, 1987

[van Renesse et al. 1988]
R. van Renesse, H. van Staveren, A. S. Tanenbaum: **Performance of the World's Fastest Distributed Operating System**, ACM Operating Systems Review, 22, 4, 1988

Virtual Memory Management in Chorus

Vadim Abrossimov, Marc Rozier and Michel Gien

Chorus systèmes, 6, ave. Gustave Eiffel, 78182 Saint-Quentin-en-Yvelines cedex (France)
Tel: +33 1 30 57 00 22, Fax: +33 1 30 57 00 66, E-mail: mr@chorus.fr

Abstract

The Chorus technology has been designed for building "new generations" of open, distributed, scalable operating systems. It is based on a small kernel onto which operating systems are built as sets of distributed cooperating servers. This paper presents the Virtual Memory Management service provided by the Chorus kernel. Its abstractions, interfaces and some implementation issues are discussed. Some examples of the use of this interface by our distributed Unix implementation are given.

1 Introduction

The Chorus[1] technology has been designed for building new generations of open, distributed, scalable operating systems. This technology allows to integrate various types of operating systems – from small real-time systems to general-purpose operating systems – in a single distributed system.

Chorus is a communication-based technology. Its minimal real-time kernel integrates distributed processing and communication at the lowest level. Chorus operating systems [11] are built as sets of independent system servers, to which the kernel provides the basic services such as activity scheduling, network transparent IPC, memory management and real-time event handling. The Chorus kernel can be scaled to exploit a wide range of hardware configurations, such as small embedded boards, multi-processor workstations or high-performance servers. Operating systems (called *subsystems*) implemented on top of this kernel currently include a full Unix System V[2] [3] and PCTE [6]. Work is currently in progress to implement object-oriented distributed subsystems [12, 5].

CHORUS-V3 is the current version of the Chorus Distributed Operating System, developed by Chorus systèmes. Earlier versions were studied and implemented within the Chorus research project at INRIA between 1979 and 1986.

This paper focuses on the description of the virtual memory management service provided by the Chorus kernel. Due to the multiple purposes of the Chorus kernel, its memory management service has been designed as a well-isolated component, offering generic interfaces adapted to various hardware architectures and to various system needs [1]. In particular, the secondary storage objects are managed outside the kernel, within independent system servers.

---

[1] Chorus is a registered trademark of Chorus systèmes
[2] Unix is a registered trademark of AT&T.

The outline of the rest of this paper is the following. In section 2 we briefly present an overview of the basic Chorus kernel abstractions. In section 3, we describe the virtual memory management service: its abstractions, interfaces, implementation issues, and some examples of the use of the virtual memory management interface by our Unix implementation.

2   Chorus basic abstractions

The physical support for a Chorus system is composed of a set of **sites** ("machines" or "boards"), interconnected by a communications *network* (in a general sense: either network or bus). A site is a tightly coupled grouping of physical resources: one or more processors, central memory, and attached I/O devices. There is one Chorus kernel per site.

The **actor** (see Figure 1) is the unit of distribution in the Chorus system. An actor defines a protected address space supporting the execution of **threads** which share the address space of the actor. Any given actor is tied to a site, and its threads are executed on that site. A given site can support many simultaneous actors.

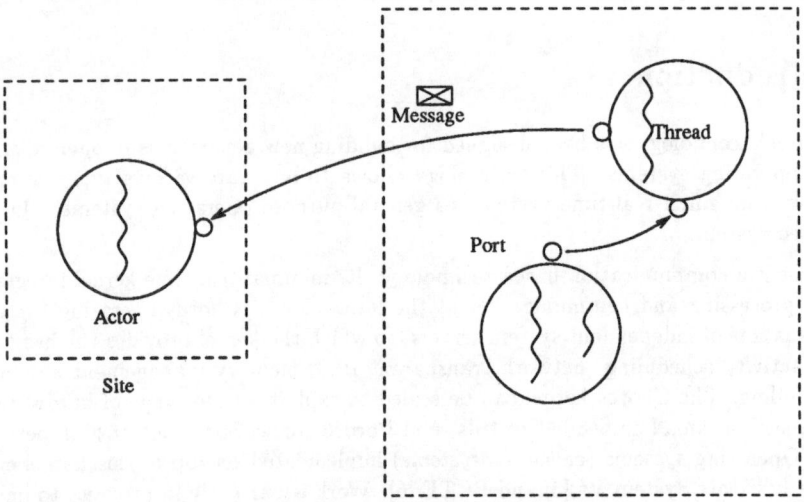

Figure 1: **Actors, threads, ports and messages**

The **thread** is the "unit of execution" in a Chorus system. A thread is a sequential flow of control and is characterized by a *context* corresponding to the state of the processor (registers, program counter, stack pointer, privilege level, etc.). A thread is always tied to one and only one actor. The actor constitutes the execution environment of the thread. Within the actor, many threads can be created and can run in parallel. These threads share the resources of that actor and no other actor. Threads are scheduled by the kernel as independent entities. In particular, threads of an actor may run in parallel on the many processors of a *multiprocessor* site.

The threads making up an actor can communicate and synchronize using the shared memory provided by the actor address space. In addition, Chorus offers message-based utilities which allow any thread to communicate and synchronize with any other thread, on any site. This is known as *IPC (Inter-Process Communication)*. The Chorus IPC permits threads to exchange messages either *asynchronously* or by *demand/response*, also called *Remote Procedure Call (RPC)*.

The principle characteristic of the Chorus IPC is its transparency with respect to the location of threads: the communication interface is uniform, regardless of whether it is between threads in a single actor, between threads in different actors on the same site, or between threads in different actors on different sites.

A **message** is an untyped string of bytes, of variable but limited size[3], called the *message body*. The *sender* of the message may optionally join a fixed size [4] string to the message body, the *message annex*. When present, the *annex* is copied from the *sender* address space to the *receiver* address space. By default, the *message body* is transferred with *copy semantics*. However, options are available to allow the transfer of the body without copying (see 3.6).

Messages are not addressed directly to threads, but to intermediate entities called **ports**. The port is an address to which messages can be sent, and a queue holding the messages received but not yet consumed by the threads. For a thread to be able to consume the messages received by a port, it is necessary that this port be *attached* to the actor that supports the thread. A port can only be attached to a single actor at a time, but can be successively attached to different actors, effectively *migrating* the port from one actor to another. This migration can be accompanied, or not, by the messages queued on the port.

The notion of a port provides the basis for dynamic reconfiguration: this extra level of indirection between communicating threads, enables a given *service* to be supplied independently of a given actor. The servicing actor can be changed at any time, by changing the attachment of the port from the first thread's actor to the new thread's actor.

A **group** of ports connects those ports to a *multicast* facility: either from one thread to an *entire group of threads* (via a group of ports); or "functional" access to a service: a server is selected from a group of (equivalent) servers. A group of ports is essentially a name to which messages can be addressed. A group is built by dynamically inserting ports into, and removing them from, the group.

Ports are globally designated with **Unique Identifiers** (UI's). A UI is unique in a Chorus network. The Chorus kernel implements a location service, allowing threads to use these names without knowledge of the locality of the designated entities. UI's may be freely exchanged in messages; the kernel does not control their transmission.

The global names for other types of objects are based on UI's, but hold more information, such as protection information. These names are called **capabilities** [13]. A capability is made of a UI and an additionnal structure, the *key*. When objects are kernel objects (e.g. actors), the UI is the global name for the object, and the *key* is only a protection key, that users must know in order to be able to modify the object. When an object is managed by some external server (e.g. segments, see section 3.1), the UI is the global name of a port of that server, and the key identifies the object within the server and holds the protection information. The semantics of keys are defined by the servers. As UI's, capabilities may be freely exchanged in messages: the kernel does not control their transmission.

---

[3] 64 Kbytes
[4] 64 bytes

3 Chorus Virtual Memory

The Chorus memory management service provides:

- separate address spaces (if the hardware gives adequate support), associated to actors. We will use the term **context** to name an address space in the remainder of this paper.

- efficient and versatile mechanisms for data transfer between contexts, and between secondary storage and a context. The mechanisms are adapted to various needs, such as IPC, file read/write or mapping, memory sharing between contexts, and context duplication.

3.1 Basic abstractions

Chorus memory management considers the data of a **context** to be a set of non-overlapping **regions**, which form the valid portions of the context. These regions are mapped (generally) to secondary storage objects, called **segments**.

Segments are managed outside of the kernel, by external servers called segment **mappers**. These manage the implementation of the segments, as well as the protection and naming of segments. They export a simple segment access interface (described in section 3.4.3) to the kernel. The subsystem running on top of the kernel must provide at least one *default mapper* to permit the kernel to create temporary segments (e.g. "swap" segments).

A region may map a whole segment, or part of one, in which case it serves as a window into the segment; the window may be caused to slide for sequential access. Protection flags (e.g. read/write/execute, user/system) are associated with each entire region. Access to different parts of a segment can be protected differently, by mapping each to a separate region.

In addition to the mapped-memory access described above, the same segment can be accessed by explicit data transfer, as decribed in section 3.3.

Concurrent access to a segment is allowed: a given segment may be mapped into any number of regions, allocated to any number of contexts; it can also, at the same time, be accessed by explicit operations, by any number of threads.

The consistency of a segment shared among actors of the same site is guaranteed by the kernel, but when a segment is shared among different sites, the segment mapper is in charge of maintaining the segment consistency, using mechanisms described in section 3.4.4.

3.2 Context management

The table 1 describes context management operations.

The rgnAllocate operation creates a new temporary segment and maps it into the context. The initial content of the segment is not defined. The real segment creation is delayed to the first mpPushOut (see section 3.4.3) operation on the segment. The rgnMap operation maps

Context management
rgnAllocate (actor, address, size, protections)   *map a region to a scratch temporary segment*
rgnMap (actor, address, size, protections, segment, offset)   *map a region to a segment*
rgnInit (actor, address, size, protections, srcSegment, srcOffset, srcSize)   *map a region to a temporary segment, initialized from another segment*
rgnMapFromActor (actor, address, size, protections, srcActor, srcAddress)   *map a region to the segment mapped to another region*

rgnInitFromActor (actor, address, size, protections, srcActor, srcAddress, srcSize)
    map a region to a temporary segment
    initialized from the segment mapped to another region

rgnCopy (actor, address, srcActor, srcAddress, size, move)   *copy data from one region to another*
rgnLockInMemory (actor, address, size)   *lock a fragment of a region into physical memory*
rgnUnlock (actor, address, size)   *permits a fragment of region to be swapped out*
rgnFree (actor, address)   *deallocate a region*

Table 1: Context Management Interface.

an existing segment to a region. The rgnInit operation creates a new temporary segment, initializes it from another segment and maps it into the context. The source segment is described by its capability. For instance, when the Unix sub-system creates a process from a file during an **exec** (see Figure 2), three regions are created: the text region, using rgnMap; the process initialized data, bss and heap, using rgnInit; and the process stack, using rgnAllocate. The file system exports two capabilities per executable file: one describing the process text and the other the process initial data.

The rgnMapFromActor and rgnInitFromActor operations have the same semantics as rgnMap and rgnInit respectively, on except that the segment is not described by its capability but rather by its address within an actor in which it has been already mapped. For instance, when the Unix sub-system creates a process during a fork, three regions are created in the child process for the text, data and stack. The text region is created using rgnMapFromActor to share the parent's text segment; the data and stack regions are created using rgnInitFromActor, to intialize the child's data and stack segments from the parent's.

The rgnLockInMemory operation permits a region fragment [5] to be fixed in real memory, so that it cannot be swapped out by a mpPushOut (see section 3.4.3) operation. The rgnLockInMemory causes mpPullIn operations to occur, for any portions of the fragment not previously in real memory. For instance, the rgnLockInMemory and rgnUnlock operations can be used by device drivers to fix buffers in the physical memory during an I/O.

---

[5] Here and subsequently, we use the term *fragment* to name a portion of a region (segment) specified by its starting address (offset) within the region (segment) and its size.

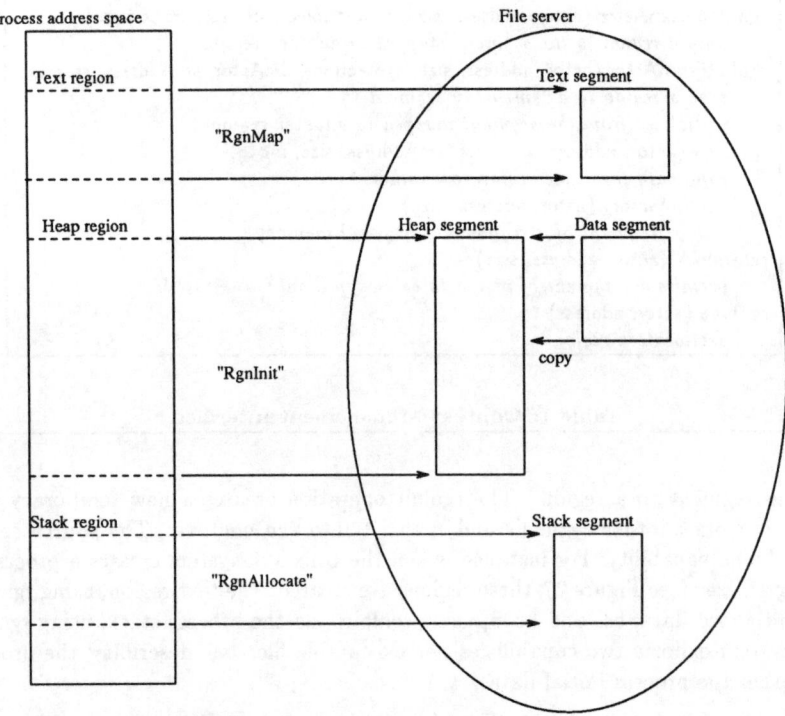

Figure 2: Exec of an Unix process

Segment operations
sgCopy (segment, offset, srcSegment, srcOffset, size, move)
copy data from one segment to another segment
sgRead (segment, offset, dstActor, dstAddress, size, move)
copy data from a segment to a region
sgWrite (segment, offset, srcActor, srcAddress, size, move)
copy data from a region to a segment
sgLockInMemory (segment, offset, size)
lock a fragment of a segment into physical memory
sgUnlock (segment, offset, size)
permits a fragment of a segment to be swapped out

Table 2: Segment Access Interface.

The **rgnCopy** operation permits data transfer between two existing regions. When the **move** flag is set, the contents of the source fragment are undefined after the data transfert. This permits the data to be remapped, instead of performing a copy or copy-on-write. This operation can be used, for instance, by the Unix sub-system to avoid extra copies from the source process address space to an intermediate buffer during **read/write** operations on pipes or sockets.

The **rgnFree** operation deallocates the region containing the specified virtual address.

3.3 Segment operations

The table 2 describes explicit-access interface for segments.

The **sgCopy**, **sgRead** and **sgWrite** operations copy a fragment of one segment to another segment. A segment can be described by its capability or by a virtual address in the actor in which it has been mapped. When the **move** flag is present, the contents of the source fragment are undefined after the data transfer, thus allowing the data to be remapped instead of copying it. These operations could be used by the Unix sub-system to implement **read/write** operations on files.

In a Unix-like system with demand-paging, there are two potential conflicts between read/write and mapped access to segments. First, the file buffers and the page buffers conflict for the real memory allocation, which can lead to a poor use of real memory. Secondly, the double-caching problem: if a segment can be both mapped and read/written, and each access has its own cache, the two caches can become inconsistent. In Chorus a given segment may be mapped in a region and, at the same time, be accessed by explicit operations. The underlying representation (see section 3.4.2) avoids the above-mentioned conflicts.

The semantics of the **sgLockInMemory** and **sgUnlock** operations are the same as **rgnLockInMemory** and **rgnUnlock** respectively.

3.4 External mappers

3.4.1 Segment capability

Segments are designated by **capabilities**, containing the mapper's port name and a key. The key is opaque for the system, and used by the mapper to manage and protect segment access.

For example, a Unix file server can construct a capability for a Unix file, by concatenating the file server port name, the file inode number and a cryptographic protection key.

3.4.2 Local caches

When the kernel decides (e.g. on a page fault or a segment operation) to make available a fragment of a segment in the form of physical memory, it extracts the segment mapper port name from the segment capability, and sends the mpPullIn request to the mapper, using the Chorus RPC mechanism. The mapper responds with a message containing the data.

The kernel encapsulates the physical memory holding portions of the segment data in a per segment **local cache** object (see Figure 3).

The same cache object is used for both the mapped and the explicit segment access, thus resolving the double-caching problem (see section 3.3).

A local cache object is designated by its capability; the server for local caches is the kernel (see section 3.4.4). Using the local cache capability, a mapper is able to distinguish between different local caches, on the different sites, of the same segment, and to implement distributed consistency maintainance protocols.

3.4.3 Mapper operations

Table 3 describes the operations, that a local cache object (in fact the kernel) may invoke on the corresponding segment mapper. The mapper is always invoked using the Chorus RPC mechanism. Any user-level segment mapper server must export all these functionals, (except for the **mpCreate** operation, which is exported only by the default mapper).

The **mpUsed** operation is invoked by the kernel when a new local cache is created. When the kernel destroys a local cache, it signals this action to the mapper with **mpRelease**.

When the kernel needs to fill up a fragment of the local cache, the **mpPullIn** operation is performed. Cached data carries the access rights defined by the **accessMode** argument; when a write access occurs to data which is cached read-only, the kernel invokes the **mpGetWriteAccess** to request write access. When the kernel needs to save a fragment of cached data, it calls the **mpPushOut** operation on the corresponding segment.

When the kernel needs to create a new temporary segment (e.g. on **rgnAllocate** or **rgnInit** operations) it performs the **mpCreate** operation on the default mapper.

3.4.4 Local cache control

Table 4 describes the operations that a mapper may perform to a local cache. This interface is sufficient for a mapper to implement a distributed virtual memory consistency maintainance protocol [4].

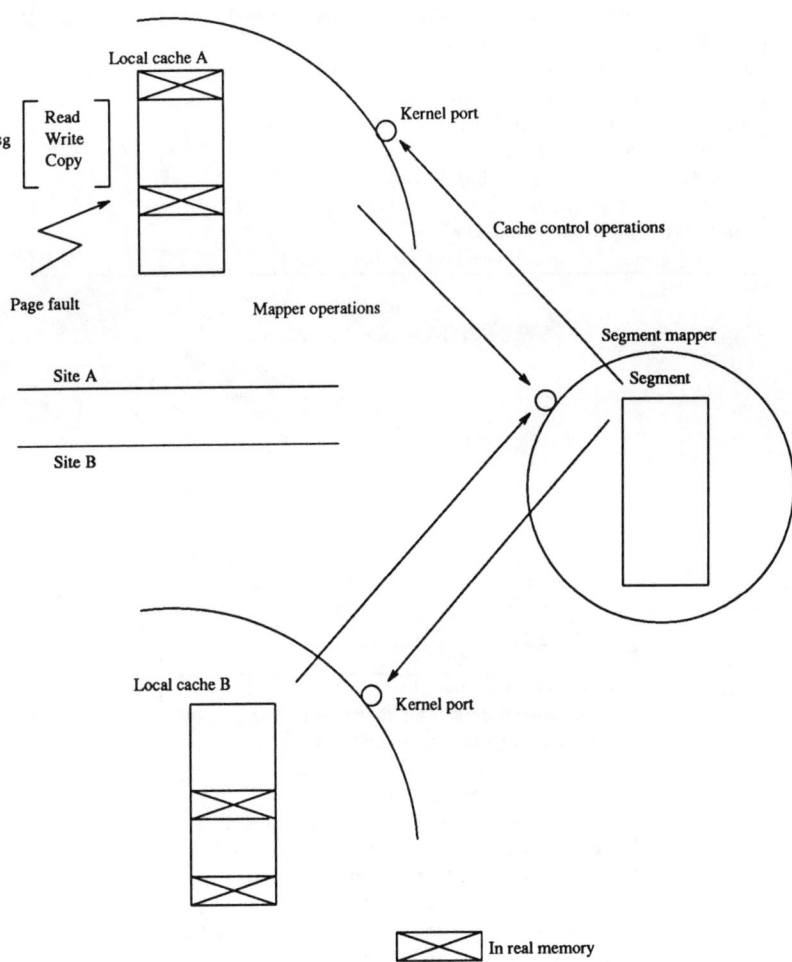

Figure 3: Local Caches

Mapper operations
mpUsed (segment, localCache)
segment will be used through a cache
mpPullIn (segment, localCache, offset, size, accessMode) → (data, realSize)
read a fragment of the segment
mpGetWriteAccess (segment, localCache, offset, size)
request write access to a fragment
mpPushOut (segment, localCache, offset, data, size)
write a fragment back
mpCreate (mapper, localCache) → segment
create a segment that will be used through a cache
mpRelease (segment, localCache)
end access to a given segment via the cache

Table 3: **Mapper Interface.**

Local cache control
chSync (localCache, offset, size)
synchronize a local cache fragment
chInvalidate (localCache, offset, size)
destroy a local cache fragment
chFlush (localCache, offset, size)
synchronize and invalidate a fragment
chLockInMemory (localCache, offset, size)
fix a local cache fragment in real memory
chUnlock (localCache, offset, size)
permit a local cache fragment to be flushed
chRelease (localCache) → ok
release the local cache, if possible

Table 4: **Local Cache Control Interface.**

The chSync operation forces all modified portions of a local cache fragment to be written back (by a mpPushOut) to the segment. The chFlush operation releases a local cache fragment; modified portions of the fragment are first written back to the cached segment. The chInvalidate operation destroys a local cache fragment, without any synchronization.

The operation chLockInMemory permits a fragment to be fixed in real memory (so that it cannot be thrown away or flushed by the kernel).

The chRelease operation demands that the kernel destroy a local cache. The destruction will be refused if the local cache is currently mapped into a region.

3.5 Segment caching

The kernel recognizes two basic types of segments: *temporary* and *permanent*. The kernel itself requests the creation of temporaries (see section 3.4.3); these correspond to "swap" areas for program data. Permanent segments correspond to user objects.

When some segment is no longer in use, the corresponding local cache could be discarded. Instead, the kernel keeps such an unreferenced local cache (of a permanent segment) as long as possible, i.e. as long as there is enough free physical memory, and enough space in the kernel tables. When a program requests the use of a permanent segment, the kernel first checks to see if there is already a local cache kept for it. This segment caching strategy has a very significant impact on the performance of program loading (Unix exec) when the same programs are loaded frequently, such as occurs during a large make.

3.6 IPC implementation

IPC messages serve to transport data, both for users and for the system. Therefore we have tried to decouple IPC from memory management, in that IPC never has the side effect of creating, destroying, or changing the size of any region. In this sense, our concepts are more similar to the V-System's view [2] than to Mach [14].

Messages are of limited size (64 Kbytes maximum in the current implementation). They are not suitable for transferring large and/or sparse data. To transfer large or sparse data, users should call the memory management operations, and not IPC.

When a message is sent, the kernel transfers its body through a temporary segment called *IPC buffer* using sgWrite operation. The kernel manages the IPC buffer as a pool of fixed-sized (64 Kbyte) slots. The number of slots is not limited: the IPC buffer is not mapped in the kernel space and is never locked entirely in physical memory. When a message is received by a thread, the kernel transfers the message body from the IPC buffer to the thread's context, using the sgRead operation. In order to avoid the data copy the move option of data transfer is used if possible.

There is one IPC buffer per site. When a message must be sent to another site, the network manager is in charge of transferring the message body between the IPC buffers. The sgLockInMemory operation can be used to fix a slot into real memory as it is being transmitted over the network.

Future optimisations will concentrate on avoiding the extra message transfer, from the source actor address space to the IPC buffer, when the message is sent by an synchronous

RPC operation, or when the receiver of the message is local and is already waiting for the message.

3.7 Deferred copy

In the implementation of the **rgnInit**, **rgnInitFromActor**, **rgnCopy**, **sgCopy**, **sgRead** and **sgWrite** operations the *history objects* deferred-copy technique is used.

Our technique was inspired by the Mach's shadow objects [9]. When Mach initializes a segment (which is called a *memory object*) as a copy of another, the source is set read-only, and two new memory objects, the shadow objects, are created (see Figure 4). The two shadows keep the modified pages of the source and the copy objects respectively; the original pages remain in the source object. So, the current state of the source and the copy are dispersed across two objects.

On the other hand, when Chorus initializes a segment as a copy of another, two new segments are created: the copy and the *history*. The copy keeps only its own modified pages, the history is to keep the original pages modified in the source segment which always keeps its current pages (modifed or not). So, the current state of the source is never dipersed, but the state of the copy may be dispersed across three segments. The advantages and performance of the history objects technique are described in detail in [1].

4 Conclusion

Like the other kernel services, the Chorus virtual memory management service has been designed as a set of basic tools, suited for versatile implementations of various system policies. In particular, memory objects are managed outside the kernel, by user-level servers. The tools provided by the kernel allow these servers to manage object caching and cache consistency with their own specific policies. All the interactions between these servers and the intra-kernel memory management services are performed via the Chorus network-transparent IPC: these servers may be distributed as needed, allowing a great variety of configurations.

The Chorus virtual memory management has been designed to be highly portable on a wide range of modern hardware architectures. It is mostly written in C++, and a small hardware-dependent part is clearly isolated from the main machine-independent part. The Chorus kernel has been ported to various hardware: Sun 3, Bull DPX 1000 (a MC68020 workstation with a Motorola PMMU), Telmat T3000 (a MC68020-based multi-processor with a custom MMU), various MC68030 boards and AT/386 PC's. Work is in progress on SPARC, MC88000 and ARM-3 based machines.

5 Acknowledgments

We wish to thank Marc Shapiro of INRIA for his ideas on virtual memory management, and for helpful comments on early drafts of this paper. Many thanks also to Francois Armand, Hugo Coyote, Corinne Delorme, Marc Guillement, Fréderic Herrmann, Pierre Lebée and Pierre Léonard who contributed, each with a particular skill, to the Chorus virtual memory specification and implementation on various machine architectures.

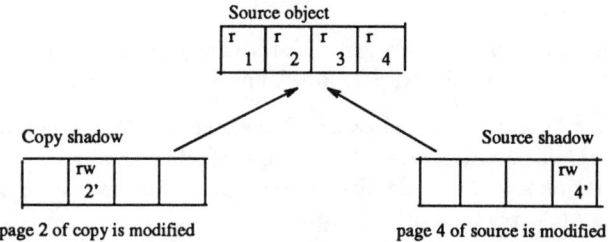

page 2 of copy is modified   page 4 of source is modified

Shadow objects technique

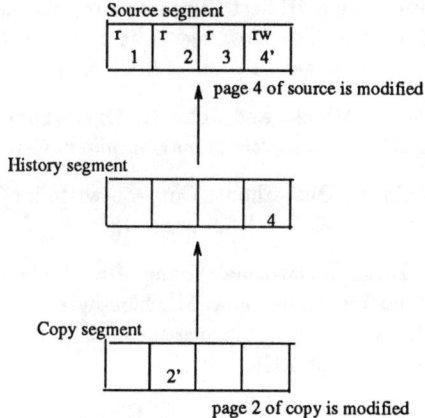

page 2 of copy is modified

History objects technique

Figure 4: Shadow and History objects

References

[1] Vadim Abrossimov, Marc Rozier, and Marc Shapiro. Generic Virtual Memory Management for Operating System Kernels Technical Report CS/TR-89-18, Chorus systèmes, 1989. Sumbitted for publication.

[2] David R. Cheriton. The Unified Management of Memory in the V Distributed System. Technical Report, Computer Science, Stanford University CA (USA), 1988.

[3] Frédéric Herrmann, François Armand, Marc Rozier, Michel Gien, Vadim Abrossimov, Ivan Boule, Marc Guillemont, Pierre Léonard, Sylvain Langlois, and Will Neuhauser. Chorus , a new technology for building Unix systems. In *Proc. EUUG Autumn '88 Conference*, Cascais (Portugal), October 1988.

[4] Kai Li and Paul Hudak. Memory coherence in shared virual memory systems. In *Proc. Principles of Distributed Computing (PODC) Symposium*, pages 229–239, 1986.

[5] Jose Alves Marques, Roland Balter, Vinny Cahill, Paulo Guedes, Neville Harris, Chris Horn, Sacha Krakowiak, Andre Kramer, John Slattery, and Gerard Vendôme. Implementing the Comandos architecture. In *Esprit'88: Putting the Technology to Use*, pages 1140–1157, 1988 North-Holland.

[6] Régis Minot, Pierre Courcoureux, Hubert Zimmermann, Jean-Jacques Germond, Paolo Alvari, Vincenzo Ambriola, and Ted Dowling. The spirit of Aphrodite. In *Esprit'88: Putting the Technology to Use*, pages 519–539, 1988 North-Holland.

[7] Michael N. Nelson, Brent B. Welch, and John K. Ousterhout. Caching in the Sprite Network File System. In *ACM Transactions on Computer Systems*, 6(1), February 1988.

[8] Michael N. Nelson and John K. Ousterhout. Copy-on-write for Sprite. In *Proc. Summer Usenix '88 Conf.*, San Francisco CA (USA), pages 187–201, June 1988.

[9] Richard Rashid, Avadis Tevanian, Michael Young, David Young, Robert Baron, David Black, William Bolosky, and Jonathan Chew. Machine-independent virtual memory management for paged uniprocessor and multiprocessor architectures. *IEEE Transactions on Computers*, 37(8):896–908, August 1988.

[10] Marc Rozier and José Legatheaux-Martins. The Chorus distributed operating system: some design issues. In *Distributed Operating Systems, Theory and Practice*, Springer-Verlag, Berlin, 1987.

[11] Marc Rozier, Vadim Abrossimov, François Armand, Ivan Boule, Michel Gien, Marc Guillemont, Frédéric Herrmann, Claude Kaiser, Sylvain Langlois, Pierre Léonard, and Will Neuhauser. Chorus distributed operating systems. *Computing Systems*, 1(4), 1988.

[12] Marc Shapiro. The design of a distributed object-oriented operating system for office applications. In *Esprit'88: Putting the Technology to Use*, 1988 North-Holland. November 1988.

[13] Andrew S. Tanenbaum, Sape J. Mullender, and Robbert van Renesse. Using sparse capabilities in a distributed operating system. In *Proc. 6th IEEE Int. Conf. on Distributed Computing Systems*, Cambridge, MA (USA), May 1986.

[14] Michael Young, Avadis Tevanian, Richard Rashid, David Golub, Jeffrey Eppinger, Jonathan Chew, William Bolosky, David Black and Robert Baron. The Duality of Memory and Communication in the Implementation of a Multiprocessor Operating System. In *Proc. 11th ACM Symp. on Operating Systems Principles*, Austin TX (USA), November 1987.

[15] Hubert Zimmermann, Jean-Serge Banino, Alain Caristan, Marc Guillemont, and Gérard Morisset. Basic Concepts for the Support of Distributed Systems: the Chorus approach. In *Proc. 2nd IEEE Int. Conf. on Distributed Computing Systems*, Versailles (France), April 1981.

Is Object Orientation a Good Thing for Distributed Systems ?

Chris Horn *
Distributed Systems Group,
Department of Computer Science,
Trinity College Dublin,
IRL - Dublin 2.

Abstract

"All animals are equal, but some animals are more equal than others", Animal Farm, George Orwell.

Object Orientation is a current hot theme for researchers and developers of distributed systems. This paper reviews the efforts of a number of such teams, and considers why, and to what extent, they have adopted a common paradigm.

1 Introduction

Many of us at this workshop are conceiving, designing, building and even using object oriented distributed systems; so are many of our colleagues worldwide. Some systems which have identified themselves with "object orientation" include Mach [Jones86], Amoeba [Mullender85], Ra [Auban87], Eden [Almes85], Comandos [Horn87], and Emerald [Black86]. Why are so many individuals and teams concentrating their efforts with this paradigm? Is it a single paradigm, or is it in fact a catch-all for a number of different perspectives? What are the key ideas in object orientation which are applicable to systems engineering? Are there any weaknesses with object oriented systems, and are the lacks an intrinsic fault with the object model? Will object oriented systems predominate in the near future?

The author is currently involved with the design and development of one of the projects identified above (Comandos, partially funded by the Esprit programme)[1]. Through the possibly biaised viewpoints of my own personal experience, I will attempt to give a perspective on the current development of object based distributed systems, and attempt to take into account the positions of other projects.

---

*e-mail: horn@cs.tcd.ie

[1]The author is also involved in a second international project, ITHACA, which is adopting object orientation: however since this project is in its infancy, it is not reported here

2   What are objects ?

To focus our attentions, let us consider a typical distributed application - possibly a little simplified so as to fit within this short discussion paper. Handling electronic mail letters is a suitable example: tools must be available to for example compose, transmit, peruse and archive letters. Initially, let us consider letters to be simple text. What might be the objects in such an application? It seems natural to treat individual mail letters as objects; also the envelopes in which they are placed for transmission, and also the mailboxes for receiving incoming letters. It is conceivable that we might place the functionality of composing, transmission, perusal and archiving into the mail letter, envelope and mailbox objects: however, following [Halbert87] we might choose to factor out some of these functions into separate service objects. This would be convenient if we later want, for example, to use the transmission service as a general distribution service for documents; or the archival service to store, for example, versions of programs as well as simple mail letters.

How do existing object oriented distributed systems provide a natural way of building such an application? We consider below several possible approaches.

2.1   Client-Server strategies

Currently there are several development teams concentrating on highly performant systems kernels for distributed systems. They all support a client-server approach, in which the servers can manage data on behalf of external clients. The V-kernel [Cheriton84], Chorus [Guillemont84], Amoeba [Mullender85] and Accent [Fitzgerald85] are all early examples: Chorus has now resulted in a supported product offered by Chorus Systèmes, and both the team at Carnegie Mellon University who are developing Mach [Jones86], and the CWI and Vrije Universiteit teams in Amsterdam who are developing Amoeba, are known to be interested in making their work widely available under appropriate arrangements.

Mach and Amoeba are both asserted to support a style of object based programming. Starting with Mach, objects are represented by *ports*, which are protected message queues, and whose names can be transmitted in messages. Ports are served by *threads*, several of which can coexist within the same virtual memory space as a *task*: only one task can serve a particular port at a time. The responsibility of serving a port can be transferred between tasks. Kernel services themselves are represented by ports which respond to particular requests. Using the Matchmaker tool, application programmers can be shielded from the intricacies of message composition, sending and reception, and instead can be offered a procedural interface for sets of typed operations upon objects. When invoking an operation on an object, the object is actually represented by a port: thus the code which implements the operation (in the "server") has to convert the name of the port through which the message was received into a suitable reference (typically a C pointer) to the data structure holding the instance data of the object. Creating a new object not only involves creating a new instance data structure, but typically also a new port to represent the object to clients.

Using the Mach facilities, it would be possible to construct our mail application. Our composition, transmission, perusal and archiving service objects would all naturally be mapped onto separate Mach tasks; each of these services would be represented by a port to which clients could issue requests. An immediate advantage is that the precise implementations of these services can be encapsulated: the only way in which to interact with them is to issue requests to their ports. A further major advantage is that the precise locations of these services can be restricted from clients: administering the system becomes easier since relocating the services to different sites need not affect clients.

Treating the mail letters themselves as typed objects, only accessible via ports, is also feasible but perhaps a little heavyweight. Usually an object is in a separate task (possibly on a remote machine) from a client which is using it. Hence a client wishing to compose a letter just might find herself using the (remote) composition service, which in turn was interacting with a separate (remote) letter object to, for example, insert text. In practice it is more likely that mail letters would not be treated as objects accessible via ports, but perhaps as pure data passed by value between the servers, so as to gain an improvement in efficiency over a pure object view. It is possible that we might choose also not to represent mail envelopes nor, perhaps, mailboxes as pure objects, for the same reason.

Would we gain advantages by adopting the Amoeba model instead? Objects are represented in Amoeba by *capabilities*, which denote both a message queue - an Amoeba *port* - and an additional protected reference. Thus ports are not first-class values in Amoeba: rather capabilities are instead. The message queue is serviced by lightweight *threads* which execute in same virtual memory space *process*. The protected data reference in the capability is mapped within the process to denote the local representation of the object represented by the capability. Thus a difference between Mach and Amoeba is that an Amoeba application might typically use one message queue to handle requests for many objects, distinguishing between the objects by their capabilities; a Mach application might use different message queues instead. Nevertheless, the mechanism to support objects, and object invocation, is still perhaps a little heavyweight, and we might still consider representing our mail letters and envelopes as data, rather than objects.

2.2 Two programming styles or just one ?

The Eden project at the University of Washington [Almes85] attempted to build a complete distributed object oriented environment for program development and execution. Rather than a port based client server approach, Eden used direct invocation of (possibly remote) objects. Each object executed in its own virtual address space, and was potentially multi-threaded. Our simple mail example could be built using Eden facilities and indeed a mail application was one demonstration built using Eden. Eden was prototyped on a Unix base, and coupled with a virtual address space per object, resulted in mediocre performance. As a result, there were occasions when objects were not used when programming an application, when in fact it would have been more natural to have done so: instead the data structure and values of a non-object language (the Eden programming language, derived from Concurrent Euclid [Holt82]) were adopted. We have hypothesised above that a similar situation might arise, under some circumstances, with both Mach and Amoeba.

The subsequent Emerald project [Black86], also at Washington, attempts to redress this discrepancy between programming in the large and programming in the small, by providing a single, uniform distributed object model, regardless of the granularities of objects, in the context of a single language. Observing that application programming can be more productive if a single style can be adopted, the Emerald team have considered how such a uniform model can be implemented efficiently. Vitally, the selection of the most appropriate representations and invocation mechanisms for an object is automatically made by their compiler, thus offering programmers a common perception of objects. From this viewpoint, Emerald would appear to offer a reasonable platform on which to base our mail application.

3 Where can objects be ?

Electronic messages are mobile entities: they are composed and then transmitted to recipients. While being composed, we would like them to be "close" to the composer; after transmission, we would like them to be "close" to their recipients. How well can mobile objects be supported in object oriented distributed systems?

3.1 Client Server approaches

Mach allows threads in the same task to communicate via ports, and hence it is in principle possible to co-locate an object in the same task as its client. Could we consider then moving the mail objects amongst the various services as and when necessary? Although ports can be freely moved between tasks, it is unclear to what extent objects accessed by the ports can likewise be. As indicated in section 2.1, a server is responsible for binding a port to its local representation of an object: if the port moves, then the pair of tasks involved may have to co-operate to pass the instance data of the object represented by the port, as well as the executable code to implement the operations provided by the object. In the case of our mail example, we could consider just passing the instance data of the mail objects (ie the text) between our servers, but this implies that each server in effect understands the behaviour of mail objects, and indeed has the executable code for this behaviour. In particular, both the composition and the perusal services must understand the structure of the message. This seems actually to be the antithesis of the object approach, since separating code and data makes it difficult to introduce new categories of objects into the system (cf section 8.1 later below).

Processes in Amoeba can easily pass ports between themselves or even share the responsibility for servicing a port. This would seem to provide a reasonable basis for handling mobile objects such as mail letters. However, as in Mach, it is not clear how best to pass the objects "behind" the ports between processes: it is insufficient to just pass an Amoeba capability if we want an object to move; we must (somehow) arrange to pass its instance data and the code which supports its methods.

3.2 Distributed Shared Memory

In both Mach and Amoeba, we have observed the benefits of the object approach to implement client-server interactions. However we have also seen some difficulties when trying to support objects, such as mail letters, which are typically lightweight, and mobile.

Researchers at Georgia Institute of Technology are considering an alternative and complimentary paradigm to the classical remote procedure call, under the Ra [Auban87] and Clouds [Dasgupta88] projects. Rather than performing invocations at the node at which an object resides, they also consider making the invocation appear local by fetching the object required for the invocation. They observe two obvious advantages: the principle of locality suggests that an invocation (or other invocations on the same object) are likely to be repeated; and that the support necessary for a slave process at the node at which the object resides is eliminated. This leads to the concept of distributed shared memory, in which segments of virtual memory can be passed between nodes, with suitable protocols (such as writing under mutual exclusion) to consistently maintain a segment. A similar idea, at the level of files, is supported by Apollo Domain [Leach83].

How could Ra/Clouds assist our mail application? One obvious benefit is that we could support our letter objects as mobile, and able to bring them to the node at which they are currently needed. For example, during composition of a letter, the letter object could be co-located with the composing tool object. In the current Ra model, an inter-object call implies a partial address space switch, which may be almost as expensive as a process context switch. The Ra team are considering special hardware support to accelerate this. Nevertheless there seem to be potential benefits over a pure client-server scheme in supporting mobile objects through distributed shared memory.

3.3 Transparency, mobility and invocation

An important goal of Eden was to support migration of objects, but in the event this was not implemented in full, partially due to the complexities in the underlying Unix support. Emerald likewise aims to support object migration. In particular the parameter passing mechanisms, used during object invocation, allow an object passed as an actual parameter to be moved (if necessary) to the site at which the invocation is taking place. Such call-by-moves are a convenient optimisation over call-by-reference, with subsequent explicit migration or a subsequent return call back to the original client.

Movement of objects in Emerald and in the distributed shared memory of Ra need not compromise network transparency. Network transparency is often cited as advantageous in distributed systems [Popek83]. Location transparency is a feature supported by all of the systems we are considering in this paper. Nevertheless there are occasions when transparency might be deliberately compromised - for example a distributed query processor cannot optimise its query strategy unless it knows the location of the data against which the query is targeted. Emerald does include facilities to determine at which node an object currently resides; to move an object to another node; to fix and unfix an object at a node, thus disabling and re-enabling mobility; and to invoke an operation at a specific node.

4 How long do objects live ?

In a classical single-user, non-distributed, object oriented environment objects can usually survive between sessions, for example by taking an explicit *snapshot* of the current state of the system into an external file, and subsequently restoring this global state in a later session.

In our mail example, our archival service would in particular be concerned about long lived objects. We would want to be able to file our mail letters away under suitable categories, and at some later stage be able to retrieve them by "name" and possibly by content. Taking a snapshot approach with respect to the total current contents of volatile memory would not be ideal: rather we would want to safely store away particular objects into the archival service.

4.1 Persistent ports ?

If we consider Mach or Amoeba, treating mail letters as objects only accessible by ports could cause problems for the archiving service. Ports are apparently essentially volatile in nature, because their lifetimes are bounded by volatile tasks: in the case of Mach, when the task which has both ownership and receive access to a port terminates, the port is destroyed. In the case of Amoeba, when all the threads servicing a port terminate, messages sent to the port will fail. Port names and capabilities cannot therefore always be safely stored on persistent storage (since the threads serving them may terminate in the interim). Further, it seems difficult to dynamically load inactive objects (addressed by ports or capabilities) from persistent storage and bring them into virtual memory as and when needed. Rather, the servers which manage object must always be operational, even if the object themselves are temporarily off-loaded to persistent storage.

4.2 Activation and Passivation

Eden considered explicit support for de-activating and re-activating objects. Rather than tying up valuable resources (such as virtual memory) when idle, an Eden object could explicitly passivate itself. Any subsequent invocation to that particular object would cause its automatic re-activation, transparently to the client.

Such a mechanism would obviously aid our mail environment generally, and in principle archiving of mail letters in particular. However the granularity of Eden objects makes it unlikely that we would actually represent our mail letters as objects (cf section 2.2), and so this passivation mechanism actually might not be applied to individual mail letters.

4.3 Management of Persistent Objects

Object orientation is not a theme soley in the domain of distributed operating systems, and nor in programming languages. As a unifying paradigm, it was adopted in the Taxis project [Mylopoulos80] to model office environments and conceptual data models. It has been applied directly in the database arena within the GemStone project [Maier86], which is experimenting with the coupling of associative retrieval techniques with Smalltalk. The Orion project [Banerjee87] is prototyping an object oriented database system which includes version control, change notification, storage and presentation of unstructured multi-media data, and dynamic changes to database schema. The Iris project [Fishman87] has developed an SQL like query language for object oriented data management systems, OSQL.

Using an object oriented data base as a foundation for archiving service would seem highly advantageous. An obvious observation is that the granularity of objects in such environments can be far more varied than those which we have considered in most of the distributed systems above. Of our distributed systems, only Emerald offers us a uniform object model, and can therefore provide us with a seamless connection between programming in the large and in the small. However Emerald does not provide us with a content or structure based persistent store. A further obvious and complementary observation is that none of the above object oriented data management systems really offer us distributed application environments: at best they may offer remote access from a workstation to information stored at a small number of object stores.

Are *persistent* objects an issue with which we, as conceivers, designers and builders of distributed operating systems, should be concerned? From the viewpoint of our users - that is, those whose job it is to build and operate distributed applications and environments - the answer must surely be yes [Balzer86]. With the advent of object orientation, and notably data whose behaviour is intrinsically encapsulated, we can no longer be content with providing untyped, essentially flat, files as the basis for persistent storage.

One project which is considering how the object approach may be uniformly be supported by programming language environments, distributed systems, and data management, is the Esprit Comandos project [Horn87], in which the author is involved. Although a uniform model is conceived, that certainly does not imply that the same run-time mechanisms are applied to all objects, regardless of their usage, or current location. Like Emerald, our support mechanisms distinguish between large and small objects; as in Eden and PS-Algol [Glasgow86] we distinguish between currently active and currently inactive objects. Objects can in principle be registered with an associative distributed store - our Object Data Management System - from which they can be retrieved by "name" or by "content". However not all persistent objects need undergo the expense of associative storage (for example, the overhead of index maintenance) and can be directly stored instead as a bit-image.

5 How can we talk to objects ?

Operation invocation in object models is usually synchronous: the code following an operation invocation is only executed once the results of the invocation are returned. Synchronous invocation conceptually leads to the creation of a "process" to handle the request (in practice invocations can be buffered, with server tasks polling an inbound message queue). In a distributed system, we should carefully consider what are threads of control, and how they may be created; also what role communication channels and streams should play.

5.1 Threads of control

In Amoeba and Mach, an object invocation usually implies the client process sending a message to a port; and then blocking, awaiting a reply, while a server process responds to the request. The *notional* thread of control thus passes between two virtual address spaces and two processes. Servers are active, in the sense that they respond to requests to perform operation invocations on the objects which they maintain: in a sense servers represent *Type Managers*, each responsible for managing all the object instances of a given type.

In Ra/Clouds, *direct* support is given to notional threads of control: when an object invocation occurs, the thread passes from the calling virtual address space to the called virtual space (possibly on the same machine). Rather than considering processes confined to single address spaces, Ra and Clouds thus consider (potentially) distributed threads of control.

Comandos also supports distributed threads of control: if an *activity* requests (synchronous) execution of an operation in of remote object, it may *diffuse* to a (possibly new) virtual address space context at the remote machine so as to use that object. It is also then possible that the activity may *re-bound* back to the original context prior to finishing the remote call. Rather than an activity diffusing, invoked remote objects may instead be fetched across the network and operated upon locally. The strategy as to when to use diffusion, and when remote fetch, is not built into the kernel, and rather is controlled by external policies. The remote fetch mechanisms are somewhat similar in principle to those of the distributed shared memory of Ra (cf section 3.2); however they have not yet been implemented in Comandos.

5.2 Asynchrony and processes

Asynchrony is also supported by many systems. In languages like Trellis/Owl [Moss87] and Hybrid [Nierstrasz87], and systems such as Comandos, asynchronous invocation can also be tied to process creation: a process is created to asynchronously invoke a specified operation on a specified object. Mechanisms must thus be made available to determine the outcome of the invocation, and its results if any: for example Owl uses the concept of an activity set, into which the "names" of concurrent activities are placed, and over which the parent activity can iterate, awaiting termination of its children.

5.3 Asynchrony and communication channels

A further mechanism of supporting asynchrony is to explicitly make channels available as objects to applications. In a similar fashion to Unix pipes and streams, channels can be used as a meta-level structuring tool to bind programs together. The word *channel* is used, rather than "pipe" or "stream", to reinforce the observation that channels ought to be typed in an object oriented framework, and thus are a little different from the bytestreams supported in Unix. In principle channels may well span an internet, and may be a natural way to reflect connection-oriented semantics at the communication layers. Further, if channels can be presented (naturally, as objects!) to application programmers, they can then establish properties such as quality of service attributes.

But is there a risk of dilemma for application programmers if we allow them a choice between synchronous and asynchronous invocation, and yet again between channels and direct invocation? When should they program objects to accept their input from channels, and send their output into a channel? Precisely which channel objects should be used when? Are channels to be (possibly implicit) parameters to every invocation? Do we have a notion of standard input and standard output?

In Comandos, we are considering channels as a typed transmission (and storage) mechanism for parameter frames for invocations. The input into a channel can be a set of actual parameter values (somewhat akin to a conventional stream), or the output parameter frame from another invocation. The output from a channel can be used as the input parameter frame to an invocation, or to a set of actual parameter results. Thus objects can be programmed independently from their possible future use with channels. Each object can be invoked directly, or via a channel, at will. It seems important to us to be able to support such meta-level structuring facilities, without compromising the objects already developed.

6 Protecting objects

Capabilities have been traditionally been associated with systems which are to a greater or lesser extent object-based (for example the Cambridge CAP [Wilkes79], IBM System/38 [IBM80], CAL [Lampson76], Hydra [Jones75]; and in particular Eden, Mach and Amoeba). They are a powerful mechanism since an administrator can easily alter the rights of an individual user, once his/her capabilities are known.

Clouds also uses capabilities as a basis for object protection. However in the first prototype of Clouds, presumably simply to speed implementation of the rest of the system, the capabilities were not themselves protected. However, even if the capabilities in Clouds are protected, there appears to be a problem with the concept of distributed shared memory. On an object invocation, the memory space containing the calling object is emptied in favour of the called object (actually, usually page tables are manipulated to efficiently achieve this effect). As we noted in section 5.1, the same thread of control is involved for both objects: the consequence is that the memory space containing the stack for the thread is preserved across the call if the call is local. Hence the called object has to be trusted not to damage (or perhaps not to even just examine) information on the stack. Invocation between objects which mutually distrust one another cannot be achieved with the reported Ra view of distributed shared memory.

Perhaps this is a slightly unfair criticism: after all, in classical systems such as Unix, we all trust the services provided. Equally though, in a distributed open environment, with minimal kernels, mutual distrust is likely to be a greater issue. Damage or perusal of invocation stacks does not occur in client-server systems, precisely because each object invocation results in a process switch from the calling object to the called object: each process has its own stack in its own address space.

In Comandos, we paradoxically hypothesise that capabilities may be too expensive a general mechanism for a distributed and persistent object-based system. Our chief objection to their use has been the increase in length that would be required for inter-object references. When objects can be fine-grained, and when collections of very many of them may be stored in associative storage, object references should be reasonably small. It is likely that many objects may actually have the same protection attributes: for example, the majority of the mail letters I might wish to archive will be limited only to my own access. If this is the case, it seems wiser to build a protection scheme which can handle groupings of objects and amortise the overheads. Further, we are concerned that scenarios of mutual distrust should be supportable if desired. Our current thinking is to consider domains of objects, each of which has a common ownership. If an object invocation crosses a domain, it must also cross a virtual address space (including using a new process stack, to avoid the problems we observed with Ra above). Not all objects belonging to a domain need be mapped into virtual memory at a time: we retain the ability to activate objects on demand, as in Eden. Objects whose ownership is changed may move across domains. Ownership is associated with a *cluster*[2] of objects. Although it might be feasible to consider two formats of object references (one of which was long and comprised a capability; the other, short and unprotected) we have instead considered how an owner can specify, using an access list, what rights other users (or groups of users) have to specific objects in the cluster, and so allow them to perform only certain invocations, and in a protected virtual address space.

7 Are new operating systems really needed ?

The operating systems which we have so far considered in this paper have all been essentially new. Only Eden and Emerald are hosted as guest layers on top of another operating system

---

[2]Clusters were introduced primarily to improve i/o and invocation performance: however it seems wise to also treat clusters as a unit of protection. Note also that a cluster may have just a single, posibly large, object in it.

(Unix); all of the others are implemented directly on native hardware. Each has, to a greater or lesser extent, considered how to provide access to classical non-object based software - in particular how to support Unix applications. An obvious issue is whether it is possible to extend, for example, a Unix system, without altering the kernel image, and using standard Unix utilities to provide support for objects.

Researchers at Purdue University [Dewan89] have built a pre-processor and series of associated libraries to support objects, using Unix with the Sun NFS, XDR and RPC [Sandberg86]. Objects have Unix like file names (which are their persistent names) and have to be explicitly initiated and passivated. Once activated, an object is given an intrinsic process which is able to respond to invocation requests on the object. An object can specify event handlers which are to be called when the object is created, deleted, activated and passivated. The resultant system DOBS is not too different in functionality from Eden and other "native" object based systems. It is interesting to note that the DOBS environment uses access lists as the basis for its protection scheme, primarily because it is built as an evolution from Unix, and can thus adapt Unix style protection model. Nevertheless, the team observe that perhaps object based systems could support protection based on access lists, rather than capabilities, because they are simpler and have been used in conventional systems. Overall DOBS has the very practical attraction of extending a familiar environment; however it has the disadvantage of not providing a uniform and seamless view of the systems and of objects.

In Comandos, our colleagues in Bull and IMAG, both at Grenoble, have likewise prototyped aspects of the Comandos platform as a collection of library routines for Unix System V (with bsd extensions for sockets) [Decouchant88]. The work did not involve alterations to their Unix kernel. Applications can call the Comandos support routines, or make direct Unix system calls. Thus, as reinforced by the Purdue experience, it appears eminently possible to evolve Unix towards an object oriented environment. In parallel, our colleagues in INESC at Lisbon and we ourselves have implemented aspects of the platform directly on IBM PC/AT and NS32000 hardware respectively. A port of the NS32000 implementation to the Digital Vax architecture is underway at the time of writing. Prototyping a complex object system on Unix, and providing feedback to native implementations, has been an extremely useful strategy within our project. The Unix System V, PC/AT and NS32000 prototypes were jointly demonstrated at the Esprit Conference in Brussels in November 1988.

8 Are object systems really object oriented ?

We have considered a variety of issues in object based distributed operating systems: remote invocation; remote fetch; persistence; mobility, and protection. There are a number of additional characteristics associated by many people with object oriented environments.

8.1 Object oriented software

A very clear characteristic of object oriented programming languages is their support for software re-use. Rather than conceiving totally new designs, they encourage a philosophy of considering how the requirements of a new application differ from the software already available: coding then proceeds by extending and tailoring the code at hand. There are three chief concepts involved, which are supported to a greater or lesser extent in various languages: subtyping, inheritance, and paramerisation. Subtyping allows interfaces to objects to be related and extended. Inheritance allows the implementations of interfaces to be related and extended - often subtyping and inheritance are combined as a single mechanism. Parameterisation, or genericity, allows type templates to be defined, which can later be instantiated to construct types, and implementations. Some examples include C++ [Stroustrup87], which combines subtyping and inheritance; Emerald, which allows multiple implementations of the same type, and supports parameterisation; Trellis/Owl, which provides a multiple inheritance hierarchy and parameterisation, and allows hand-crafted operations for component access; Eiffel [Meyer88], which supports multiple inheritance and parameterisation, and adds pre- and post-conditions as constraints on operations, and a mechanism to propagate re-declaration of types when re-using code, using "anchors"; and Modula-3 [Cardelli88], which treats procedures as first class values, thus like Emerald allowing different implementations of the same type: however its subtyping rules are less general (and perhaps easier to apply).

How might the issues of subtyping, inheritance and parameterisation effect us as designers and implementors of distributed operating systems? The ability to extend a system to handle changed requirements is often suggested as a benefit of the object oriented approach. Returning again to our mail application example, it may appear that many of the issues I have considered in this paper are largely superficial *if*, as we stated in the introduction to section 2, mail letters are just simple text. Simple text can be represented using a flat file: our composing, transmission, perusal and archiving services could all easily manage a flat file, and could pass it by value between them as required. Having conceived and perhaps even built such an application accordingly, however it might not be very easy to extend it to handle structured documents. The perusal service might know how to display a flat file: it might find it more difficult to display a composite structure, having component sections divided across a number of objects. Instead a composite document, built using the object philosophy, might "know" how to display itself. Such a document might be, for example, a conference report, as a particular kind of general report; it might adopt most of the methods of displaying itself as would a general report; and it might be used to construct, as a parameter, a sealed letter object. Further, another document might be composed and sent tomorrow, which included the ability to interactively select different graphics images: interaction with the recipient so as to select the presentation of the graphical images would be a function of a component object in the document. It soon becomes clear that we must place at least some functionality (that which is specific to different mail letters) in the mail letters themselves. The other services can be responsible for functions which are independent of mail letters. Further, as a particular mail letter is sent, and stored, and later retrieved, it must (conceptually at least) carry its behaviour along with it. There may potentially be numerous such letters, very many of them having different behaviour and structure. We cannot expect to maintain all of them "active" at once: we must be able to passivate and store them when not in current use.

Although Emerald offers us a seamless transition from small to large objects, it is probably infeasible to consider providing just a distributed environment supporting just a single language. I have mentioned several object oriented languages above: there are probably many more, and naturally any practical system must also provide support for non object languages. The heterogenity problem extends beyond hardware concerns such as byte ordering and instruction sets, and includes differences in programming language conventions, and objects semantics: for example, can complex number objects, which uses rectangular co-ordinates, programmed in C++ and with appropriate arithmetic operators, be used in a graphical vector display package, programmed in Eiffel, and using polar co-ordinates? Tools such as Matchmaker are an early step, but surely it remains a major challenge to develop a canonical object oriented type model, with mappings to and from a range of widely accepted programming languages.

8.2 Object oriented modelling

We noted earlier in section 4.3 the desireablity of including support for persistence into the general mechanisms for object oriented programming. Integrating general programming languages with data base management is traditionally a difficult issue. One stumbling block has often been the notion of intensional and extensional typing: the concept of a class in, eg C++, as a holder for the behaviour of a number of object instances, is different from that of a class in, eg Galileo [Albano87], where it defines a collection of objects having similar properties. Another is defining a common type and data model, so that the data passed to and from the programming and database environments can be kept consistent. Projects such as GemStone [Purdy87] and O_2 [Barbedette87] are experimenting with common object models so as to achieve this coupling.

The coupling of a database environment with an operating system is historically a further problem. [Stonebraker85] describes problems encountered with a proprietary recoverable file store when trying to host Ingres, including inefficient use of the recovery log. Other problems include controlling buffer caches; ability to write-through; lack of structured files; and often poor support for fine grained locking and recovery [Stonebraker81]. Object oriented operating systems realistically need to achieve a close coupling with data management systems, in an open and extensible fashion. In Comandos, we have found the work of Exodus [Carey86] particularly stimulating, as the philosophy of modular, and modifiable, database systems is attractive. The low level stores of the two projects, as uninterpreted byte sequences of arbitrary sizes, are similar; some of the functionality of the Exodus type manager and E language support reappear in Comandos. Yet a further problem is how to store objects for efficient retrieval [Valduriez86] [Deppisch86]. It seems clear that any realistic system must support the ability to tailor storage mechanisms to the requirements of particular application services.

9 Can it all be brought together ?

Is it really possible to build an integrated development and operational environment, based on object invocation? We have alluded to facets of the challenge in this paper, and particularly noted the problems faced in attempting to unify distribution, persistence and general programming. We have ignored further issues, such as:

- concurrency control, atomicity and recovery: what are reasonable models for concurrency in distributed object systems? How should atomicity be supported? Can the concurrency and recovery mechanisms implemented in the persistent environment be made generally available to application programmers?

- fault tolerance: are models such as ISIS [Birman87] a reasonable basis for building resilient object systems? Can the ISIS concepts of *virtual synchrony* and *process groups* be applied in a uniform object model?

- operational management: does object orientation materially improve, or even effect, the problems of management, particularly of large scale systems?

- standards: can object invocation evolve existing de facto standards, such as X/Open? Can distributed object systems exploit OSI protocols, such as ROS? Can they be used as a basis of application layer implementations, such as X.500? Can the ODP workitem provide a canonical computational, and even a canonical type, model?

- performance: despite Simula-67, object oriented programming languages such as Smalltalk-80; object oriented distributed systems such as Eden; and object oriented data management systems such as GemStone, all have historically had mediocre performance on conventional hardware. Is this an intrinsic fault with the paradigm, and is it overly ambitious to seek an integrated environment? The performance of systems such as Mach and Amoeba are generally excellent and perhaps this is precisely due to careful attention to engineering tradeoffs. Yet reasonable performance has also been reported for Emerald. Our own preliminary results in Comandos have also been encouraging [Marques88], but these were for incomplete implementations.

The challenges remain. An integrated development and operational distributed environment is aesthetically, and industrially, desireable: the degree to which we, as researchers and developers, can achieve it in a realistic and useable manner is currently an intrigue.

10 Acknowledgements

A large number of talented people have contributed greatly to the Comandos project. In thanking them here, I would also note that the views expressed in this paper are my own, and that therefore these views may not reflect those of my colleagues: nor can my colleagues be blamed for any inaccuracies made in this paper.

Within TCD, I would greatly acknowledge the work and input of Sean Baker, Vinny Cahill, Donal Daly, Alexis Donnelly, Ahmed El-Habbash, Eddie Finn, Andre Kramer, Damien Lynch, Maurice Martin, Faris Naji, Annrai O'Toole, John Slattery, Gradimir Starovic, Brendan Tangney, Bridget Walsh and Iseult White. Finally all the TCD team owe our special thanks to the work of Neville Harris as TCD project director.

I am also conscious of my indebtedness to my many colleages outside of TCD with whom we have collaborated in Esprit Comandos. I would in particular express my appreciation to Jose Alves Marques, Roland Balter, Elisa Bertino, Richard Cooper, Dominique Decouchant, Paulo Guedes, David Harper, Sacha Krakowiak, Helmut Meitner, Marie Meysembourg, Andreas Ness, Paulo Pinto, Andrew Redman, Xavier Rousset de Pina, and Gerard Vandome.

Finally, I would like to thank Robbert van Renesse for clarifying some of my understanding of Amoeba: I take full responsibility if there remain any inaccuracies with respect to its presentation in this paper.

References

[Albano87] A. Albano, G. Ghelli, M. Occhiuto and R. Orsini "A Strongly Typed Interactive Object Oriented Database Programming Language" *1986 International Workshop in Object Oriented Database Systems*, pp94-103, Sept 1986.

[Almes85] G. Almes, A. Black, E. Lazowska and J. Noe, "The Eden System: A Technical Review", *IEEE Software Engineering*, Vol SE-11, No 1, pp43-58, Jan 1985.

[Auban87] J. Bernabéu Aubán, P. Hutto and M. Yousef Khalidi, "The Architecture of the Ra Kernel", *Technical Report GIT-ICS-87/35*, Georgia Institute of Technology, 1987.

[Balzer86] R. Balzer "Living in the next generation Operating System" *Proceedings of IFIP 10th World Congress*, Sept 1986.

[Banerjee87]   J. Banerjee, H-T Chou, J. Garza, W. Kim, D. Woelk and N. Ballou "Data Model Issues for Object-Oriented Applications", *ACM Transactions on Office Information Systems*, Vol 5, No 1, pp3-26, January 1987.

[Barbedette87]   G. Barbedette, C. Lécluse, P. Richard and F. Velez "Connecting the O_2 Data Model to Programming Languages" *Rapport Technique Altair 13-87*, November 1987.

[Birman87]   K. Birman and T. Joseph "Exploiting Virtual Synchrony in Distributed Systems" *Technical Report TR87-811*, Department of Computer Science, Cornell University, February 1987.

[Black86]   A. Black, N. Hutchinson, E. Jul and H. Levy, "Object structure in the Emerald system", *University of Washington*, Seattle, TR 86-04-03, April 1986. (also in proceedings of OOPSLA '86, Portland Oregon, Sept 1986 reproduced in ACM SIGPLAN Notices, Vol 21, No. 11, Nov 1986).

[Cardelli88]   L. Cardelli, J. Donahue, L. Glassman, M. Jordan, B. Kalsow and G. Nelson "Modula-3 report" *Digital Systems Research Centre*, August 1988.

[Carey86]   M. Carey et al., "The Architecture of the EXODUS Extensible DBMS", *proceedings of the 1986 International Workshop on Object-Oriented Database Systems*, IEEE Computer Society Press, Asilomar California, Sept 1986

[Cheriton84]   D.R. Cheriton, "The V. Kernel: a software base for distributed systems". *IEEE Software*, Vol 1 No2, pp19-43, April 1984.

[Dasgupta88]   P. Dasgupta, R. LeBlanc and W. Appelba "The Clouds Distributed Operating System", *Proceedings of the Eighth IEEE Distributed Computing Symposium*, pp2-9, June 1988.

[Decouchant88]   D. Decouchant et al., "Implementation of an Object-Oriented Distributed System Architecture on Unix", *proceedings of Autumn EUUG Conference*, 1988, Cascais Portugal, October 1988.

[Deppisch86]   U. Deppisch, H.B. Paul, and H-J Schek, "A storage system for complex objects", *proceedings of the 1986 International Workshop on Object-Oriented Database Systems*, IEEE Computer Society Press, Asilomar California, Sept 1986

[Dewan89]   P. Dewan and E. Vasilik "Supporting Objects in a Conventional Operating System" *Proceedings of Usenix Winter'89 meeting*, pp273-285, February 1989.

[Fishman87]   D. Fishman, D. Beech, H. Cate, E. Chow, T. Connors, J. Davis, N. Derrett, C. Hoch, W. Kent, P. Lyngbaek, B. Mahbod, M. Neimat, T. Ryan and M. Shan "Iris: an Object Oriented Database Management System", *ACM Transactions on office Information Systems*, Vol 5, No 1, pp48-69, January 1987.

[Fitzgerald85]   R. Fitzgerald and R. Rashid "The Integration of Virtual Memory Management and Interprocess Communication in Accent" *Proceedings of Tenth ACM Symposium on Operating Systems Principles*, December 1985.

[Glasgow86]   Persistent Programming Research Group, "PS-algol reference manual - third edition", *Persistent Programming Research Report 12*, Department of Computing Science, University of Glasgow and Department of Computational Science, University of St. Andrews, November 1986.

[Guillemont84]   M. Guillemont, H. Zimmermann, G. Morisset and J.S. Banino "Chorus: une architecture pour les systèmes répartis" *INRIA Rapports de Recherche*, No 274, March 1984.

[Halbert87]   D. Halbert and P. O'Brien "Using Types and Inheritance in Object-Oriented Programming", *IEEE Software*, September 1987.

[Holt82]   R.C. Holt "A short introduction to Concurrent Euclid", *SIGPLAN Notices*, Vol 17, No 5, pp60-79, May 82.

[Horn87]   C. Horn and S. Krakowiak "Object Oriented Architecture for Distributed Office Systems", *Proceedings of 1987 Esprit Conference*, North Holland, September 1987.

[IBM80]　　　　IBM, *IBM System/38 Technical Developments*, July 1980.

[Jones75]　　　A. Jones and W. Wulf, "Towards the Design of Secure Systems", *Software Practice and Experience*, Vol 5, pp 321-326, 1975.

[Jones86]　　　M. Jones and R. Rashid "Mach and Matchmaker: Kernel and Language Support for Object-Oriented Distributed Systems", *Proceedings OOPSLA '86*, pp 67-77, September 1986.

[Lampson76]　　B. Lampson and H. Sturgis, "Reflections on Operating System Design", *Communications of the ACM*, Vol 19, No. 5, May 1976.

[Leach83]　　　P. Leach, P. Levine, B. Douros, J. Hamilton, D. Nelson, B. Stumpf "The Architecture of an Integrated Local Network", *IEEE Journal on Selected Areas in Communications*, pp843-857, Vol SAC-1, No 5, November 1983.

[Marques88]　　J. Alves Marques, R. Balter, V. Cahill, P. Guedes, N. Harris, C. Horn, S. Krakowiak, A. Kramer, J. Slattery, and G. Vandome, "Implementing the Comandos Architecture", *Esprit'88: Putting the Technology to Use*, pp1140-1157, 1988 North-Holland.

[Maier86]　　　D. Maier, J. Stein, A. Otis and A. Purdy "Development of an Object Oriented DBMS", *Proceedings of ACM OOPSLA '86* Portland, Oregon, pp472-482, Sept 1986.

[Meyer88]　　　B. Meyer "Object Oriented Software Construction", *Prentice Hall*, 1988.

[Moss87]　　　J.E. Moss and W. Kohler "Concurrency Features for the Trellis/Owl Language" *Proceedings of ECOOP'87*, Springer-Verlag, June 1987, pp223-232.

[Mylopoulos80]　J. Mylopoulos, P. Bernstein and H. Wong "A Language Facility for Designing Data Intensive Applications", *ACM Transactions on Database Systems*, Vol 5, No 2, pp185-207, June 1980.

[Mullender85]　S. Mullender, "Principles of Distributed Operating System Design", Mathematisch Centrum, *Vrije Univeriseit*, Amsterdam, October 1985.

[Nierstrasz87]　O. Nierstrasz "Hybrid - a Language for Programming with Active Objects" *Objects and Things*, Centre Universitaire d'Informatique, Genève, March 1987.

[Popek83]　　　G. Popek and B. Walker "Transparency and its Limits in Distributed Operating Systems" *Personal Computer Workshop*, sponsored by Digital Equipment Corporation, San Francisco, June 1983.

[Purdy87]　　　A. Purdy, B. Schuchardt and D. Maier "Integrating an Object Server with Other Worlds" *ACM Transactions on Office Information Systems*, Vol 5, No 1, pp27-47, January 1987.

[Sandberg86]　　R. Sandberg "The Sun Network File System: Implementation and Experience", *Proceedings of EUUG Spring 1986 meeting*, Florence.

[Stonebraker81]　M. Stonebraker "Operating System Support for Database Management", *Communications of the ACM*, Vol 17, pp412-418, July 1981.

[Stonebraker85]　M. Stonebraker, D. DuBourdieux and W. Edwards, "Problems in supporting Database Transactions in an Operating System Transaction Manager", *ACM SIGOPS*, pp6-14, January 1985.

[Stroustrup87]　B. Stroustrup "The C++ Programming Language" *Addison-Wesley*, 1987.

[Valduriez86]　P. Valduriez, S. Khoshafian and G. Copeland, "Implementation Techniques of Complex Objects", *Proceedings of the Twelfth VLDB*, pp101-109, August 1986.

[Wilkes79]　　　M. Wilkes and R. Needham, "The Cambridge CAP Computer and its Operating System", *Computer Science Library*, 1979.

Experiences with a Portable Network Operating System

K. Geihs and H. Schmutz

IBM European Networking Center
P.O. Box 10 30 68
6900 Heidelberg
W-Germany

Abstract

DACNOS (Distributed Academic Computing Network Operating System) is a prototype network operating system that facilitates cooperation in heterogeneous multi-vendor computing environments. It is an add-on software system that does not replace nor interfere with the existing host operating system, but enables resource sharing with integrated access control and resource management across the network of heterogeneous computers. We describe the DACNOS design goals and the resulting architecture. Our main focus is on our experiences with the development and use of the prototype. In particular we comment on the portability of the system and the experience with newly written applications. It has been shown that DACNOS is a powerful and convenient application enabling platform for distributed computing in heterogeneous environments.

1. Introduction

The main goal of the DAC (Distributed Academic Computing) project was to provide support for distributed computing in an academic environment. There - and in most historically grown computing infrastructures - one typically finds a rather heterogeneous collection of computer systems. This heterogeneity encompasses machine architectures, operating systems, data communication networks and access control and management. DACNOS is a prototype for a network operating system that facilitates protected resource sharing between autonomous heterogeneous computers.

The need for resource sharing was felt strongly, but the available system support, i.e. transport level interfaces, made the development of distributed applications a difficult task and only a few specialized distributed applications existed before DACNOS. With DACNOS most of the added complexity of distribution and heterogeneity is handled by the NOS. It provides a high degree of transparency such that the development of a distributed application is very similar to a non-distributed one. The productivity of an application developer is significantly increased through relieving him from dealing with e.g. communication protocols, communication error handling or data conversion.

One possibility to tackle the heterogeneity is to enforce a single operating system onto all machines. In the historically grown heterogeneous academic computing environment we could not do so, and in many large organizations this would not be a choice either simply because it is economically infeasible to replace the existing base of applications. Therefore, our objectives were:

- The native user interfaces of the participating Operating Systems should remain unchanged. Applications of the native system should continue to run unmodified (Coexistence).

- Users should be able to access remote resources from their own native environment without having to learn anything about the remote system. Ideally, the users would access remote resources in the same way as local resources (Access Transparency). For example, the user of system A should be able to edit a file from remote system B with the native editor of system A.

- Node autonomy should not be affected. It should be easy for the owner of a node to grant access to selected remote users. It should be at least equally easy to prevent access from unauthorized users. Clearly, in an environment with open access to computing equipment the question of identifying accessible resources, of authorization, of resource management and of accounting need to be solved systematically in a way which preserves node autonomy.

- The developed solution should be integrated with local systems in a way which reduces the complexity of portation of the system to another system (Portability).

- There should be no dependency on specific underlying network architectures and protocols. Concepts and Services for the transport of messages should be based on open, public network architectures. To achieve a maximum of connectivity, these services should be offered independent of the underlying network architecture.

The main focus of this paper is on the experience with the development and use of the DACNOS prototype. Other publications [1.,2.] present more information on the DACNOS design philosophy, software architecture and implementation structures. Related work is discussed in [3.]. Section 2 of this paper contains a brief overview over the DACNOS design. Section 3 presents implementation aspects and experiences with the portability of the system. Section 4 shows results and interpretation of a performance analysis. Finally, in Section 5 we talk about our conclusions and the lessons that we learned from working on and with DACNOS.

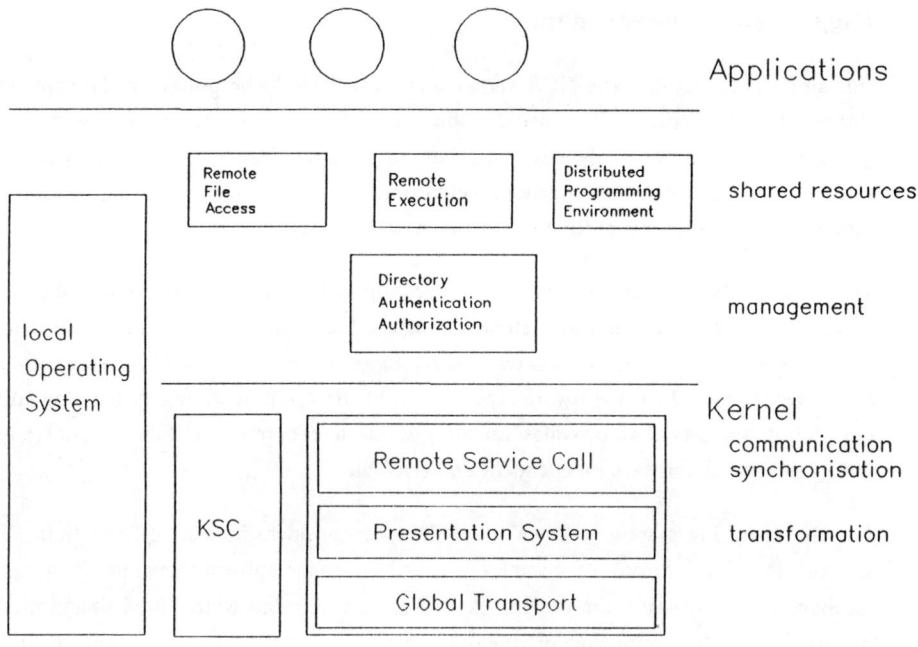

Figure 1: The Components of the DAC Network Operating System

2. Design Overview

Figure 1 shows the component structure of a DACNOS node. The NOS is an extension of and coexists with the host operating system. Application programs have access to the operating system services and to the NOS extension. The NOS consists of the kernel and of system services. Applications may use the available system services and - at the lowest level - the Remote Service Call interface in order to achieve and manage distributed cooperation. A service is a distributed application consisting of clients and of one or more servers residing at - in general - dedicated nodes.

The kernel is "resident" in each logical DACNOS node. It consists of the following functional units: the portability environment (Kernel Service Call and Global Transport), the Remote Service Call (RSC) including the data presentation component, the management oriented system services (e.g. directory, authentication, authorization, accounting) and services to share system level resources (e.g. files, remote execution, remote libraries). The system services are implemented as applications on the NOS kernel.

Host System Independency

Our aim was to develop the NOS kernel such that it could be ported to different machines with little effort. We consider this not only to be a software engineering requirement and economically desirable, but an integral design goal for a *systematic* solution for arbitrarily heterogeneous environments. Modularity and separation of functions were (once more) the keys to the system design.

The kernel software makes use of a) the operating system services and b) the data communication services of the host system. These are the main issues when discussing host system dependencies. Our approach to solve these problems is "to add coherent interfaces", i.e. we introduce a software layer on top of the given operating system and communication services that provides on all systems a coherent interface and therefore makes the kernel software independent and portable.

For the operating system "surface" the following considerations were important. To support the development of complex, layered protocol software one needs suitable mechanisms to structure the design. A well-understood and widely used design methodology is the decomposition of functions into a set of processes that perform independent tasks concurrently. They are particularly useful for layered architectures where it is important to facilitate the handling of asynchronous events, e.g. device driver interrupts or timeouts. Heavy weight processes, i.e. processes with their own address space, are not useful. Instead, required are *light weight processes* which are characterized by shared memory and efficient, low overhead inter-process communication and dispatching. In addition some form of timer support and a convenient way to wait for and handle multiple asynchronous events were considered to be very helpful.

The Kernel Service Call (KSC) offers this functionality coherently on all machines. According to our design goals KSC does not interfere with existing operating system services and applications. KSC basically multiplexes the (heavy-weight) "user process" among many (light-weight) "KSC processes" and provides an object-based interface to the communication and synchronization of KSC processes [1.].

For the data transport service we had to find a common interface to a variety of transport protocols and networking hardware. Our Global Transport (GT) component offers a simple datagram-style send/receive interface with a global addressing scheme that hides the actual network structure. Depending on the available communication support between two nodes the GT e.g. initiates virtual circuits, routes messages through gateways or does error control. The GT interface hides all the details of the actual data transport, and thus creates a basis for the independence of RSC from the communication aspects. In any case, the programmer of a distributed application on DACNOS does not see any details of the GT interface (except for some transport addresses) since he is only using application related RSC operations.

Remote Service Call and Presentation

The key component of the DACNOS kernel is the *Remote Service Call (RSC)*. RSC provides an uniform interface for the implementation of distributed applications in a heterogeneous environment. Network transparent inter-program communication together with integrated access control and resource management is achieved via cooperating RSC entities. The interface to these functions is based on objects which are used as building blocks for the cooperation of distributed application processes in accordance with the client-server model.

The programmer's interface of RSC is built on familiar concepts and constructs that are commonly used in operating systems, but modified for the distributed heterogeneous environment. For example, there is a port object which is an access point for requests to some service, i.e. a "meeting point" for service requests and service providing processes. Because of the heterogeneity it carries a format description to enable the correct data translation for requests that are sent to the port. Another example is the window object that represents a data buffer. The programmer will only once have to specify the data formats of a window, and all access is done by *read* and *write* operations whereby the RSC kernel takes care of all the data transport considerations and format conversions.

A major guideline for the NOS kernel design was *object sharing* which is one of the basic paradigms in local systems. However, extending the notion of shared memory to the NOS would violate our autonomy requirement. Imagine the case of a large network in which every workstation has access to all of the addressable memory in the network. To substitute for the shared memory, access controlled object sharing was selected as an adequate solution in the presence of distrust between network nodes. From an RSC application point of view, objects reside in a single global object space. Logical nodes need first to obtain access rights before they actually can perform operations on an object. An RSC object may be accessed, i.e. shared, only if each accessor has obtained the access right for the object.

System Management Services

As part of the DACNOS we developed a number of management services to be the basis for the various applications in achieving location independence, transparency, security and charging for resource usage. Three services are available: Directory, Authentication/Authorization and Accounting. The directory service maintains, distributes and protects information about network resources and services [7.]. The binding functions of the directory are *name to property* ("White Page Service"), *property to set of names* ('Yellow Page Service') and *name to set of names*. In addition a number of client controls are supported. One of them, for example, allows clients to restrict the extent of searches for required information, thereby limiting the costs of information retrieval.

The Authentication/Authorization Service (AAS) was designed to satisfy the following requirements: provide for mutual identification of interacting partners, assist applications in controlling access to their objects and close the security gap introduced by freely accessible workstations. Our design relies on a password based authentication scheme and on access control lists in servers to control the user access [8.]. Subject descriptions are kept in the directory and maintained via the directory client interface. A user that wants to identify himself to the DACNOS specifies apart from his name and password an AAS server capable of performing the authentication. If the specified server is unknown to the user's local AAS server its address is obtained via a special search request. The user's authentication request is then transferred to the specified server which tries to verify the purported identity. Authorization and maintenance of access control lists lies in the responsibility of the respective application servers.

In a local system a service will usually be charged to the account of the user who had requested the service. Also process state and system information is kept in control blocks. This information identifies the user and is used by system services like dispatching, authorization, resource management and accounting. In DACNOS we have provided the RSC *Account* object to extend this concept for the distributed environment. The account object uniquely identifies a service requestor and can be used to support fine grain authorization. Each process is associated with an account object which is automatically appended to all requests issued by the process. Thus the NOS is aware at any time who is to be charged for a service. The server shares the account object of the client during the processing time of the request and accumulates accounting, dispatching and system information into the client's account. Similar to local system facilities the user need not be aware of this mechanism. The account object of a requestor may also be passed to other nodes, e.g. subservers if they are involved in the request. At the end of a request the accounting data is sent to an Account Server [4.] who maintains a resource usage data base. This can then be used as a basis for network-wide scheduling and resource management. (The Account Server has been implemented; a network scheduler is on the way.)

Resource Sharing Services

So far we have sketched those DACNOS components that are needed to provide a controlled cooperation for autonomous computers in a heterogeneous distributed environment. On top of this services we have implemented services that allow a sharing of network resources among the authorized user community [5., 9., 10.]. Remote File Access (RFA) is a particularly important example, since it has been developed mostly in parallel to the DACNOS kernel and had influence on the design of the kernel interface.

RFA is a global homogeneous file system for heterogeneous networks. The file naming structure is hierarchical; the running prototype supports sequential record oriented files. The RFA file system is partitioned into multiple RFA file servers, each being responsible for a subset of RFA files. RFA Servers use the local file systems of the host operating systems. This technique minimizes the effort needed to port RFA servers to different operating systems. It also allows to store the data of global files in local files, thus allowing easy exchange of files between RFA and the local file system and easy maintenance of global files through local utilities [5.].

RFA users run the RFA Client software, which is an extension and - optionally - a modification to the local operating system. The *extension* offers access to the global RFA files through a procedure and a command interface. The *modification* opens the local file system interfaces for the global RFA files. Sets of global files can be bound ("mounted") into the local file system as "virtual volumes". A table driven file name translator associates local alias names to global file names. Global files can be accessed transparently via their local aliases in the same way as local files. Existing application programs can use global files without any change.

3. *Implementation*

Most of the DACNOS implementation was written in the programming language C. Only for KSC we had to code some very low-level routines in assembly language. A few numbers on the amount of code produced for the NOS kernel (excluding the DACNOS System Services) shall illustrate the development work: the KSC component (for VM/CMS) has about 7000 lines of code, half C and half assembly language. The GT for VM/CMS consists of 6500 lines of C code. Both figures vary depending on the host operating system. The NOS kernel, i.e. RSC including the data presentation, has roughly 55000 lines of code and occupies 160K Bytes of memory under VM/CMS. It took roughly 50 person-years to build the current prototype which runs on VM/CMS, VAX/VMS, PC-DOS, OS/2 and AIX.

Obviously, portability also requires that the involved systems have a C compiler. However, using C does not necessarily mean that the software is portable, as will be shown in the following paragraphs.

Implementation Language

C has turned out to be an adequate choice for our needs, although we do not feel enthusiastic about some of its properties. Programs written in "C" are portable to a high degree with the exception of two problem areas.

- The runtime environment is not subject of the language standard. There may be different names for the same function or different numbers or types of function pa-

rameters. In the worst case some functions do not exist at all in a certain environment.
- It is easy to declare and use nonportable data structures, e.g. the order of bit fields and their boundaries is non-standard, only primitive access to bit fields guarantees portability. Unions used to overlay different data structures on the same storage area have to be considered carefully, since different lengths of their substructures on different machines could make them nonportable.

Some problems arrived through deviations between compilers on different machines sometimes even with the use of a new version of a compiler. Just to give an idea, a list of possible aberrations follows :

- The maximum length of names for preprocessor-, local- or external variables (hopefully the compiler warns you when detecting a duplicate definition).
- Default types - an integer may be a short integer or a long integer.
- Sign extension - for example on shift operations.
- Automatic type conversion which is associated with the last item.

Besides these problems we also discovered a few bugs in the compilers which caused quite some delay in the development process on certain machine types.

From all of this experiences with "C" we derived two implications. First we defined a set of additional conventions to be obeyed by implementers of system software. Second there is a constant need for better compilers with cross module parameter checking and extended support for symbolic debugging. In addition the code generated by some compilers is not very efficient, it leaves ample room for optimization. Since "C" is more and more accepted as a standard for portable system programs, we look forward to a new generations of improved "C" compilers.

Implementation of KSC

As outlined in Section 2 KSC provides a coherent, communication software oriented surface on top of the host operating systems. The portation of RSC is basically the portation / implementation of KSC. The amount of work varies depending on what is available in the host operating system.

For DACNOS on VM/CMS each virtual machine (VM) is a "logical node" and represents an independent RSC entity with several internal and potentially many user-defined processes. We therefore had to add a transparent, coexistent light-weight multitasking system to a VM which originally does not offer support for multiple processes. It is important to note that KSC must not interfere with existing applications. Before KSC is added, the "CMS user process" is the only active thread in the VM. With KSC this view of the machine is still supported, but it is possible to create additional processes and thus multiplex the VM.

For VAX/VMS a logical node corresponds to a VMS process. With KSC this process can be split up into light-weight processes that share the process' address space. This implementation is analogous to the VM/CMS version, i.e. a VM in VM/CMS corresponds to a VMS process. The AIX version of KSC is also along this guideline, whereas OS/2 offers suitable facilities (light-weight multitasking with shared memory) that make the implementation of KSC basically a functional mapping.

PC-DOS was in many respects a system with special features and requirements. A PC was considered a single logical node in DACNOS. KSC was implemented by mapping the KSC process constructs onto a multitasking system that was internally available in IBM for the PC. Although this was relatively easy, later on the PC gave us a hard time because of memory size restrictions and lack of memory protection. It is safe to say that the PC under PC-DOS is not suited for a fairly large software extension such as DACNOS. Though we succeeded to port DACNOS to PC-DOS and implemented e.g. the RFA transparent file access client for the PC file system, the applicability of such a PC is rather limited due to the lack of memory. (DACNOS plus RFA client leave less than 70K main memory in a fully equipped PC). We therefore did not further invest into the PC-DOS version of DACNOS.

4. Performance

Achieving good performance of the NOS Kernel was a main goal though it was not the most important one compared to heterogeneity and autonomy. DACNOS is an extension that uses the given services of the host machine, i.e. it is not built directly on the hardware, which usually promises superior performance in terms of execution time for remote requests.

Communication is rather expensive in our data transport network where diverse networking facilities, e.g. token ring, Ethernet, leased lines, standard protocols, proprietary protocols, are connected by gateways to form a global communication system. Therefore RSC was designed to minimize the number of protocol messages sent. For example, we could not use frequent multi- or broadcast operations.

Nevertheless, measurements of elapsed times and instruction path lengths indicate that the performance of DACNOS is well within acceptable response time limits and that the overhead introduced for remote requests is relatively low. To illustrate the performance we have measured the execution time of a service request cycle, i.e. a request is sent to another node, accepted and inspected there, and immediately returned to the sender who waits for the return of the request. Measurements were taken during regular daytime with medium load on the hosts. First we measured three different "local configurations", i.e.

- two RSC entities on one IBM/370 (type 4361),

- two RSC entities on one DEC VAX (type 8600),
- two RSC entities on two PC-ATs on a token-ring.

Then we examined a remote interaction between

- two IBM/370 computers (4361 and 3083), connected by a 64 Kbps line and IBM internal transport protocols,
- two VAX VMS computers (8300 and 8600), connected by an Ethernet LAN and DECnet protocols,
- an IBM PC-AT and a VM on an IBM 4361 connected by a token-ring and IBM internal transport protocols.

The following table shows the results for a basic two-way request cycle:

REQ. CYCLE	VM to VM	VMS to VMS	PC to PC	PC to VM
local	50 ms	200 ms	165 ms	---
remote	125 ms	500 ms	---	345 ms

We were also very much interested in the overhead introduced by the DACNOS kernel compared to the basic, unenhanced inter-process communication facilities of the host system. This is best expressed in the approximate number of machine instructions. For a round trip request the RSC client performs 6000, the server side 8000 instructions. GT (including KSC, but excluding the transport protocol itself) adds another 1500 instructions for a send operation and 6000 for receive. For the above mentioned scenario with the client on a IBM 4361 (1.5 Million instructions per second (Mips)) and a server on a IBM 3083 (5 Mips) this amounts to roughly 12 milliseconds for RSC and GT, a number we were quite satisfied with. If both, client and server, are located on the 4361 and only VM/CMS internal communication is used the processing for RSC and GT takes roughly 20 msec and process switches, interrupt handling, data copy operations etc. take the rest, i.e. 30 msec.

5. Conclusions

With DACNOS the problems of distribution and heterogeneity are handled in the kernel of the NOS. Therefore, the resulting design has to be fairly complex. It is our claim however, that the efforts to do it "once for all applications" greatly decreases the threshold to the programming of distributed applications and thus increases the programmer productivity. Otherwise, there is a great danger to re-invent the wheel over and over again.

This claim was partly proven by students who wrote applications on DACNOS without having much programming and no distributed system experience at all. Within a few weeks they were able to implement applications like remote data base access and and a distributed mailbox service. The convenience and power of RSC lets programmers concentrate on their particular application problem without dragging their attention to e.g. communication error handling, data conversion problems or authentication protocols.

The RSC object interface has been found to be an adequate abstraction for the facilities that are needed to achieve and manage cooperation. It simplifies the view onto the remote interactions significantly, and provides independence of applications from particular implementation decisions in the kernel. The style of the RSC interface is not necessarily tied to the DACNOS environment. We can very well imagine to have such an abstract, generic platform for distributed applications on top of other data transport and operating system environments.

The DACNOS prototype demonstrates the feasibility of our rather ambitious approach to build support for distributed cooperation of heterogeneous systems on the basis of distribution transparency and the local system paradigm. With DACNOS the development of distributed applications takes little more than the development of non-distributed ones.

Acknowledgements

Many people at the University of Karlsruhe and at IBM, too numerous to mention them all, have contributed to DACNOS. We are grateful to all of them.

References

1. K.Geihs, R. Staroste and H.Eberle, "Operating System Support for Heterogeneous Distributed Systems", in *Proceedings of the GI/NTG Conference "Communication in Distributed Systems", Aachen/W-Germany, Springer (1987)*

2. K. Geihs, B. Schoener, U. Hollberg, H. Schmutz and H. Eberle, "An Architecture for the Cooperation of Heterogeneous Operating Systems", in *Proceedings of "IEEE Computer Networking Symposium", Washington/USA, IEEE (1988)*

3. K. Geihs and U. Hollberg, "A Retrospective on DACNOS - a Network Operating System for Heterogeneous Computers", *IBM ENC Internal Report, Heidelberg (1989)*

4. G. Harter and K. Geihs, "An Accounting Service for Heterogeneous Distributed Environments" in *Proceedings of "8th International Conference on Distributed Computing Systems", San Jose/USA, IEEE (1988)*

5. U.Hollberg, H. Schmutz and P. Silberbusch, "Remote File Access: A Distributed File System for Heterogeneous Networks" in *Proceedings of the GI/NTG Conference "Communication in Distributed Systems", Aachen/W-Germany, Springer (1987)*

6. G. Krueger and G. Mueller, "HECTOR", *Vol. I and II, Springer (1988)*

7. B. Mattes and H. v. Drachenfels, "Directory and Orientation in Heterogeneous Networks", in *HECTOR, Vol.II: Basic Projects, Springer (1988)*

8. B. Mattes, "Authentication and Authorization in Resource Sharing Networks", in *HECTOR, Vol.II: Basic Projects, Springer (1988)*

9. R. Oechsle, "A Remote Execution Service in a Heterogeneous Network", in *HECTOR, Vol.II: Basic Projects, Springer (1988)*

10. B. Schoener and B. Kieser, "Transparent Database Access in a Network of Heterogeneous Systems", in *Proceedings of the GI/NTG Conference "Communication in Distributed Systems", Stuttgart/W-Germany, Springer (1989)*

On the Implementation of Abstract Data Types in BirliX

Wolfgang Lux, Hermann Härtig, Winfried Kühnhauser

German National Research Center For Computer Science (GMD)

St. Augustin

Abstract

The BirliX operating system provides abstract data types to its users. All kinds of system resources are accessed by calling type-specific operations on instances of abstract data types. On top of BirliX, the Berkeley 4.3 UNIX[1] interface is implemented by a small set of UNIX-tailored abstract data types. Abstract data types are implemented by an universal implementation structure, called team. A team, representing one instance, joins active and passive resources to one cooperating functional unit. Depending on their role within the team, the active resources are divided into agents and natives. While agents perform the type-specific operations on the instance, internal activities are executed by natives. Administration of teams, i.e. creation and deletion of its components, is done by a team manager. The implementation of teams exclusively uses active resources via light weight processes and passive resources via segments, which both are offered by lower system levels.

---

[1] Unix is a trademark of AT&T Bell Labs

1 Introduction

The objective of the BirliX operating system is the support of distributed, fault tolerant, and secure application programs in a hardware scenario of networks, multiprocessor architectures, and large main memories. In an environment of loosely coupled computer nodes, application programs under BirliX are distributed among the nodes either explicitly as directed by application programmers or implicitly by embedded policies for performance or reliability improvement. In distributed applications the probability of failures grows with the number of affected nodes, if application programs do not explicitly deal with partial system failures by moving system components from failed to non-failed nodes. Failure detection and recovery are major features of the BirliX architecture. Security is a key problem yet, even in centralized systems; distributed systems add still a new dimension to the security problem. A major goal in BirliX is a security scheme providing a high and classifiable level of security.

To achieve a system open for functional enhancement, we constituted two design principles. First, mechanisms instead of complete policies are provided, e.g. BirliX does not provide a transaction system but its basic recovery mechanism supports the implementation of different fault tolerance policies. Secondly, the BirliX design is based on few but powerful concepts, i.e. general solutions are used intensively throughout the whole system.

Abstract data types are the essential concept at the system interface of BirliX. Momently, the Berkeley 4.3 UNIX interface is emulated by the a small set of abstract data types such as file, directory and socket. All kinds of system resources are accessed by calling type-specific operations on instances of abstract data types. Any application program is a set of cooperating instances of different data types. At the user level instances of all data types are named via pathnames. Pathnames are symbolic identifiers within a global hierarchical names space. At system level each instance is assigned exactly one identifier unique in space and time.

Instances are the unit subject to distribution, recovery, and protection. Instances belonging to an application program are distributed among a network of machines. The actual physical location of each instance may depend on policies to increase availability, security, or performance (e.g. load balancing). To this end naming, access, and use are uniform and location transparent for every data type thus providing the essential transparency of network architectures. Transaction management facilities and related fault tolerance policies are supported by operations to checkpoint and recover individual instances and by operations to reestablish their cooperation. Security mechanisms are based on the autonomy of instances and on the authenticity of their cooperation. On that base instances individually protect themselves, thus permitting the implementation of different security policies.

The system is open to future requirements by a facility for integrating new abstract types, both on application and on system level. Integration is supported by providing a primary type, which defines operations inherited by all data types. This concept avoids system disintegration by functional expansion and easily outfits new operating system facilities with the distribution, fault tolerance, and security standards of the system.

Obeying these design principles all abstract data types are implemented by an uniform implementation structure called team. A single team represents one instance. Cooperation between instances is implemented by communication between the representing teams. Hence an application program is a set of communicating teams. In the following the concept of teams is presented in detail. After a short survey of the BirliX system architecture, the implementation of teams within the BirliX system is described.

2 Concept of Teams

2.1 Team Structure

A team joins cpu-like active resources and memory-like passive resources to one cooperating functional unit. To consider the different scopes of executing externally called operations and of internal team activity, the active resources within a team are divided into respective roles of agents and natives.

Every caller of type-specific operations, called client, is represented within a team by one agent. Besides administrating the client specific state of the implementing instance the agent is responsible for checking the access rights of the client and performing the type-specific operations on the instance. An agent is logically divided into a common part, which performs the primary type operations, and a special part, which performs the type-specific operations. As manipulation of instances can only by done via the synchronized accesses of agents, the autonomy and consistency of instances are guaranteed.

Natives represent internal activities of an instance. Examples are garbage collection within a list type or interrupt handlers within device handling types. While a UNIX-process type is represented by an abstract data type with a single native, each task in an ADA-program is represented by a corresponding native.

To increase the cooperation within one team and to defend different teams, agents and natives within one team share a common address space. The passive resources within this address space are a team descriptor and segments. While a team descriptor collects the administration information about the instance, segments contain its proper data.

As an example the team of database type has the following structure: requests to the database are handled by the agents. The natives are responsible for reorganization of data base records. The team descriptor contains the structures for access synchronization and database organization. The database records are stored in the segments.

Depending on the activities within a team, a team is either active or passive. If there are one or more agents or natives within the team, its state is active; otherwise its state is passive. First access to a passive team causes a transition to active. If during passivation of a team its implemented instance is not reachable within the global name space, the team and thus its instance is deleted. State transition is done by the team manager, which renders access to teams by establishing communication connections between clients and agents.

2.2 Team Communication

Communication within one team is derived straightforward from the team structure. Agents and natives in the same team communicate via their shared address space in a synchronized way.

Disjunct address spaces make team-to-team communication a little bit more complicated. The client-/agent-relationship suggests communication via fixed connection. One end point of this connection is the so-called access descriptor in the client team, the other end point is the agent in the called team. All access descriptors of a client are part of its team descriptor (Figure 1). Establishing and removing of communication connections is done by a type-independent team manager during activation and passivation of teams.

To create a new instance of a data type, the client calls the team manager operation Create, which demands a data type as parameter. The team manager creates an initialized team with one agent. Initialization means: an address space is provided and filled with the newly created team descriptor and segments of the team. After activation of the team the agent awaits further communication of its client. The result of the Create-operation is a communication connection

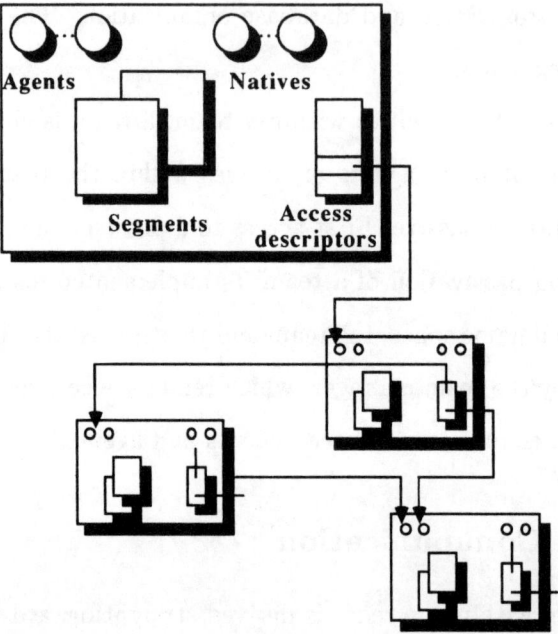

Figure 1: Team Communication

between the clients' access descriptor and the created agent. The returned access descriptor contains the unique identifier of the created instance and the identifier of the agent.

To establish a connection to an already existing instance, the client calls the Open-operation, which needs the unique identifier of the requested instance. If the team is passive, i.e. there is no other agent and no native in the team, the team manager activates the team, i.e. provides an address space and fills it with the existing team descriptor and segments of the team. If the team is already active, only the agent is created and the team descriptor is updated. After the team manager has identified the client as authorized user of the instance, the agent awaits further communication of its client. Again the result of the Open-operation is a communication connection between the clients' access descriptor and the created agent.

Using the returned access descriptor, the client calls operations by communicating with its agent. After the agent has checked the access rights concerning the requested operation, it performs the operation by accessing the team descriptor and the segments.

Depending of the abstract data type natives are created by the team manager during team activation or by agents during execution of the operation.

To terminate accesses to the instance, the client directs the Close-operation to the agent. If there is no other agent or native in the team any more, the team manager passivates the team: if the instance is still visible in the global name space, its descriptor and segments are written to permanent storage. Otherwise passivation of the team means deletion of the instance and its resources. The result of the Close-operation is the shutdown of the communication connection, i.e. the clients' access descriptor becomes invalid.

2.3 Adding New Abstract Data Types

The functionality of the system is easily extended by adding new types, which inherit the predefined common operation of the primary type. New abstract data types are added to the system in the same way new programs are installed in any conventional operating system. Activation and passivation of the teams implementing the new type is still done by the team manager. After the access rights are checked by the common part, the created agents perform the type-specific operations in the address space of the team. As team-to-team communication crossing address spaces is more expensive than communication within one address space, implementation of data types is divided into user teams and kernel teams. While user teams still have separate address spaces, kernel teams share a single kernel address space.

Kernel teams optimize the access to instances by deleting the boundaries of address spaces. This also deletes the boundaries of fault and security. Therefore only a trusted team can become a kernel team. The implementation then becomes part of the BirliX system code. The BirliX system provides kernel team implementations for a set of commonly used data types such as file, directory and some devices.

User teams render the user to extend the functionality of a system by adding abstract data types. Depending on the type definition there is one address space for all teams of a type or for a single team. The user teams implementation makes use of kernel services, e.g. activation of teams and checking access rights, with the guarantee, that neither the kernel address space nor the address space of other abstract data types can be disturbed. So each agent in a user team has a kernel part maintaining the kernel data structures and a user part performing the user specified actions. The kernel part type-independently handles communication, security, and recovery, which are implemented by the system once.

2.4 Distribution

Teams are tailored to distributed environments. Team-to-team communication does not only cross boundaries of address spaces, but also that of local systems. Distributed application programs are easily implemented by communicating teams distributed among the nodes within a network. As instances are the unit of distribution, a whole team resides on one node. To administrate the teams scattered over the network, one team manager exists at each node.

BirliX users need not be aware of the actual location of their data types, but can use the type-independent, distributed naming and locating mechanism. On user level instances are identified by pathnames in a global hierarchical name space. Pathnames do not reflect any location information, they are neither unique in space nor in time. The system constructs the global name space by instances of type context. Contexts contain relationships between instances, e.g. parent/child for processes, directory references for files. To implement network transparency a reference in a context instance consists of an unique identifier and a locating advice. The number of references to an instance is reflected in each instance. Pathnames are interpreted by successive searching through instances of contexts. The last step of identification results in the system unique identifier of the instance. Using the unique identifier the binding facility locates the instance and the team manager establishes the connection between the client and its agent on another node. Besides the unique identifier and the agent identifier, the locating advice is also held in the access descriptor. While the unique identifier of a team is location-independent, the identifier of the agent contains the location of the agent. Once a connection is established, the team implementation uses the network transparent communication provided by lower layers of the system.

As network communication is more expensive than local communication, there are two optimizations in establishing a connection. First, the team is not activated at the node its passive representation resides, but at its first clients node. Additional clients must still communicate over the network, as shown in Figure 2. If a remote activation occurs frequently, a team can be migrated from one node to another. Migration is done by checkpointing the team to its segments, sending the segments to the other node, and activating the team from the checkpointed segments on the other node. Checkpointing a team and activation of checkpoints are operations provided by the recovery mechanism of BirliX. While pathnames and unique identifier are not changed by migration, the locating hints in the context teams are updated and the agent identifiers become invalid. Teams can also be migrated by system embedded strategies or by users explicitly.

A communication connection can be interrupted by migration or by a system crash. To reestablish existing communication connections, the team managers

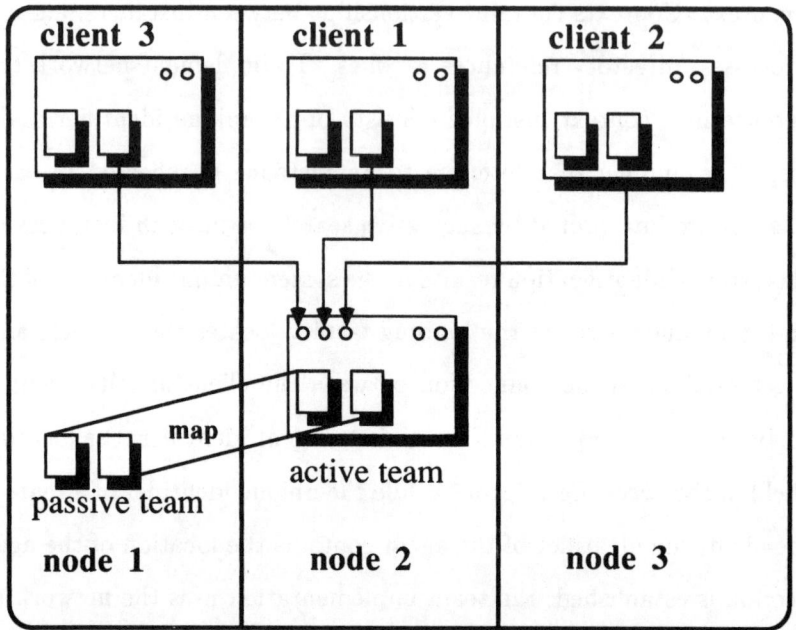

Figure 2: Communication within the Network

provide the Reopen- operation. Reopen connects a client with its agent, which has a new identification and possibly resides on another node.

2.5 Security

In a distributed environment security is a key problem. Autonomy of teams and authenticity of their communication are the basis for security policies, that guarantee the security of instances. Autonomy is achieved by enforcing operational data type access via agents only. Depending on the implemented security mechanism, access control lists momently, the connected agent identifies the client and checks the access rights concerning the called operation. Authenticity of team communication is simply achieved by using the communication primitives of BirliX. These primitives add to each communication an unforgeable characterization of the client.

2.6 Recovery

BirliX provides primitives to recover single data type instances and rebuild communication connections between instances. These primitives can by used by various policies recovering complete application programs.

To recover single instances the primary type exports common Checkpoint- and Recover-operations. When checkpointing a team, its agents and natives are suspended and a passive team representation is put to secondary storage. After a failure the Recover-operation uses the checkpoint to reset the instance to the previous state.

The one-to-one connection between access descriptor and agent facilitates rebuilding the communication connection between teams by using the Reopen-operation. The implementation of idempotent communication calls allows a simple retransmission of interrupted calls.

3 Implementation of Teams

3.1 General System Structure

To put the team implementation in its proper place, the general system structure of BirliX is presented first. As shown in Figure 3 the system consists of four system layers and an emulation layer, which provides the Berkeley 4.3 UNIX system call interface.

The system nucleus integrates single and multiprocessor architectures by providing active resources via threads (light weight processes) and thread communication. Thread administration covers its creation, synchronization, scheduling, and deletion. To synchronize threads that access a shared address space, the nucleus provides monitors [Hoa74]. Thread communication without shared address space is realized via synchronous message passing, which is transparent within the net-

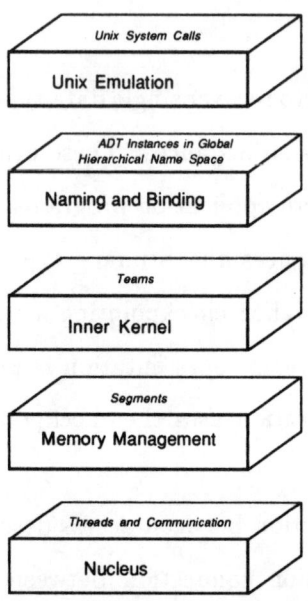

Figure 3: System Structure

work. The basic hardware interrupt handling and the software exception handling are also implemented within the nucleus.

The memory management layer provides large virtual address spaces and segments as single abstractions from storage resources. This abstraction achieves independence of properties of particular memory management units and transparency within the network. Segments are accessed by mapping them locally or remotely into address spaces of threads, hence segment access and paging across networks is a natural property.

The inner kernel joins resources provided by the nucleus and memory management to the implementation structure team. Besides the teams and the team manager, which will be presented in the next section in detail, the inner kernel administrates the kernel address space and an unique identifier data base, which supports the binding between the unique identifier of an instance and the passive representation of the implementing team.

The outer kernel supplies distributed naming and binding of instances within the global hierarchical name space common to all data types.

Abstract data types performing user system calls, i.e. accessing instances via pathnames, are implemented in the emulation layer. The current UNIX emulation layer provides the UNIX system call interface, i.e. the UNIX process team maps the UNIX system calls to operations on BirliX instances.

The implementation language of the system is Modula-2.

3.2 Team Representation

The active resources of a team are represented by nucleus threads. When creating a thread the team manager binds the execution code of the agent or native to the thread. While threads in different teams communicate via message passing, threads within a team synchronize their accesses to the team descriptor by monitor operations. The data structures of an agent are collected in its agent descriptor.

The passive resources of a team are represented by memory management segments. During team activation the team descriptor is copied from the root of its segments (associated segment) to the system heap. The team data are mapped from its segments into the team's address space. When a team is passivated, its segments are unmapped and closed, and the team descriptor is copied to the associated segment.

3.3 The Manager

On each node within the network there is one team manager, which activates and passivates teams locally. The team manager is implemented by a nucleus thread created during node initialization. Most of the time the manager thread awaits messages from clients. Once a message is received, the manager thread activates or passivates a team depending on the operation requested in the message. To exonerate the team manager bottleneck, its work is reduced to the necessary. The manager thread only creates an agent thread and forwards the messages to the created agent thread. The agent takes over the manager operation and replies to the client. Analogously, the agent thread performs the manager Close-operation and forwards the Close-message to the manager thread. The manager thread deletes the agent thread and sends the reply message to the client. As native activities are concurrent to agents, natives are created and destroyed by the team manager. Native creation may be requested by an instance during its initialization on creating or opening or explicitly by agents or natives. Deletion of a native is triggered by itself during its termination. This results in the general implementation structure of a manager thread (Figure 4). The manager operations delegated to agent threads administrate the manager data structure called active instance table. The active instance table is a synchronized hash table containing for each active team an active instance descriptor. An active instance descriptor contains the unique identifier of the instance and the address of its team descriptor.

The way the active instance table is manipulated is exemplary demonstrated at the Create-operation. The parameters of Create are the access descriptor of the client, the access control list for the created instance and the user identification of the client. Execution starts with creating an unique identifier for the instance and obtaining a locked entry in the active instance table. Type-specific team and agent descriptors are obtained and initialized then. When initializing the team descriptor, the associated segment of the instance is created. After the unique identifier and the address of the team descriptor are registered in the active instance descriptor, it is unlocked. As the general structure, i.e. obtaining and locking entries, is analogous for the remaining manager operations, only their deviating parts are described.

```
BEGIN
  LOOP
    MessageAccept((*OUT*) ClientThreadId,(*OUT*) Message,(*OUT*) OpCode);
    CASE OpCode OF
      Create, Open, Reopen, Recover:
        AgentThreadCreate((*IN*) AgentProcedure,(*OUT*) AgentThreadId);
        MessageForward((*IN*) AgentThreadId,(*IN*) Message,(*IN*) OpCode,
                       (*IN*) ClientThreadId)
      | Close :
        AgentThreadDelete((*IN*) Message.AgentThreadId);
        MessageReply((*IN*) ClientThreadId,(*IN*) Message);
      | NativeThreadDeleteC :
        NativeThreadDelete((*IN*) Message.NativeThreadId);
    END;
  END(*LOOP*);
END;
```

Figure 4: Manager Code

The Open-operation renders access to already existing instances, i.e. the unique identifier is provided by the client. If the unique identifier is not registered in the active instance table, the instance must be activated. The location of the passive team is determined using the unique identifier data base and a new entry for the team descriptor is obtained. The address of the team descriptor is registered in the active instance descriptor. When initializing the activated team, its associated segment is opened and mapped from the passive team's location. If the team is already active, only its team descriptor is locked. After the team descriptor is updated, all descriptors are unlocked.

When executing the Close-operation, the instance descriptor and team descriptor are locked and the team descriptor is updated. If the team is passivated, the associated segment is unmapped and closed. Closing an associated segment means also copying the team descriptor into the associated segment. As the agent descriptor is not needed any more, it is deleted. When the team is passivated, its team descriptor and instance descriptor are released, otherwise they are unlocked.

The NativeCreate-operation locks the active instance descriptor and the team descriptor. Then a nucleus thread, executing the native program, is created and the descriptors are unlocked.

The NativeDelete-operation locks the active instance descriptor and the team descriptor. If there is no more agent or native, the team is passivated and the entry containing the team descriptor is removed from the table, otherwise the team descriptor is updated and unlocked. Finally a message is sent to the manager thread, which will delete the native thread.

The Reopen- and the Recover-operation are similar to Open. Reopen does not create a new agent descriptor, but uses the agent descriptor of the interrupted client-agent connection. Recover does not use the finally closed associated segment, but a checkpointed version of the segment.

3.4 Kernel Teams

In this section the kernel team implementation is presented. As kernel team operations work on kernel address space, they are completely executed in kernel mode. All agent threads performing the operations have the same program structure: A newly created agent thread first awaits the forwarded message sent by the team manager. After initializing the team, the agent thread sends the reply message to the client and awaits further requests. Subsequently, the client sends its request directly to the agent thread, which performs the operation depending on the operation code. If the operation code specifies a primary type operation, it is executed directly, else the mechanism to execute type-specific operations is activated. The result of the operation is sent back to the client. When receiving a close request the agent thread performs the manager operation and forwards the message to the manager. As already mentioned the manager will then delete the agent thread.

The data structures manipulated by an agent are its agent descriptor and team descriptor. Both descriptors have a primary part and a type-specific part. While the primary operations only access the primary part, the type-specific operations use both parts. The primary structure of the agent descriptor contains the granted access permissions, dispositions for execution of operations, several client identifications needed for security checks and failure detection with respect to distribution and recovery, and a pointer to the team descriptor. The state information in the team descriptor is divided into a volatile part, which is only needed by active teams, and the permanent part, which is needed by active and passive ones. The main components of the volatile part are references to its agents and natives and the ranges of the mapped segments. The permanent part contains the unique identifier of the team and its data length. Besides protection relevant informations like the creator and the access control list, there are several time values registering the executed operations. A reference counter summarizes the number of references by context instances. Additional parameters render efficient disk usage.

The primary type operations working on these descriptor parts are used during team activation and passivation by the manager operations. As an exemplary the manager operation Create uses primary operations to initialize the components of the corresponding descriptors. On the other hand the primary type provides operations to the clients. Most operations are status-/control-operations, which read or modify the status of the whole instance or parts of its descriptors. There are status/control-operations for the access control list, the set of granted access rights, and the disposition set. When calling the Checkpoint-operation, a passive representation of the active team is created, i.e. the representation includes the state of agents and natives. This checkpointed representation can be used by a policy to recover a former state. The AgentDuplicate-operation creates a new agent, which has the same state as the original agent. Changes of context references are notified in the referenced team via ModifyReference, which updates the reference counter.

The primary type descriptors and operations are used to add abstract data types to the system. Each type implementation consists of the inherited primary part and an additional type-specific part. The type-specific part of the agent descriptors and team descriptors contain the data structures needed for the additional operations, e.g. an agent descriptor of type file contains a pointer to the currently read byte and a team descriptor of type pipe contains pointers to the first and last byte within the cyclic data buffer. The descriptor references of an active team are shown in Figure 5.

As the implementation language lacks an inheritance mechanism, an empty image is used for implementing new kernel types. To tailor the image to a new type, special code, that implements the type-specific operations, is added. As example the directory type adds the code for InsertReference, RemoveReference, LookUpReference and ReadNextReference. The image pattern supports definition of the specific message structure and transferring procedure parameters to the message structure and vice versa. Execution of the team operations is prepared by deriving agent and team descriptors from the access descriptor, permission checks, locking of the team descriptor, and updating the primary parts of the descriptors.

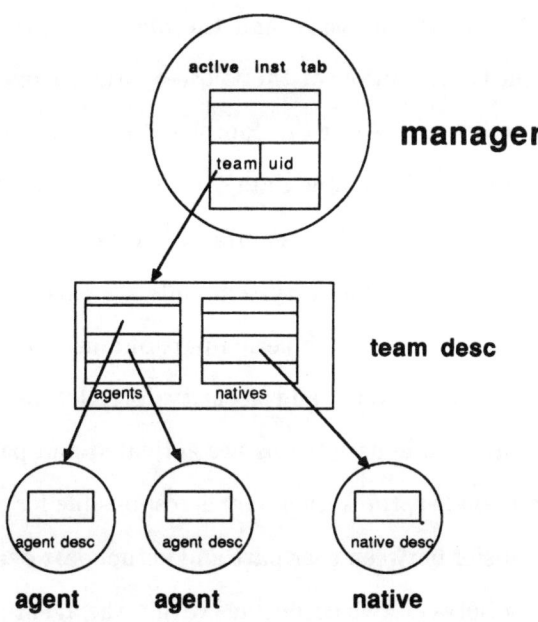

Figure 5: References of an Active Team

3.5 User Teams

If a user wants to provide system services to other users, he creates a new abstract data type by defining the user part of a user team. Similar to a system programmer implementing a kernel team, the user adds a type-specific part to a system provided pattern. The user part contains its type-dependent data structures in a team descriptor and one agent descriptor per client. The user-defined operations are performed by the user part of an agent thread, whose general structure is similar to the type-independent kernel part. First, the agent receives a call to initialize its descriptors by an user-defined Create- or Open-operation. Besides initialization, the operations can contain an additional security mechanism defined by the user. After returning control via system call to its kernel part, the user part awaits calls of type-specific operations. Depending on the identification contained in the message the operations are executed one after the other. The results of execution are notified in the message and the message is transferred via system call to the kernel part. Execution of the Close-operation releases the descriptors and terminates the user part. After the completed pattern is compiled and linked, users can create instances of the new data via the Create-operation.

To handle user access to system-maintained data structures, the kernel provides additional system calls. These system calls are executed by the user team-kernel team, which administrates the kernel part of a user team. This kernel team handles communication, recovery, and security for all types of user teams in a type-independent way. While user teams are activated and passivated in cooperation with the team manager, the kernel part is responsible for execution of primary type operation. Transfer between user part and kernel part of a user team is implemented by switching between two coroutines within the agent thread. Cooperation of the coroutines is illustrated by presenting the execution of a Create-operation.

- Via a system call the client executes the Create-operation to create a new user team. Besides the parameters of the kernel team creation, he specifies the instance containing the loadable code for the user team.

- The system call mechanism copies the parameters from the client's address space into a message within the kernel address space and sends the message to the team manager. The team manager creates an agent thread with one coroutine executing the kernel part and forwards the message to the created thread.

- The agent thread initializes the kernel part of the user team. During initialization the agent thread is extended by a coroutine executing the user code in a newly created address space. While the address space is notified in the special part of the kernel team descriptor, the agent descriptor contains a description of the user coroutine. Then the agent thread copies the message into the user team address space and transfers control to the user part of the agent.

- The user part initializes its type-specific part as shown above and transfers control via system call to the kernel part of the agent.

- The kernel part copies the reply message into the kernel address space, updates its descriptors, and activates the system call mechanism.

- Finally, the system call mechanism copies the data to the clients address space and returns the system call of the client.

Subsequent operations to the instance use the established connection between the client and the user part of the agent analogously. During the Close-operation the address space is deleted, if there are no more agents or natives in the team.

Not only agents, but also natives may operate in user and kernel mode. One example is the implementation of the UNIX-process team, whose user part executes the user program and whose kernel part performs the system calls of the user program within the kernel.

4 Conclusion

Teams combine active and passive resources to a homogeneous implementation structure for abstract data types, that is tailored to distribution, recovery and security. By adding new abstract data types the functionality of the system is easily extended without disturbing its remaining system structure. This extentability renders the openness for changing requirements to systems. As new data types take automatically possession of distribution, recovery, and security qualities of the system, the implementation of the kernel part of user teams is a place for tuning and proofing correctness of large-scale algorithms. Few concepts increase understanding and maintaining of the system.

5 Related Systems

Most related systems offer lightweight processes in shared address spaces. They mainly differ in the respective roles of these processes and the kernel integration of their services. In the V system [Che88] processes communicate via shared memory within a V-team and via network transparent, synchronous message passing between different V-teams. Because of this analogy the notation of teams was taken over to BirliX. V system services are implemented by service modules outside a small kernel, which is reduced to process communication. This diverges from the BirliX kernel, which implements the common parts of the services, e.g. distribution, recovery and security. Abstractions of physical resources are supported by the Mach kernel [TR86] in a similar way. Threads within a Mach task share a common address space. Threads in different task communicate by massage passing via ports. The functionality of ports, which are kernel protected reference objects, is achieved by agents in BirliX. In Argus [L+87] abstract data types are implemented by guardians, which combine lightweight processes similar to BirliX teams. Handlers of a guardian are comparable to natives. While transactions are built into the guardians, team recovery is open for different recovery policies. Distributed team activation was inspired by LOCUS [PW85], which distinguishes between using, synchronizing and storing sides.

References

[Che88] David R. Cheriton. The V Distributed System. *Communications of the ACM*, 31(3):314–333, March 1988.

[Hoa74] C.A.R. Hoare. Monitors: An Operating System Structuring Concept. *Communications of the ACM*, 17(10):549–557, October 1974.

[L+87] B. Liskov et al. *Argus reference manual.* MIT Laboratory for Computer Science, Cambridge, Mass., 1987.

[PW85] G.J. Popek and B.J. Walker. *The LOCUS Distributed System Architecture.* Computer Systems Series. The MIT Press, 1985.

[TR86] A. Tevanian and R.F. Rashid. MACH - A Basis for Future Unix Development. In *EUUG Conference Proceedings*, Manchester, 1986.

MONITORING AND MANAGEMENT-SUPPORT OF DISTRIBUTED SYSTEMS

Dieter Haban, Dieter Wybranietz and Amnon Barak

Abstract - This paper describes a tool for on-line monitoring of distributed systems. The tool consists of a hardware component and software level, i.e., a hybrid monitor, which is capable of presenting the interactive user and the local operating system with a high-level information and performance evaluation of the activities in the host system with minimal interferences. A special hardware support, which consists of a test and measurement processor (TMP), was designed and has been implemented in the nodes of an experimental multicomputer system. The main function of the TMP is to execute software for monitoring the local system behavior and to measure the performance of both the resident operating system and the application software. The TMP can also be used to execute low level operating system functions, to manage local resources and to trigger time driven events in order to reduce the overhead of the host operating system. The operations of the TMP are completely transparent to the users with a minimal, less than 0.1%, overhead to the hardware system. In the experimental system, all the TMPs were connected with a central monitoring station, using an independent communication network, in order to provide a global view of the monitored system. The central monitoring station displays the resulting information in easy-to-read charts and graphs. Our experience with the TMP shows that it promotes an improved understanding of run-time behavior and performance measurements, to derive qualitative and quantitative assessments of distributed systems.

Index Terms--Distributed systems, multicomputer, distributed operating system, real-time monitoring, measuring, management, events, user interface, graphical display, load balancing.

1. INTRODUCTION

Distributed systems have desirable capabilities such as improved reliability and availability, ease of modularity, incremental growth, configuration flexibility, and high performance. New technologies, increased research, and demand for improved performance, communication, and productivity yield new architectures and commercial systems. A few examples are the Hybercube [18], the Butterfly [4] and the Transputer [8]. Research in distributed operating systems and adequate programming languages are also under way [15, 20]. Despite these increased activities, there is a substantial lack of development of methods and tools for monitoring and measuring distributed systems

---
D. Haban is with the International Computer Science Institute, 1947 Center Street, Berkeley, CA 94704.
D. Wybranietz is with the Department of Computer Science, University of Kaiserslautern; D-6750 Kaiserslautern, W. Germany.
A. Barak is with the International Computer Science Institute, 1947 Center Street, Berkeley, CA 94704, on leave from The Hebrew University of Jerusalem, Israel.

which aid in verifying the above features, assisting in detecting and locating abnormal behavior such as performance bottlenecks, and exploiting new functions that can be performed by the monitoring sub-system.

In this paper, we describe an experimental hybrid monitoring system that was built as part of the INCAS [16] multicomputer project. Hybrid monitoring means a dedicated hardware device (attached processors) that can extract data from the host machine and can then execute software to process and evaluate that data, concurrently and independently of the host system. The specific monitoring system that we present is designed to perform three main functions. First, it monitors the host machine in a transparent manner, with minimal side effects. This function is used primarily to extract raw data. Second, the monitoring system can measure the behavior of the software in the host system by tracing its execution, evaluating its performance, and providing insights about this execution to the interactive user and the resident operating system. The third function that the monitoring system can perform is the execution of several routine tasks to assist the resident operating system in managing the increased number of operations which results from the distributed environment.

Traditionally, monitoring and measurement have been fundamental techniques in hardware engineering. The increased complexity of present computer systems necessitates such tools for software development as well. In most existing computers, the hardware and software systems are not designed to be monitored, although monitoring tools in the form of stand-alone hardware devices, programs, and hybrid tools have been available for many years. Measurement and monitoring become even more difficult in distributed systems, since these systems feature asynchronous concurrent activities, nondeterministic and unreproducible behavior and communication among processes that introduces unpredictable delays. The measurement task is further complicated due to a lack of central control, precise global time and accurate global state, since measurements have to be performed simultaneously in different nodes and the results must be collected and evaluated in some reasonable form, preferably in one location, in order to provide users with a meaningful view of their software.

Monitoring tools can be classified into pure hardware, pure software and hybrid monitors. A hardware monitor is a device that is not a part of the monitored system. Although such devices can be designed to have minimal or no effect on the host system, they generally provide only limited, low-level information about the activities of the host system. In contrast, software monitors can present information in an application-oriented manner. These monitors are usually contained within the measured system, sharing with it the same execution environment, thus producing some degree of interference in both the timing and space of the monitored program. Therefore, pure software monitors are not adequate for on-line monitoring and for real-time measurements during the execution time.

Hybrid tools [7,19] can be designed to benefit from the advantages of both hardware and software monitors with minimal effects on the monitored system. Such monitors typically consist of an independent hardware (device) which can perform the low level monitoring, i.e. information gathering, and a software level which is executed by this device capable of measuring, evaluating and displaying the performance of the host system. The monitoring system described in this paper is a real-time hybrid monitor which, in addition to the above mentioned function can also interact with the host system. One feature of this monitor is the small amount of its interference with the application level. Another feature is the ability of several monitoring devices placed in different nodes of a multicomputer system to cooperate by communicating with each other.

The ability to combine on-line information and display execution patterns creates a powerful tool for evaluation and management of programs which are executed concurrently on several processors. The monitoring tool described in this paper allows the user to perform on-line observations of communication patterns, to detect bottlenecks and inactive processes, assistance in debugging and in general, they provide a multi-level view of the application and zooming capability with several degrees of granularity. The monitoring system can also combine local monitored data with remote information and knowledge about other nodes, then evaluate this information and make it available to the operating system of each node, thus supporting it in managing its tasks. Examples of such tasks are load balancing, locating resources and orphan management. These tasks become important in a system with a large number of nodes where efficient management requires knowledge the entire system or parts thereof and frequent evaluation of local and remote parameters.

In the next section, we specify the objectives which guided the design of the TMP monitoring system. Sections 3 and 4 describe the TMP software and hardware components. In section 5 we discuss means to improve the users' understanding of their distributed applications using the TMP concept. Section 6 demonstrates how the TMP system can be used for management support at the operating system level.

2. DESIGN OBJECTIVES

Monitoring program execution may require a significant amount of an application programmer's efforts, since the insights it provides cannot be replaced by those obtained from static analysis of program texts [17]. In addition, monitoring activities can be used to support the operating system's tasks. The role of on-line monitors becomes even more important in a multiprocessor environment when many threads of a program may execute concurrently. The design objectives which have been accomplished in the TMP monitoring system are aimed to assist the interactive user to gain better knowledge about the run-time behavior of their applications and the host operating system in the performance of its low level tasks. The specific objectives are:

- **Interference**: the interface between the monitoring device and the host system is transparent, it does not change the system behavior and has minimal effects on its performance.

- **Continuous Monitoring During Operation**: the monitoring sub-system can trace the host system, evaluate and supervise the execution of certain applications, and display information in real-time about their progress. We note that this service is particularly important when monitoring long-running (concurrent) processes, complex distributed programs with dynamically changing structures and when considering real-time programs that control critical systems such as a nuclear power plant or an airborne system.

- **Application-oriented Presentation**: the monitoring and measurement tool provides a user-friendly, graphic interface which can be used by application programmers and not only by experts. This means that, for observation purposes, the large amount of monitor and performance data is interpreted, evaluated, and presented in an application-oriented manner which reflects the semantics and organization of the application programs. In addition, the processing, evaluation and display of this vast amount of monitored data does not cause any overhead in time and space.

- **Preserve Data for Off-line Analysis**: the information gathered by the monitoring system can be recorded to provide more detailed measurement results about past execution and for further, off-line analysis.

- **Integration and Ease-of-Use**: the instrumentation of the monitoring system is incorporated into the hardware system during its design phase, resulting in an integrated approach. This feature allows the users to take advantage of these tools during the development, debugging and execution of their applications. Since this monitoring scheme is transparent to the application level and requires minimal overhead, this approach is better than temporary instrumentations which change the system behavior upon removal.

- **Flexible Hardware and Software**: the monitoring hardware and software can easily be customized to various environments and application requirements. The tools are not tailored to one specific hardware or application. During operation the monitoring hardware and software can be interactively adapted to changing needs.

- **Feed-Back**: in order to allow the monitored system to dynamically respond to the results of the measurement, the monitoring sub-system is capable of funnelling its results back to the monitored system. This provides the host system with up-to-date information about its own activities, and can be used for fine performance tuning.

- **Operating system management support**: the monitoring system can execute routine, low level, operating system tasks, such as the local load or network management, thus reducing the overhead of the host system.

3. THE TEST AND MEASUREMENT PROCESSOR

In this section, we present the concept behind the Test and Measurement Processor (TMP). In the next section, we describe its hardware realization.

3.1. The TMP concept

The main goal of the TMP is to perform efficient monitoring of the application software. This goal is accomplished by using events generated by the application software; then these events are categorized, time-stamped, processed, and displayed by the TMP hardware. By using semantic information about the monitored programs provided by the compiler, the monitoring software is able to present evaluated data in an application-oriented manner. The TMP is also capable of executing local software for various processing and evaluation needs for its host. In an environment that consists of several nodes, each TMP can receive data from any other TMP over a network; symmetrically, each TMP is able to send data to other TMPs. Ideally, the TMPs communicate via their own network, thereby avoiding disturbances to the application level. However, the communication among the TMPs can also be accomplished by the communication facility of the host system. In Figure 1 we illustrate the principles of the TMP.

A key point of the measurement procedure is the identification of the type of events which should be monitored. Then the problem is how to insert these events into the monitored software. In the current study, we identified events which represent significant trends in the behavior of the system, e.g., process creation and deletion. The triggering points for these events are placed in the operating system kernel which then provides continuous information about the system behavior. We note that additional triggering points may also be inserted at the application level. Initial experiments with the INCAS [16] multicomputer system, showed that, typically, 600-800 such events were generated each second on each node. We note that the host overhead caused by the TMP is lower than 0.1%, thus it becomes a permanent part of each node.

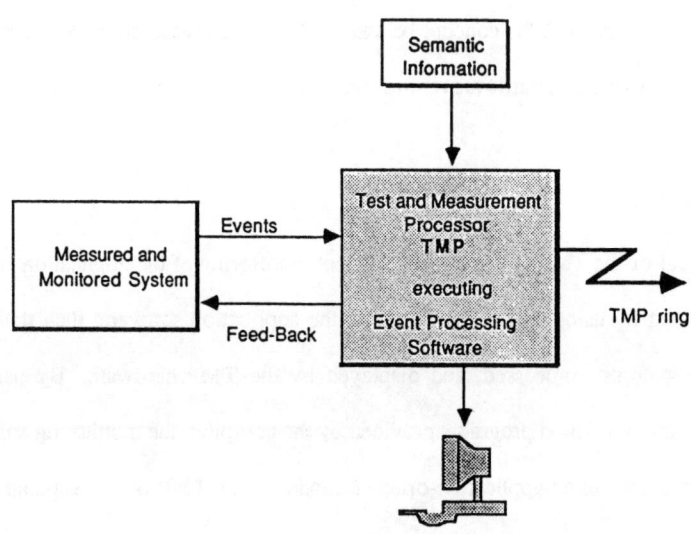

Figure 1: Principles of the TMP

3.2. Instrumentation of the host system

An event is defined as a special condition that occurs during the normal system activity, such that it can be made visible to the TMP. As such, events represent changes in the behavior of the system. There are two kinds of events, standard and optional. Standard events are permanent and integral parts of a system. They are triggered by the kernel software, the communication subsystems, and the supporting software. Standard events are intended to support monitoring and measuring during the normal system execution. Note that since standard events are an integral part of the operating system, monitored software need not be recompiled or relinked. Optional events are associated with the application programs. They are generated by the compilers or are placed manually into program code. Optional events serve for debugging purposes.

The instrumentation of standard events is an integral part of the operating system. In this case the minimal monitored activities should include the dispatcher, the kernel activities and the communication sub-system. Note that several degrees of desired details can be obtained. In a multicomputer system with a dynamic structure, additional events have been added to reflect the increased number of activities. Examples of standard events for a distributed system are listed in Table 1. For each event, we list the event class, followed by a list of parameters.

Dispatcher Events	Communication System Events
start process <procID> <procNo>	receive message <portID>
stop process <procID>	send message <portID>
assign process <procID>	**Kernel Events**
resign process <procID>	
ready process <procID>	I/O init <queueID>
block process <queueID>	wait queue <queueID>
migrate process <procID>	send queue <queueID>
	receive queue <queueID>

Table 1: Examples of Standard Events

Dispatcher events trace the operations of the operating system dispatcher. The general model of a dispatcher is depicted in Figure 2. It includes events which reflect the following states of a process: ready, blocked, running, migrated, killed. The parameter *procID* (see Table 1) identifies the process object, and the parameter *procNo* identifies its type. Kernel events describe low-level activities of the operating system. These include initialization of queues for I/O devices, communication sub-system and synchronization mechanisms.

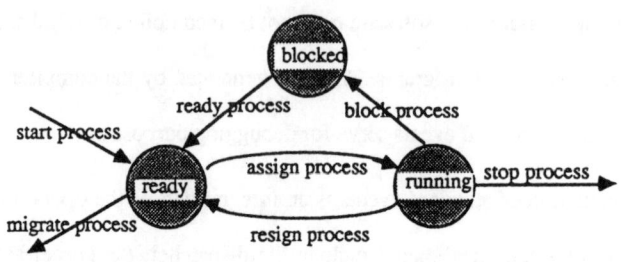

Figure 2: Events representing Operations of the Dispatcher

Communication events allow insights into the activities of the communication sub-system activities, including inter-process communications. The minimal types of operations that are monitored include sending and receiving of messages. The corresponding operations are *send message <portID>* and *receive message <portID>* events.

3.3. Processing of local events

The evaluation of global events is performed in two stages. First, the TMP software processes incoming events at each host, then it transfers condensed data to a central station. The second stage is done at the central monitoring station which combines all the obtained results to provide the user with a global view of his applications (this is further explained in a section below). We note that the central station provides a consistent global state by ensuring the causality relationship [12] among the locally collected activities. Another algorithm incorporated into the monitoring system ensures that the received measurement data are collected at close time intervals by synchronizing the length and the overlapping of these intervals at the TMPs, as suggested by [9].

The monitoring software in each TMP is responsible for collecting data about the behavior of its host. Upon system startup, the monitoring software keeps track of initialization of waiting queues and creates a table of wait conditions (see Table 1). The entries of this table, which are accessible via a hash function over the *queueID*, contain necessary semantic data and evaluated execution summaries such as the name of the wait condition, average queue length, and maximum queue length.

To demonstrate a typical sequence of events and the corresponding TMP activities, we now follow the operations of the dispatcher. Initially, the event *start process <procNo> <procID>* informs the TMP that a process of a type *<procNo>* has been created and placed in the ready queue. Upon occurrence of the event *assign process <procID>*, the monitoring software is informed that the process has been activated (running); thus all the subsequent events result from the activities of that process until the next *assign process* event. Since each event is stored with a local time stamp, the TMP software can measure elapsed times between activities accurately. For example, the time difference between *assign process* and *resign process* or *block process* determines the elapsed time of a process. The time difference between *block process* and *ready process* determines the blocked time of a process. Cumulative execution and blocked times are stored in information tables for each process. In particular, for the idle loop, the idle time is accumulated. Due to the vast amount of accumulated information, execution times of procedures are kept only during debugging. Upon receipt of an event *block process <queueID>*, the length of the corresponding queue is incremented. In this case the parameter *<queueID>* enables the TMP to identify the wait condition and to measure the duration which the process spent in the blocked queues. Finally, upon receipt of event *ready process <procID>*, the corresponding length of the waiting queue is decremented.

The communication system events *send message* and *receive message* enable the TMP to keep track of the number of messages each process exchanges with other processes. Additional communication events include failed messages, retransmissions and timeout for send/receive operations. We note that in each case the size of the message is also measured.

Based on the above monitoring, the TMP software measures the host machine load, including the CPU utilization, the idle time, length of queues, times that processes spent in the queues, rate of

I/O and the communication traffic. This list can be further extended pending the desired degree and the purpose of the measurement. We note that additional evaluation algorithms and new events can easily be integrated into the current software.

3.4. Event generation

The mechanism for generating an execution-time event consists of an instruction that is inserted at a specific, well-chosen point in the application code. Each event is marked by one store instruction which writes through the local processor cache. Therefore, each event is immediately visible on the system bus. The format of the instruction is:

STORE ADDR, VALUE

Each address represents one event class. In the current implementation, there are 256 different event classes, and therefore the range of the address field is bound to 256 addresses. Examples of event classes are:

start process

block process

The VALUE of the store instruction serves as a parameter which specifies one event within each class. For example:

start process   <*processID*>

block process   <*queueID*>

In some cases, a standard event may require two parameters. For example, the event *start process* <*procNo*> <*procID*> is triggered by two instructions, one for each parameter. In this case, the operating system kernel ensures that these events are treated as one atomic operation.

In the current implementation, the TMP has 32 standard and 26 optional monitoring events. Most of the standard events are related to the initialization procedure and the startup configuration. Thus, upon system initialization, there is a burst of standard events with information about queues, process creations, establishment of communication channels, etc. During actual operation of the system, the majority of the standard events are related to the dispatcher and communication sub-system activities.

4. THE ARCHITECTURE

The TMP is a hardware device that was designed to be an integral part of each node in a multi-computer system. Typically, such a node consists of one or more processors, memory, I/O and communication devices. The TMP may be viewed as an additional device responsible for monitoring, recording, and evaluating the activities of the host node as well as its communication activities. The TMP can send its findings to the host operating system, to other TMPs and to a central monitoring station. The central station, which may be connected to all the TMPs, is used for interactive monitoring, global measurements, and distributed debugging. To further reduce the interference of the TMPs with the monitored system, all communication among the TMPs is done via a separate network. The scheme of the TMP architecture is given in Figure 3.

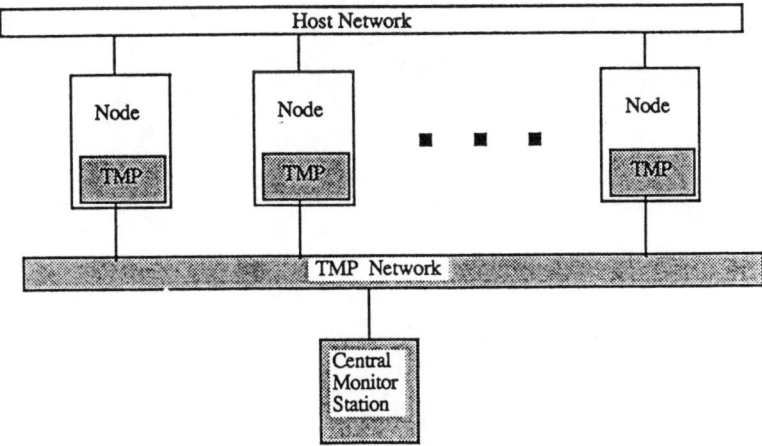

Figure 3: TMP Architecture

4.1. Hardware implementation

The design of the TMP hardware was aimed to allow implementation in any computer system. It is connected to a system bus and monitors events on this bus with negligible impact on the measured system. Figure 4 shows the TMP hardware and its integration into a node of the INCAS system [16]. The bus interface is a separate module which does not effect the other parts of the TMP. This module can be developed for use in any bus architecture.

The specific parts of the TMP hardware consist of a M68000 based processor with 1 MByte of local memory, a dual RS232 port for local interactions, a network interface to other TMPs, and an Event Processing Unit (EPU). The processor is used for the execution of monitoring software. This includes low-level monitoring and evaluation routines which are resident in the memory. Higher-level evaluation software as well as operating system functions can be loaded onto the TMP's memory. This software makes use of the preprocessed data condensed by the lower-level monitoring software. In the current implementation, this software can collect and process up to 10,000 events per second.

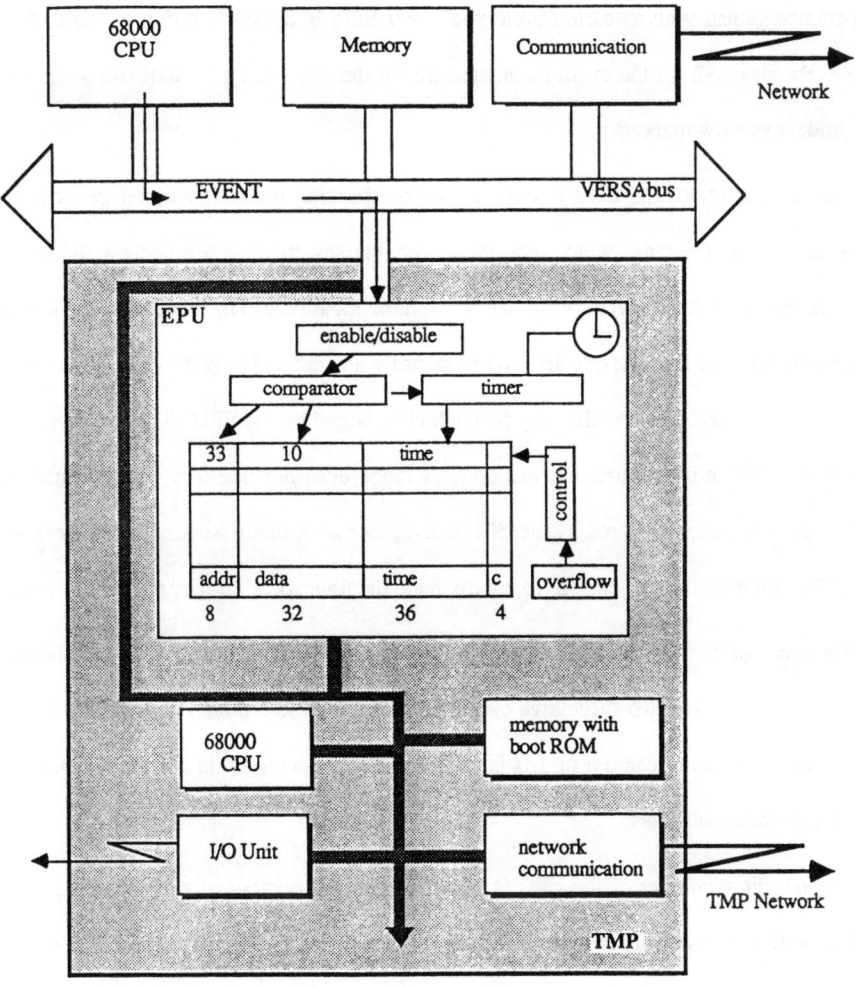

Figure 4: The TMP Hardware

The EPU consists of a local event buffer, a comparator, a clock and an overflow counter. The local event buffer of the EPU is used as a FIFO for collecting sequences of events. The depth of the FIFO is 16 entries. This depth was tuned to cope with a high arrival rate of events, and is based on an experience gained with an earlier prototype. Each entry in the event buffer consists of 80 bits: 8 for the event class; 32 for the event parameter; 36 for the time stamp (in µs); and 4 bits for control (CPU mode, overflow marker).

The comparator of the EPU is responsible for checking the addresses on the host bus. If an address falls within the range which represents event classes, the matched address and the next data on the bus are stored in the event buffer, along with the local time. The location of the address range can be adapted to the actual hardware environment by a switch. The last byte of the address determines the event class; thus it is the only byte which is stored by the EPU. The low level implementation of the TMP must ensure that this address range does not interfere with the main memory. Another function which is stored by the EPU is the processing mode (supervisor or user) of the host system. This information can be used to approximate the time spent for user or kernel modes.

The timer of the EPU is tuned to measure the time difference between events. The rate of this timer guarantees that no two successive events will have the same time. For example, in the current implementation, a time quantum of 1µs is used, thereby allowing up to 19 hours of measurements before the counter overflows.

The overflow counter of the EPU is used to count the number of events lost due to a buffer overflow. Although the specific type of each event is lost, the TMP software is aware of this inconsistency. In order to detect the occurrence of an overflow, the first event placed in the buffer after such an overflow is marked in its control field. The contents of the overflow counter can be accessed by the TMP software using the *read overflow counter* and *reset overflow counter* commands.

Other commands for controlling the EPU include *enable EPU, disable EPU, reset EPU, set time slice, set timer, reset timer, mask events,* and *read next event*. For example, the commands *enable EPU, disable EPU* are used to enable or disable the collection of events by the EPU. Similarly, the command *mask event* is used to disregard events which are not relevant to a given application. Finally, we note that the TMP has access to the memory of the host processor. This property is used for debugging activities which can run on the TMP and for redirecting information gathered by the TMP to the host operating system.

It is possible to insert more than one TMP into one node without disturbing each other. Thus, each TMP may run different event processing software concurrently to perform different analysis tasks. The TMPs may also run the same event processing software, but each TMP is responsible for different event classes, resulting in their sharing the work. In both cases, the monitoring instrumentation and the application processes need no further preparation. In addition, the collection of data done by the TMP might include hardware monitoring, such as measuring the bus and I/O devices load. These measurements do not cause any interference with the operation of these hardware components and do not need any additional instrumentation.

5. IMPROVING THE UNDERSTANDING OF DISTRIBUTED PROCESSING

In this section we show how the monitoring sub-system can be used to help users to manage and actually improve their understanding of the run-time patterns of their applications, and the system programmers to gain insights about the performance of the operating system level. A discussion of further operating system management support by the monitoring sub-system is given in the next section. In the sequel, we refer only to the application level users, although the benefits to the system programmer are obvious.

Distributed programs may be viewed as a set of modules (processes), where each module may consist of other modules or processes. During the execution time these modules are dispersed among the nodes and are executed concurrently. Our goal is then to provide the users with sufficient information for observing the run-time behavior of their modules. Our basic assumption is that by these observations the users can gain better knowledge about execution patterns of the application software. They can then perform further analysis, perform more measurements and tune the execution patters. We note that the monitoring system cannot automatically improve the performance of the application level, it can only assist the application level user to do so.

The information which is collected by the monitoring sub-system includes the following: process creation and deletion, context switches; process execution times, process blocked and ready times; performance of I/O operations, including sending and receiving messages; total communication volumes and establishments of new links; length of queues; machine load and idle times; counts of events, etc. Evaluation of this information, with several degrees of granularity, can then be used for process profiling and measurements, debugging, animation, identification of bottlenecks, zooming on a particular activity and for load distribution.

5.1. Visualization of Program Behavior

From the user point of view, the monitoring system consists of several layers. The lowest level is that of the individual TMPs which are placed in the nodes of the system for information gathering. After an initial filtering, this information is sent to the central monitoring station. The second level is a rule-based evaluation module capable of performing specific operations based on the information received, including generic operations, i.e., a sequence of prespecified operations. Specific examples are given later in this section. The third part is the display monitor and the user's point of interaction module. The display module, like the evaluation module, is a rule-based software which is responsible for displaying the results of the evaluation module on the screen. It uses a set of symbols and control tables, so that for each type of information, an appropriate display icon is used, i.e., graphs, charts, etc. The interaction module is responsible for interpreting the user commands and then relaying the appropriate control commands to the other layers.

The first step in the monitoring process is to gain knowledge about the internal structure of the application program and its semantics. This is accomplished by using information which is extracted during the compilation of the monitored program. This information includes the internal organization of the program, communication links, names and types of the program sub-modules, and how these components are linked to each other. This information is compiled when a program is load/linked and is then stored in the program specific data base of the central monitoring station. Then, during the execution of the monitored program, this data base is updated continuously by the evaluation module, following the dynamic changes of the program modules, along with additional execution summaries obtained.

We now describe a simple example to illustrate how the monitoring system is used. Consider a program which consists of four interacting modules, see Figure 5 for details. Our first goal is to display a general overview of these modules, then to add the communication links (and volumes), and finally the performance of each module. Using a menu-driven interface, the user initially requests a display of all his program modules. At this time the user also specifies his preferred mode of display, e.g., graphs, icons, colors. Note that this is stored in the user's display data base for future use. After processing the first request, the central monitoring station obtains the names, types and locations of each program module from the program specific data base. Note that the TMPs provide information about all their respective activities continuously, thus the central station needs only to identify and filter the requested information. It then displays these modules on the screen using the display mode specified by the user's display data base. Next, the user requests the addition of the communication activities. This is done by the menu on the display module, which then activates the corresponding TMPs to transfer relevant information to the central station. At this time the communication lines will appear on the screen, including the total number of messages exchanged. We note that most of the work is done at the local TMP in each node and that only specific requested information for display is passed to the central station. Finally, upon another request by the user, the performance activity of each module is transferred by the TMPs to the central station, which then draws the bar graphs displaying CPU utilization, I/O rate, communication usage and accumulated time in the ready queue.

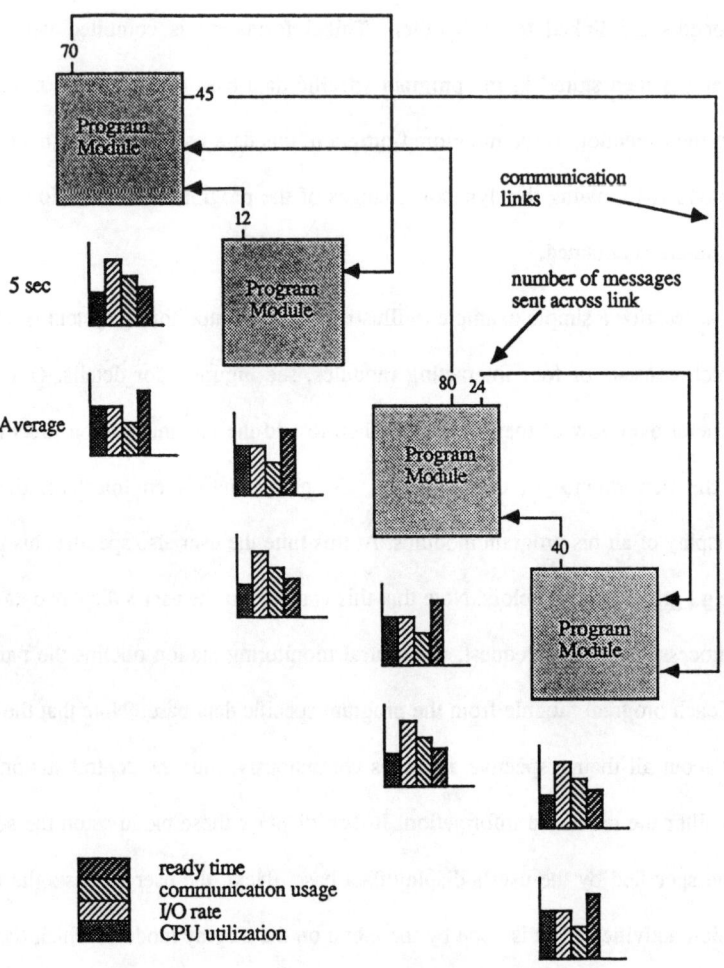

Figure 5: Graphic display of interacting processes

In the remainder of this section, we give a brief overview of some specific areas that may benefit by using our monitoring tools.

5.2. Communication

As a result of the measurements that the TMP performs, it is possible to gain knowledge about each process' communication volume and targets, starting from such low-level information about the message sizes, rate of transmissions, time spent in performing communication tasks, establishment of links, IPC, communication buffer usage, rate of retransmissions and network failures. It is also possible to obtain knowledge about the system-wide communication activities or any subset of machines or processes.

It is evident that, normally, the user does not need all these details, therefore a ruled-based menu is provided to select specific requests. This menu also allows the definition of threshold functions which then trigger display of irregular communication patterns, i.e., stray messages or overloaded links. Note that in this last case, an average function is used by the evaluation module.

5.3. Synchronization, bottlenecks and deadlocks

From the monitoring point of view, synchronization problems, bottlenecks and deadlocks are states to which some processes lend themselves and are thus either saturated or not executing at all. Although these processes may look like any other processes in the system, nevertheless they may cause performance degradation or even system failure. Unfortunately, few mechanisms allow transparent detection of such cases, and thus the user's involvement is critical. The monitoring system can help in locating these kinds of irregularities, then allow further zooming on each cause separately, thus simplifying the evaluation process.

Specific states that trigger this part of the monitoring system includes: a prolonged idle or blocked process; improper clustering of sets of processes, i.e., many waiting for one; overloaded process due to improper allocation of communication buffers; improper balance between internal mechanisms, e.g., the speed of the communication controller and the software which interact with it. In such cases, heuristic threshold functions given by the user may assist in detecting such abnormalities.

5.4. Zooming through the program structure

Based on the evaluated measurement data, the user may interactively zoom through the hierarchical program structure and focus on parts of the programs, a single machine, a single processes, or even a sub-module. At each of these levels, it is possible to obtain measurements about the monitored modules displayed in charts and graphs [21]. Another service provided by the monitoring system is on-line information gathering for off-line analysis.

5.5. Debugging

The monitoring tool is a natural aid in the debugging process. To begin with, the user is informed about the state of execution of each process: failed, blocked or starved. Error detection using the TMP becomes a simpler job with the possibility of inserting optional debugging events to the programs. When executing such a program, and particularly when the program includes many threads, the centralized display of the debugging information is the only adequate source of on-line information [10].

5.6. Load balancing

Load balancing is a simple byproduct of the monitoring system. For proper performance, this algorithm needs to know the execution profile of each process, its I/O and communication requirements, as well as the combined load of all the processes in each node. For systems with static or user controlled load balancing, the monitoring system can provide this information, on-line and in real-time. It can also provide the user and the system manager with information about irregularities in the distribution of the load. In integrated systems, where load balancing is done automatically, by the operating system [2,3], the monitoring system can help the host system to manage its duties. This is discussed in the next section.

6. OPERATING SYSTEMS MANAGEMENT SUPPORT

Due to the capability of the TMP to monitor and interact with the host node, it is possible to use it to carry certain operating system tasks, thus reducing the amount of overhead of the host processor. In this section, we describe three such tasks: the load balancing algorithm, which is responsible for dispersing the load among the nodes; the remnant collection algorithm, responsible for removing any remnants due to remote node failures; and the process location algorithm, which helps in re-establishing communication links between processes.

The algorithms described in this section represent a class of tasks that are performed by a system with a large number of nodes. Each such algorithm consists of several low-level tasks, e.g., monitoring the I/O rate of a process or sending *keep alive* messages, and a higher level tasks, e.g., process migration. The high-level procedures, which are invoked with a relatively low frequency, involve decision making that in many cases depends on some threshold functions. Updating these threshold functions requires that the system carry the low-level tasks, which in turn are executed with relatively high frequency. It is at this level of activity that the TMP services are needed most. Since the TMP can monitor the node activities with minimal overhead, it can relieve the host processor of carrying many of these functions, particularly network-related chores. The TMP performs the monitoring and the initial processing of the results. Then it may decide to initiate certain activities by triggering the operating system of the host processor or simply by updating its threshold functions for future use. The TMP can also send and receive information from other TMPs over the network, containing information about their respective hosts.

6.1. Load balancing

In distributed systems, load balancing algorithms are used to improve the overall system performance by transferring processes from overloaded machines to less loaded machines. Despite the overhead which is incurred by these algorithms, it has been shown that their execution can significantly improve the performance of the system [11]. Many existing algorithms for load balancing use distributed control, i.e., each machine performs the algorithm independently of the other. Typically, these algorithms consist of four main parts: local information gathering, information exchanges among the nodes, matchmaking and the actual process migration [3].

In the first part, each node gathers information about the length of the internal queues and monitors the processes' activities. Close examination of this monitoring reveals that, in order to make good load balancing decisions, it is also necessary to profile each process, i.e., to record its CPU usage, rates of I/O and Inter Process Communications (IPC), the node locations to which remote operations are targeted, ratio of remote vs. local operations, the process size, etc. Furthermore, this profiling must be done frequently due to possible changes in the characteristics of the processes.

The task of profiling all the host system processes results in a considerable amount of overhead for the operating system. Due to its causes, this overhead increases with the number of processes, thus further reducing the efficiency of the system. We note that it is due to this kind of overhead that many multicomputer operating systems will grind to a halt when required to handle a configuration beyond a certain size. A hardware device, such as the TMP, is one way to reduce this overhead.

The second part of the algorithm includes load information exchanges. Using the communication links of the TMP, this load information can be exchanged among the TMPs by using some dissemination algorithm [1, 6], while at the same time, each TMP makes the information received available to the local operating system. The matchmaking part is done by comparing the information about the local load to that of other nodes, and by using some pre-specified decision (threshold) parameters [14]. The role of the TMP at this level is limited to triggering process migrations due to special requirements by individual processes.

6.2. Remnant collection

In a distributed system, processes executing in one site may have allocated resources such as entries in system tables in remote sites. As nodes and communication links are inherently unreliable, failures may disconnect processes from such remote objects. After such a failure, these objects are futilely allocated, without actually being used, thereby wasting their site's resources. Essentially, they have become remnant in the same sense that inaccessible objects allocated from a heap storage are termed garbage [5]. As crashed sites are seldom able to notify other sites of their failure, these resources have to be actively detected and reclaimed for reuse.

The following remnant collection scheme is implemented in MOS [2]. When an object is allocated, a timer is attached to it. Processes are responsible for resetting the timer of the objects they use. This is done whenever an object is accessed, or when it receives a special *keep alive* message. A remnant collection process periodically scans all the objects, and releases those whose timers have expired. The timers are implemented by tagging each object with a unique creation time, and using a fixed upper limit on objects' lifetimes. Resetting the timer is done by resetting the tag. The special *keep alive* messages are periodically transmitted by each node to all accessed objects.

The role of the TMP in the remnant collection algorithm becomes clear when we consider all the operations involved. Initially, the operating system is responsible for allocating the resources and for setting their timers. This includes registration of the initiating process in the local TMP (in the node that hosts the process), and registration of the active object, including its timer, in the TMP of the remote node. This "remote" TMP is then responsible for updating the timer of the object, while the "local" TMP is responsible for sending the *keep alive* messages, validating from time to time that the process is still active. Note that if the original process migrates from one node to another, then part of this migration procedure includes updating of the TMP at the new site. Also note that if the object is migrated, then in addition to updating the TMP at the new site, it is necessary to inform the original process(es) about the object's new location. An algorithm that performs this task is described in the next section. The other activity which is carried by the "remote" TMP is removal of the object if its timer is expired. This can be accomplished using several additional safety measures, such as further negotiations among all the TMP involved.

6.3. Process detection

In a distributed system, a user's process may initially be assigned to one node, and later, as a result of load balancing considerations, be migrated to another node. In order to support IPC and to preserve the user's interface, the operating system must maintain up-to-date information about the location of all processes. A simple scheme to maintain such information is to establish a *"home"* site for each process, naturally in the node where it was created, and to continuously maintain in this location information of its whereabouts.

Suppose that a node which contains the home of a process is crashed, losing as a result all information about that process. Despite the crash, if the process has migrated to another site, then it may not be affected, and normally there is no reason to stop its execution. We call such a surviving process an *orphan process*. The existence of an orphan process has several undesirable implications. First, if an orphan process cannot be located, then this may lead to a violation of the user's interface, since the user may lose control over his processes. Similarly, IPC to an orphan process can not be performed despite the fact that this process exists and may communicate with other processes.

A simple, probabilistic scheme to overcome the single home site failure is used in MOS [2]. This scheme is intended to reduce the likelihood that a process becomes orphan by using multiple homes in a fixed set of nodes called the home pointer sites, and by sending *keep alive* messages between the process and its home pointer sites. More specifically, for each new process a set of pointer entries is created and placed in the home pointer sites. Note that the number of these sites depends on the hardware reliability and the required degree of fault-tolerance, and does not depend on the size of the configuration. The specific locations of the home pointer sites are determined by a universal hash function (on the process number), which is known to all the nodes.

The algorithms that are executed in order to maintain communication between each process and its home pointer sites includes establishing the entries when the process is created, then after each process migration and at fixed time interval, sending *keep alive* messages from the process to its home pointer sites. To locate a process, one need only contact its home pointer sites, using the process number and the hash function.

It is evident from this scheme that the algorithm for locating process relies on replication of links and on time dependent,*keep alive* messages. The first part requires a fixed amount of overhead and may be considered part of the process creation routine. In contrast, the *keep alive* messages require a considerable amount of overhead, since this part of the algorithm is executed as long as the process exists. If the time interval between two consecutive messages is small, then the overhead of maintaining this service is increased. If this time interval is decreased, it may slow down the detection process and eventually effect some processes. The role of the TMP is sending the *keep alive* messages and updating the timers at the home pointers entries. The TMP is also responsible for informing the host system when a timer expires, thus triggering the remnant collection algorithm.

7. CONCLUSION

The underlying philosophy of the TMP concept is to view monitoring as an integral part of a computer system. The TMP combines the advantages of software and hardware monitors while overcoming their deficiencies. The monitoring system does not change the behavior or the performance of the monitored software, and operates with minimal overhead to the host hardware. The algorithms running on the TMP operate in a decentralized mode and manage their node autonomously; thus the TMP concept can also be applied in a system with a large number of nodes.

Experience with the TMP shows an an improved understanding of run time behavior and system performance, and it promotes qualitative and quantitative assessments about the execution of distributed applications. It can also be used to perform management support to the operating system, thus releaving it from this kind of low-level routine task.

Our experience is that real-time monitoring implies a separate monitor processor that operates completely transparent to users. The advantages of our monitoring architecture are worth the additional hardware costs since the monitoring system reduces the software costs which occur when developing, debugging and monitoring complex (distributed) systems. In the future, a TMP-like facility may become an integral part of any node, thus helping to improve the reliability, availability, flexibility, and performance of systems, particularly systems with a large number of nodes.

ACKNOWLEDGEMENTS

The authors wish to thank the contributions of many participants from the INCAS and MOSIX projects, especially M. Abel, A. Gabel, T. Gauweiler, J. Lichtermann, F.Mattern, R. Reske, K. Rohleffs and A. Shiloh. Thanks also to A. Collison for the editorial assistance.

REFERENCES

[1] N. Allon, A. Barak, and U. Manber, "On disseminating information reliably without broadcasting," *Proc. 7th Int. Conf. on Distributed Computing Systems*, pp. 74-81, Berlin, Sept. 1987.

[2] A. Barak and A. Litman, "MOS: A multicomputer distributed operating system," *Software Practice & Experience*, vol. 15, no. 8, pp. 725-737, Aug. 1985.

[3] A. Barak and A. Shiloh, "A distributed load balancing policy for a multicomputer," *Software Practice & Experience*, vol. 15, no. 9, pp. 901-913, Sept. 1985.

[4] C. Brown et al., "Research with the butterfly multicomputer," *Computer Science and Computer Engineering Research Review* 1884-1885, University of Rochester, 1985.

[5] J. Cohen, "Garbage collection of linked data structures," *ACM Computing Surveys*, vol. 13, no. 3, pp. 341-367, Sep. 1981.

[6] Z. Drezner and A. Barak, "An asynchronous algorithm for scattering information between the active nodes of a multicomputer system," *J. of Parallel and Distributed Computing*, vol. 3, no. 3, pp. 344-351, Sept. 1986.

[7] D. Ferrari and V. Minetti, "A hybrid measurement tool for minicomputers," *Experimental Computer Performance and Evaluation*, D.Ferrari and M. Spadoni (eds), North-Holland Publishing Company, 1981.

[8] K.A. Frenkel, "Evaluating two massively parallel machines," *Commun. ACM*, vol. 29, no. 8, pp. 752-758, Aug. 1986.

[9] R. Gusella and S. Latti, "TEMPO- A network time controller for a distributed Berkeley UNIX system," *Distributed Processing Tech. Comm. Newsletter*, IEEE, vol. 6, no. 2, pp. 7-15, June 1984.

[10] D. Haban and W. Weigel, "Global events and global breakpoints in distributed systems," *Proc. 21st Hawaii Int. Conf. on System Sciences*, vol. 2, pp. 166-175, Jan. 1988.

[11] P. Krueger and M. Livny, "A comparison of preemptive and non-preemptive load distributing," *Proc. 8th Int. Conf. on Distributed Computing Systems*, San Jose, CA, pp. 123-130, June 1988.

[12] L. Lamport, "Time, clocks and the ordering of events in a distributed system," *Commun. ACM*, vol. 21, no. 7, pp. 558-565, 1978.

[13] J.E. Lambert and F. Halsall, "Program debugging and performance evaluation aids for a multi-microprocessor system," *Software & Microsystems*, vol. 3, no. 1, pp. 2-10, Feb. 1984.

[14] K.J. Lee and D. Towsley, "A comparison of priority-based decentralized load balancing policies," *Proc ACM SIGMETRICS Conf.*, pp. 70-77, 1986.

[15] B. Liskov, "Primitives for distributed computing," *Proc. 7th Symp. Operating System Principles*, pp. 33-42, 1979.

[16] J. Nehmer, D. Haban, F. Mattern, D. Wybranietz and D. Rombach, "Key concepts of the INCAS multicomputer project," *IEEE Trans. on Software Engineering*, vol. 13, no. 8, pp. 913-923, Aug. 1987.

[17] B. Plattner and J. Nievergelt, "Monitoring program execution: A survey," *IEEE Computer*, pp. 76-93, Nov. 1981.

[18] C.L. Seitz, "The Cosmic Cube," *Commun. ACM*, vol. 28, no. 1, pp. 22-33, 1985.

[19] L. Svobodova, "Online system performance measurements with software and hybrid monitors," *Operating Systems Rev.*, vol. 7, no. 4, pp. 45-53, Oct. 1973.

[20] A.S. Tanenbaum, "Operating systems: Design and implementation," Prentice-Hall, Inc., Englewood Cliffs, New Jersey, 1987.

[21] D. Wybranietz and D. Haban, "Monitoring and performance measuring distributed systems," *Proc. ACM SIGMETRICS*, Santa Fe, in: *ACM Performance Evaluation Review*, vol. 16, no. 1, pp. 197-206, May 1988.

DAPHNE

Support for Distributed Computing in Heterogeneous Environments

Klaus-Peter Löhr, Lutz Nentwig
Freie Universität Berlin

Joachim Müller
Universität Bremen

Abstract

The DAPHNE system is a collection of tools and run-time support creating a network operating system interface for distributed programming using Modula-2. DAPHNE accomodates hardware and operating system heterogeneity without necessarily unifying heterogeneous system features. In describing the essentials of the DAPHNE approach we concentrate on the semantics of heterogeneous distributed programs and on the difficulties encountered in implementing DAPHNE on top of standard operating systems. Several requirements for the functionality of system interfaces are derived.

1. Introduction

1.1 Traditionally, the user's view of a computer network has been determined by the *network services* provided in addition to local system services and utilities: remote login, file transfer, and the like. In this setting the individual systems in the network keep their autonomy, the user is aware of the different systems, and the network services provide new functionality.

More recently, fast LAN technology has allowed for disk-related operating system functions to work across the network; examples include not only file access but also program loading, page swapping, and process migration. This scenario is common in workstation environments and special multi-computer configurations (usually homogeneous). The user is not aware of the machines involved. Typically, these are controlled by a *distributed operating system* [Tanenbaum/van Renesse 85] which hides the network from the users. In a network of autonomous machines, the operating systems can be enhanced to form a *network operating system* which makes remote system services and utilities available locally. This works both for homogeneous and for heterogeneous networks. Two more recent examples for accommodating heterogeneity are the HCS project at Seattle [Notkin et al. 88] and the DACNOS project at Karlsruhe/Heidelberg [Geihs et al. 88].

Networked systems may or may not support *distributed computing* in the sense that the code of user programs is distributed across the network. Network operating systems do not usually support this. Distributed operating systems often provide for distributing the processes of a concurrent program among different nodes in order to achieve speedup by parallel execution.

1.2 In a heterogeneous environment with different operating systems there is an incentive to partition programs and distribute them across the network, even in the absence of concurrency: complex programs often have "heterogeneous" demands, i.e., different program parts may have different preferred system environments. A typical example is a program that has a sophisticated graphical user interface, employs a number crunching component, and uses data base support. It is this scenario that is addressed by the DAPHNE system - a network operating system for *d*istributed *a*pplications *p*rogramming in *h*eterogeneous *net*works. In DAPHNE, a program with the described behaviour would preferably be partitioned into three *components*, each being assigned to a computer system best suited for its execution.

The reference language of DAPHNE is Modula-2. The module concept of Modula-2 defines the distribution granularity: programs are partitioned along module boundaries (there is one important exception that will be described later); a component may include several modules. Inter-module calls that cross machine boundaries are supported by a remote procedure call (RPC) mechanism that copes with the autonomy and heterogeneity of the systems involved.

The overriding concern of the DAPHNE approach is not to meddle with, duplicate, or usurp features of the native systems software. In particular, we do not introduce special network agents like file servers, mail servers, time servers, accounting servers etc. As respective local system services are offered anyway, a properly designed RPC will make them easily accessible from remote sites. Likewise, we take the view that questions of authorization, mixed-language programming, even concurrency, have nothing to do with heterogeneous distributed computing. They have to be resolved locally, exploiting whatever native system support is available.

1.3 The basic concepts and mechanisms of DAPHNE have been described in [Löhr et al. 88]. We will give a comprehensive survey in section 2. The reader is assumed to be familiar with the RPC paradigm and the relevant terminology [Birrell/Nelson 84] [Tanenbaum/van Renesse 88]. Section 3 deals with implications of autonomy and heterogeneity for the Modula-2 RPC semantics. With respect to implementation, it turns out that operating systems do not usually offer the functionality that is required for building efficient and secure RPC support on top of standard communication protocols. The trouble spots are identified in section 4, and recommendations for suitably amended system interfaces are given. Section 5 gives a conclusion and an outlook on future work.

2. Concepts and Mechanisms of DAPHNE

2.1. Heterogeneous distributed processes

A distributed sequential program as described above is executed by a *distributed process*, an abstraction that comprises the processes executing the different components of the distributed program on different nodes of the network. Each component is administered as a regular user process by the underlying operating system. (For the sake of simplicity, we will not always distinguish between a program component and the corresponding "process component".) Note that if heterogeneous systems are involved we may have widely varying process concepts which have to be accomodated by the distributed process abstraction. We assume single-threaded address spaces on all machines.

If we watch a single-threaded distributed process in action, we usually see a sequential computation which crosses machine boundaries once in a while; at most one component is active at any time (except in special circumstances - see below). Inter-component transitions are caused by remote procedure calls/returns. We say that a *client component* calls a *server component*.

Introducing the abstraction of a distributed process does *not* mean that a network-wide canonical process concept is superimposed on the existing heterogeneous process concepts. We feel that process attributes and operations on processes can vary between systems to such an extent as to make any attempt to "homogenize" process concepts unrealistic. *Exception handling* is a point in case. In the absence of special provisions in the program (e.g., *signal* on a Unix system), each component uses the local default handlers. This does not preclude remote exception handling if desired. (Modula-2 does not support exceptions, but the exception concepts of the underlying operating systems can be imported through library modules, and calling exception handlers is covered by the RPC design; see section 3.3).

2.2. Loading a distributed program

Components of a distributed process are brought into being on demand. Execution of a distributed program is started by loading and starting the root component, i.e., the component containing the main module. Typically, this will be done on behalf of an interactive user. As the computation proceeds, the first call upon a remote module will

(1) locate the component containing the module, i.e., locate a certain program file on a certain machine;
(2) create a process on that machine, loading the component code and starting its initialization sequence;
(3) generate an RPC address to be used in all subsequent remote calls to the module;
(4) using this address, execute an RPC for the desired procedure.

Further calls upon one of the modules contained in the new component will only involve step 4 (and possibly step 3). In due course, the distributed process may expand by creating further components, either directly from the root component or indirectly from one of the other components. Knowledge about the component structure is kept in the run-time system, replicated among all components. Thus, if component A has created component B, another component C that calls upon one of the modules in B will not re-create B.

Creation of a component is a *dynamic linking* activity, and steps 1-3 mentioned above are the last steps in a multi-stage name resolution process. The overall effect of this process is to map a module name into an RPC address. Step 1 is the crucial step here. If the stub generator has substituted a <machine name, file name> pair for the module name, it is easy to locate the server component. This technique, however, is too static to be generally applicable. We will discuss alternative techniques below.

Step 2 is initiated by a process server or *spawner* [Brownbridge et al. 82], i.e., a special process on the target machine. Note that it is not enough to just create a thread of control (or to assign one from a pool of pre-fabricated threads) to execute in an existing module instance. The module (and its enclosing component) is private to the program, so a module instance has to be created and initialized. Thus, the component process created by the spawner is necessarily a heavy-weight process, carrying one or more initialized module instances in its address space.

Successful component creation depends on passing a number of checks, first and foremost the local authorization procedure (as for authentication, see 4.4): the user associated with the client component must be registered on the local system. The server component is then endowed with the rights defined for that user. Likewise, all other process attributes are set according to the standard values specific to the user. Note that the file name for the program component to be loaded is interpreted in the context of the newly created process.

In passing the user identity of the client component to the spawner, forgery is prohibited. This implies that if the client component is authentic, there is no need for authentication by the spawner. Now, a root component running on a system with proper authentication is authentic; thus, any directly or indirectly created components will be authentic by induction. If the root component runs on an unprotected system like a PC it has to authenticate itself by means of a special *login* service provided by the spawner before any remote module calls are accepted. This scheme is safe because the spawners know the network addresses of the trusted (i.e., protected) systems.

2.3. Heterogeneous program management

In a heterogeneous environment, different language systems and different linkers are involved in the construction of a distributed program. We do postulate that a certain language standard is supported throughout the network, but we do not postulate that a unique (ported) compiler is used at all sites. DAPHNE's stub generator is written in Modula-2 and produces Modula-2 stubs from Modula-2 definition modules. It doesn't matter where a stub is generated, but it has to be compiled on the proper target machine where it is to be linked with user modules, other stubs, and the RPC run-time support to form a component.

Enforcing interface consistency across machine boundaries is outside the realm of the local linkers. For each module processed, the stub generator attaches a unique number to the client and server stubs. During run-time, when the server component is created, the corresponding client and server stubs are checked for matching numbers (this is one of the checks mentioned in 2.2). Together with the local checks performed by the Modula-2 linkers, this ensures the desired consistency.

As described in [Löhr et al. 88], a distributed program is prepared, configured, and installed using a set of tools on a workstation. This is in itself a distributed activity as compilers and linkers on different machines are involved.

3. The Programmer's View of Distribution and Heterogeneity

3.1. Distributed Modula-2

If a programming language has not been designed with distributed computing in mind, it is virtually impossible to add an RPC facility without altering language semantics. This has nothing to do with concurrency issues; it is caused by the presence of several disjoint address spaces. Modula-2 does suffer from those problems [Almes 86]. As we were unwilling to sacrifice efficiency for keeping the exact semantics, we decided to live with the following consequences:

(1) (Exported variables) Exported variables cannot be used for inter-component communication.
(2) (Variable parameters) Remote variable parameters are passed by value/result.
(3) (Pointers in parameters) Pointers in RPC parameters must not be dereferenced by the recipients[1].
(4) (Procedure parameters) Procedure parameters in RPCs are not supported. Note, however, that this does not preclude remote procedures to be passed as parameters in local procedure calls; also, "backcalls" to exported procedures are possible.
(5) (Module initialization) As mentioned in 2.2, a module is only initialized when the enclosing component is created. (This is not an important restriction; while it is possible to write initialization code that influences the behaviour of other modules - by calling their exported procedures - this is certainly neither common nor is it good programming practice.)

The treatment of Modula's *opaque pointers* is worth mentioning. (3) is not a handicap in this case because an opaque pointer cannot be accessed outside its manager module anyway. For transmission purposes, the pointer is replaced with a small cardinal which can be represented on all machines.

Object managers may be implemented as *distributed modules* which span several components. Each component contains a copy of the module code and several objects managed by this code. (If the module has local data, their "copies" in the different components are independent of each other - see 3.3.) In this case, the small cardinal representing the pointer outside the module serves as an index to a table of <RPC address, local address> pairs maintained by the stubs (for non-distributed modules only the local address has to be recorded). The client stub uses the RPC address to direct an RPC to the proper component.

If we take an object-oriented view, the parts of a distributed module are like different subclasses of the superclass defined by the definition module. Each object is of a specific subclass type; therefore, an object reference must necessarily contain a reference to its class (i.e., the RPC address).

---

[1] In a language with mandatory pointer initialization, it would make sense to "flatten" linked data structures for transmission, so that a recipient could at least read from a dereferenced pointer.

3.2. System interface modules

DAPHNE hides the heterogeneities of hardware and basic communication protocols from the application programmer. We feel, however, that it is neither possible nor desirable to completely mask the operating system heterogeneities. After all, a demand for different functionalities is the reason for having heterogeneous systems in the first place.

System services are offered to the Modula-2 programmer through a collection of library modules. Each operating system has its own specific library of services which can be used both locally and remotely. As for remote access, library modules are just like any other modules.

The most important example of system services are file system operations. A distributed program dealing with several file systems at the same time can use different approaches:

(1) The homogeneous case (i.e., identical file systems) is a prime application of the distributed module concept introduced in 3.1. A distributed *file system module* serves as an interface to a homogeneous collection of file systems which is thus turned into a coherent distributed file system. The channels used for reading and writing are the abstract objects referred to by opaque pointers. Opening a file amounts to creating a channel object on the system where the file resides.

(2) In the heterogeneous case, the programmer may intentionally use file systems with different functionality. This simply amounts to referring to several definition modules, each representing a different file system.

(3) The abstraction of a homogeneous distributed file system may be superimposed on different file systems, creating the effect of (1).

3.3. Independence of component states

It should be kept in mind that side effects of calling a system function will never affect a component other than the currently active one. Likewise, if the effect of a system function is dependent on the current settings of process attributes, the executing component's settings are used.

As an example, consider the notion of a *current directory* as known from Unix. Each component has its own current directory (if the notion is supported by the local file system) and a *change directory* operation will only influence the executing component. Thus, a distributed program using a distributed file system may have several current directories at the same time; when control crosses a component boundary, a different current directory may become effective. Note that this is a subtle semantic difference between the centralized and the distributed version of a file system module.

Another example is exception handling. Each component of a distributed process has its own local settings for exception handlers, according to the palette of exceptions supported by the local operating system. This does *not* mean that an exception occurring in a component is necessarily handled within this component; a *signal* operation (à la Unix) may have specified a remote procedure for handling that exception, and this procedure will be activated through an RPC. The point is that *signal* affects the local component only. Thus, crossing a component boundary may cause different exception handling strategies to become effective.

4. What DAPHNE demands from Operating Systems

DAPHNE intentionally renounces the option of modifying the underlying operating systems. Ideally, the DAPHNE tools, run-time support, and the spawner code should be portable, so that any kind of system could be easily accommodated. Problems arise, however, with the run-time support and the spawner code. We tried to minimize these by hiding the operating system dependencies in special interface modules. But, set aside heterogeneity, the trouble is that a few functions are required that are usually not offered at all at system interfaces.

4.1. Achieving RPC efficiency

We set out to produce a system usable for fine-grain distributed computing, in spite of heterogeneity. A fast RPC is of paramount importance for this. Degradation of RPC performance is caused by different data representations (to be accomodated by a presentation mechanism) and slow lower-level communication protocols. It is obvious that we cannot expect our RPC to bear comparison with similar mechanisms in distributed operating systems for homogeneous hardware. But we can do pretty well by (1) transmitting the internal representations of simple data values if identical for client and server component and (2) employing a genuine DAPHNE protocol suite that evades the inefficiencies of standard protocols.

Achieving high commmunication efficiency boils down to the question of whether the underlying operating system offers a suitable transport service at the system interface. If not - or if no communication services are offered at all - the only resort is to incorporate a (new) network driver into the system (which hopefully supports such amendments).

The portable part of the RPC protocol is built on top of an unreliable DAPHNE transport service. To implement this service, a small module has to be written for each system; the module uses whatever suitable transport service is available at the system interface (e.g., UDP, or a custom-made network driver). This "raw" transport service need not be reliable, but should be of sufficient quality.

4.2. Efficient and reliable multicast

Behind the scenes, several DAPHNE functions have to be supported by multicast communication. Internal *multicast RPCs*, not available to the user, are used for
(1) locating systems and services by talking to the spawners,
(2) updating replicated state information in a distributed process (the list of components, the pointer tables, etc.).

Version (1) is a well-known technique for soliciting an answer from a distributed service. It can be implemented efficiently on LANs - if the system interface includes a suitable broadcast function whose destination is a set of "well-known ports" with identical port numbers on all systems.

Version (2) does not deliver a result, nor is an acknowledgement expected. Reliability is achieved through the RPC protocol: on entering a component the process checks whether the replicated state information is up-to-date; if not, it is patched from the previous component (where the state information is up-to-date by induction [Isle et al. 86]). The destination of the multicast message is "all components of the executing distributed process". We have to issue a broadcast message that will be relayed to the destination components on the relevant systems, but will be discarded on other systems. The protocol must know about the association of components with distributed processes. We use a unique *dpid* for each distributed process, attach it to all its components, and establish a mapping from *dpid*s to port numbers of components on each machine. Note that this cannot be done completely above the system interface.

4.3. Process management

If an operating system is unable to create processes dynamically it cannot be used as a host for DAPHNE servers. Ideally, all systems should be able to create a user process in response to a request arriving over the network. This means that all systems should support a *process service* that does not stipulate specific protocols for data transmission.

In the absence of such system support, a spawner is needed as an operating system extension that can be addressed using the RPC protocol. The spawner is the least portable part of the DAPHNE software. It must be able to fulfill the usual duties of a process server: to create a server process for a certain login name (that of the client), establish a communication path between client and server, and start the server with a certain program (as requested by the client).

Note that the spawner is also a *component manager*. It is responsible for all bookkeeping on the local components and has to be notified about component termination (normal or abnormal) by the operating system. A client can ask the spawner about the status of a server (e.g., "is it alive?"). Also, spawners cooperate in tearing down a distributed process when one of its components has terminated.

4.4. Security requirements

The DAPHNE RPC protocol is implemented as part of a program's run-time support; it is not incorporated in the protected operating system. Therefore, we have to cope with potential security threats.

First, communication between components of a distributed process must be protected from interference by other processes. Eavesdropping is not a problem because a component cannot alter its transport address. Talking to an "alien" component (i.e., a component of a different distributed process) can be prohibited by making transport addresses or *dpid*s unforgeable. We chose to encapsulate tables of *pid/dpid* associations in our custom-made drivers because the *dpid*s have to be known to the drivers anyway (according to 4.2). A driver attaches the *dpid* associated with the current process to a message; so the receiving driver will get an authentic *dpid* and will never forward a message to an alien component.

Both the *dpid* and the login name of a component are set during component initialization by means of a special system call that is available to the spawner only.

5. Concluding remarks

DAPHNE is a language-oriented approach to distributed computing and exploits the module concept of Modula-2 for accommodating heterogeneous systems software. It is important to remember that *heterogeneous computing* is at the core of our notion of distributed computing, not concurrency issues.

The DAPHNE approach is of course not tied to Modula-2, neither is it confined to sequential programs. Our tools support Modula-2 and the currently used RPC version supports single-threaded components only. The tools are language-dependant, but the RPC support is not - although it has been designed with module-oriented languages in mind. Presently, we are exploring the expansion of the DAPHNE design towards object orientation and light-weight processes. An object-oriented language to replace Modula-2 has not been chosen yet.

Acknowledgements

It is our pleasure to thank Yin Zhao-lin for his excellent work on an improved version of the DAPHNE stub generator.

References

[Almes 86] G.T. Almes: The impact of language and system on remote procedure call design. Proc. 6. Int. Conf. on Distributed Computing Systems, Cambridge, IEEE 1986

[Brownbridge et al. 82] D.R. Brownbridge, L.F. Marshall, B. Randell: The Newcastle Connection or 'Unixes of the world unite!'. Software - Practice & Experience 12.12, December 1982

[Birrell/Nelson 84] A.D. Birrell, B.J. Nelson: Implementing remote procedure calls. ACM TOCS 2.1, February 1984

[Geihs et al. 88] K. Geihs, B. Schoener, U. Hollberg, H. Schmutz, H. Eberle: An architecture for the cooperation of heterogeneous operating systems. Proc. Computer Network Symposium, Washington, IEEE, April 1988

[Isle et al. 86] R. Isle, J. Müller, L. Nentwig: Maintaining the state of a distributed Unix process. Proc. EUUG autumn '86 Workshop, Manchester, September 1986

[Löhr et al. 88] K.-P. Löhr, J. Müller, L. Nentwig: DAPHNE - Support for distributed applications programming in heterogeneous computer networks. Proc. 8. Int. Conf. on Distributed Computing Systems, San Jose, IEEE 1988

[Notkin et al. 88] D. Notkin, A.P. Black, E.D. Lazowska, H.M. Levy, J. Sanislo, J. Zahorjan: Interconnecting heterogeneous computer systems. Comm. ACM 31.3, March 1988

[Tanenbaum/van Renesse 85] A.S. Tanenbaum, R. v. Renesse: Distributed operating systems. ACM Computing Surveys 17.4, December 1985

[Tanenbaum/van Renesse 88] A.S. Tanenbaum, R. van Renesse: A critique of the remote procedure call paradigm. In R. Speth (ed.): Research into Networks and distributed applications. Elsevier 1988

Distributed Computing with a Processor Bank

J M Bacon, I M Leslie and R M Needham

*University of Cambridge Computer Laboratory,
New Museums Site, Pembroke Street, Cambridge CB2 3QG, UK*

The Cambridge Distributed Computing System (CDCS) was designed some ten years ago and was in everyday use at the Computer Laboratory until December 1988. An overview of the basic design of CDCS is given, an outline of its evolution and a description of the distributed systems research projects that were based on it. Experience has shown that a design based on a processor bank leads to a flexible and extensible distributed system.

1. The Cambridge Distributed Computing System

CDCS [Needham82] was designed some ten years ago and was in everyday use, as the main research environment at the Computer Laboratory, over many years. It is based on the Cambridge Ring (CR) local area network and employs the "pool of processors" approach to distributed computing. CDCS provides a number of common services such as file storage and printing, which may be invoked from the heterogeneous systems running in processor bank machines. It also provides a naming and authorisation infrastructure and management of the processor bank.

Typical usage of CDCS is for a user, via a terminal server, to ask the Resource Manager for a processor from the processor bank. The user specifies a software system to be loaded into the acquired processor, is authenticated to this system and to CDCS and then runs applications on this single machine. Although the user is free to acquire more than one machine, CDCS originally provided virtually no support for users to spread a task across a number of machines. Processor bank machines may be loaded with public operating systems, which may be used to run public utilities, or private research systems.

1.1. Evolution of CDCS

CDCS was initially implemented on a single Cambridge Ring and was extended to operate over three bridged Cambridge Rings on two sites. Project Universe [Leslie 84] further extended the basic system design to CR-based systems connected by satellite over a wide area.

The program development environment provided through the processor bank and file server, which for practical reasons were small research systems, was augmented by two Vax Unix™ systems, with local discs, and a number of Ethernet-based MicroVax2s. Sun and Xerox distributed systems also use the Ethernet [figure1]. The recent development of the Cambridge Fast Ring (CFR) gives potential for systems research based on an order of magnitude increase in LAN speed.

CDCS was originally programmed in an ad-hoc way and in 1982 the Mayflower project was set up to develop a language and environment for programming distributed services and applications. A concurrent programming language Concurrent CLU (CCLU) including a language level remote procedure call (RPC) facility was produced and used for development of a number of services, tools and applications.

2. CDCS Design Overview

2.1 LAN Medium and Protocol Hierarchy

The Cambridge Ring is a slotted, 10Mbps ring with anti-hogging and indication of success or failure of delivery at the lowest (minipacket) level [Wilkes 79]. The recent Cambridge Fast Ring, designed to operate at 100Mbps follows this tradition but with a larger packet size [Hopper 88]. A protocol hierarchy was designed for CDCS with a Basic Block protocol above the CR and a choice of a Single Shot (request-response or transaction) Protocol and a Byte Stream Protocol at the next level. Above this, specialised application protocols were developed for sevice bootstrapping, file service and garbage collection, above SSP and for terminal connections above BSP. CDCS was an early example of the use of lightweight protocols in a reliable, high speed, high bandwidth LAN environment.

2.2 Software System Structure

A processor bank may contain heterogeneous hardware which may be loaded with heterogeneous software systems. Each system may have its own implementation of naming, protection, reliability, etc. An aim of CDCS was to allow such systems to share common services such as printing and disc storage and common utilities such as electronic mail.

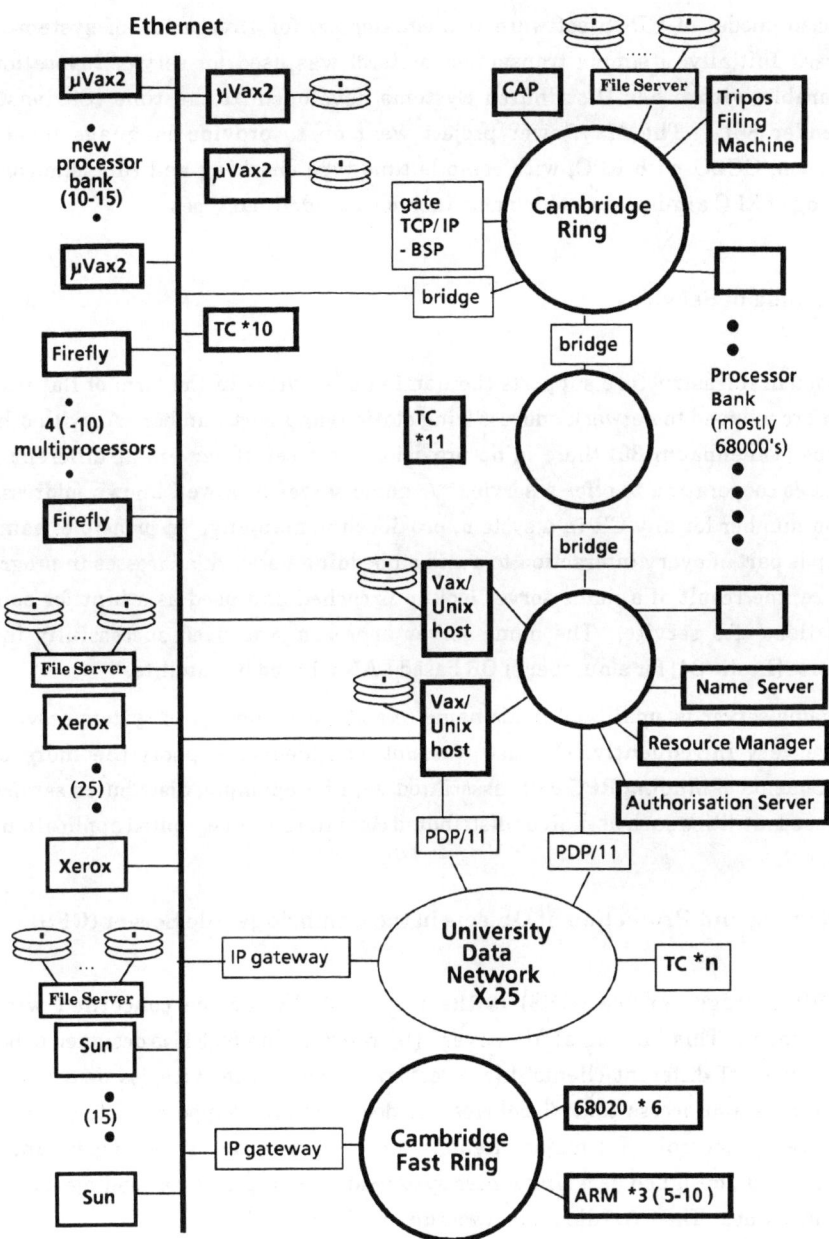

FIGURE 1. Part of the Distributed Computing Research Environment (to December 88). The Cambridge (old) Ring world is now being dismantled.

The basic model of CDCS software is *client-server,* for invocation of system-provided services. Initially, a simple transaction protocol was used for service invocation (SSP), comparable with other Distributed Systems developed at the time [Shrivastava 82, Mullender 86]. The Mayflower project went on to provide language level service invocation, CCLU with RPC, with compile time type checking and run time consistency checking of RPC arguments, which may include user-defined types.

2.3 Naming of Services

The system infrastructure supports the naming of services in the form of flat text names which are mapped to network address (ring station) and port number. As with other early systems [Tanenbaum 85] there is no provision for a set of servers at different network addresses cooperating to offer a service. A name server at a well known address, a fixed station number for any CR in a system, provides the mapping. In principle, name server lookup is part of every interaction to avoid embedding network addresses in programs. In practice, the result of a name server lookup is cached and used as a hint for subsequent invocations of a service. The name server approach was used successfully in Project Universe [Leslie 84] for a number of CR based LANs linked by satellite.

The name server is small and holds name to address mappings of system services which change very infrequently. Its use was not extended to support the more dynamic requirements of binding RPC calls associated with for example, distributed services being developed, utilities such as mail or distributed compilers, or distributed applications.

2.4 Naming and Protection of Objects in the Cambridge File Server (CFS)

The file storage service (CFS) is the major CDCS service concerned with object management. This "universal file server" [Birrell 80, Dion 80,81] is designed to be used by any number of different clients' file directory servers, each with its own text naming conventions and access control policies. It does however support existence control and concurrency control. Its major client in practice was the Tripos Operating System [Richards 79], designed as a single user system and appropriate for loading into processor bank machines. The CAP file system was also replaced by CFS.

CFS thus provides a low level storage service. It supports the primitive types *byte* and *id* and the single type constructor *sequence.* A file is a sequence of bytes and an *index* is a sequence of id's. Every file and every index has an *id.* Indexes may be used by clients to mirror their directory structures. The CFS interface is such that creation of an object is combined with storing its *id* in an index. The CFS existence control policy, that an object exists while it is reachable from the root, is supported by a garbage collection mechanism which CFS initiates to run asynchronously in a processor bank machine.

CFS was designed to support filing systems as its clients. It may also be used directly by services or utilities and an evaluation of its design for this style of use is given in the references cited in section 3 .

Mandatory concurrency control, typically multiple reader single writer locks on whole files, is often argued to be inappropriate at the lowest level of distributed systems, since clients will often be multiple instances of the same program, able to synchronise their access to shared objects at a higher level. A more flexible approach is to provide a separate lock primitive and possibly to support finer grained concurrent write sharing [Burrows 88].

The Tripos directory service was initially provided as part of the Tripos system loaded into processor bank machines. Such systems cannot be trusted to carry out access control. The Tripos Filing Machine [Richardson 83,84] was developed to function both as a trusted directory server for Tripos systems and as a caching machine to improve the performance of the file service.

2.5 Authorisation for Service Use

Each processor bank operating system carries out its own user authentication but must register its current user with a CDCS authorisation server, the Active Object Table manager (AOT). AOT issues a session key, with a random component, which, together with information on the category of the user, functions as a capability for service use, in that a server may check with AOT that a request comes from an authenticated user. Users loading private software systems into processor bank machines must also be authorised to use public services by registering with AOT.

2.6 Reliability

Each service may take its own independent approach to reliability, for example, CFS provides atomic transactions on special files, typically used for client file system metadata.

The infrastructure was designed for rapid rebooting through the boot server. The network interfaces and node software provide facilities for remote control and debugging.

A dead man's handle technique is used to monitor allocated processor bank systems.

The CCLU RPC system is a communications facility and is not concerned with application level issues such as orphan extermination and server restart. The default RPC semantics are *at most once* but an option may be specified which offers *exactly once* semantics in the absence of server crashes and prolonged network failure.

3. CCLU and the Mayflower Project

The Mayflower project was set up in 1982 to provide an environment for developing and running distributed applications and services. It comprises a language, CCLU, a communications protocol, RPC, integrated into the language system, and an operating system, the Mayflower supervisor. Details are given in [Hamilton 84] and [Bacon 87].

3.1 Sequential CLU

CLU [Liskov81] was selected and extended by the Mayflower group. CLU is object orientated in style and provides procedures for procedural abstraction, iterators for control abstraction and clusters for data abstraction. It is strongly typed and supports user defined abstract types. It has separate compilation facilities and the compiler generates and checks interface specifications. Parameterised clusters go some way towards providing the facilities usually associated with a polymorphic typing system.

3.2 Concurrency Features in CCLU

CLU was extended with a fork primitive to support the dynamic creation of lightweight processes sharing an address space, allowing the construction of high performance services with internal concurrency (multi-threaded servers). Semaphores and monitors were added for process synchronisation. It was found, in a systems environment, that classical monitors unduly restrict concurrency in large systems [Cooper 85] and a critical region construct, with programmer specified locking, was added. This allowed the critical code to be kept to a minimum while modular structure was maintained by the use of clusters.

3.3 CCLU RPC

CCLU RPC is a type-checked, type-safe, language-level construct incorporating dynamic binding under program control. Arbitrarily complex objects of practically any type in the CLU language, including user-defined abstract types, can be passed in arguments to RPCs. The philosophy of Mayflower RPC is not to hide from the programmer that certain processing is remote and the peculiar semantics and overhead of remote operations are made explicit. The language was therefore modified to add new syntax for the definition and call of remote procedures, rather than using the method of preprocessing and stub generation often associated with transparent RPC [Birrell 84]. The programmer may use the default communications semantics of *at most once* or may select reliable *exactly once* semantics in the absence of node crashes and prolonged network failure. CCLU RPC operates through bridges and across a ring-ethernet gateway.

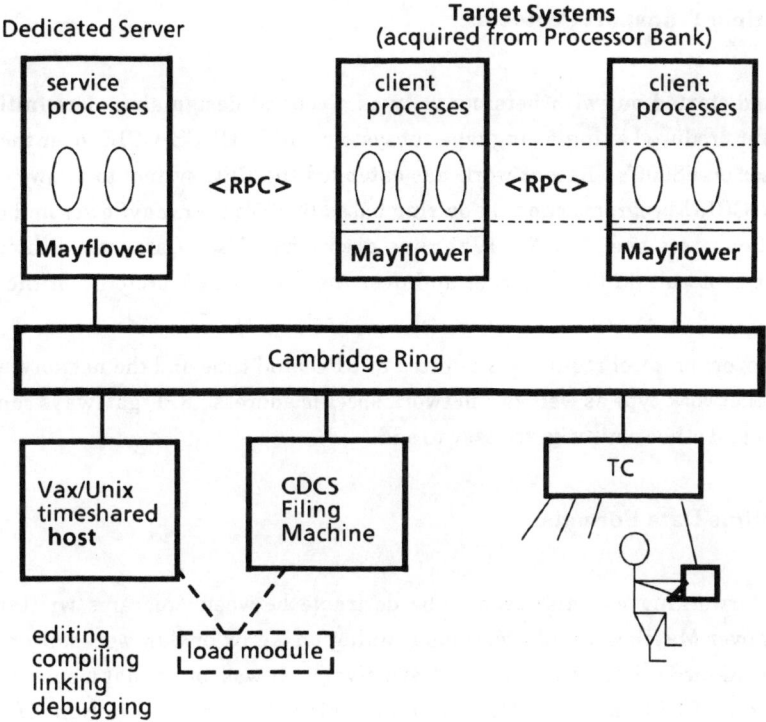

FIGURE 2.   Mayflower on CDCS

3.4 The Mayflower "Lightweight" Kernel

The Mayflower kernel was designed for implementing high performance services for distributed systems. It supports lightweight processes running in a shared address space (a Mayflower domain) hence supporting what are often called multi-threaded servers. Resources are allocated to a domain and are shared by all processes therein. Multiple domains per node may be used but inter-domain communication is by (expensive) RPC.

System development is carried out in CCLU on (Micro)Vaxes under Unix and target code runs on processor bank MC68000s under the Mayflower kernel and, for preliminary testing, on Vaxes under Unix. CDCS infrastructure, services and applications can be written in CCLU to run under Mayflower and have RPC interfaces [figure 2]. The CDCS authorisation server AOT was reimplemented and a new processor bank manager was designed [Craft 85].

3.5 Multiple Transport Protocols

CDCS had started out with heterogeneity as a central design aim. The initial phase of Mayflower produced a single language subsystem within CDCS; CCLU over the Mayflower supervisor on 68000's. Recent work has extended the RPC system to allow interworking between CCLU programs running on ring based 68000's over Mayflower and on Ethernet based Microvaxes over UNIX. RPC runs over UDP (User Datagram Protocol) and IP (Internet Protocol) on the Ethernet and over the Basic Block protocol on the Cambridge Ring.

The transport protocol required is selected at RPC bind time and the network address now includes network type as well as a network specific address. RPC gateways can be written in CCLU and other networks are easy to add.

3.6 Multiple Data Formats

Some interworking was also seen to be desirable between programs written in CCLU running over Mayflower and programs running on Xerox or Sun workstations written to use Xerox Courier RPC and Sun RPC respectively. It was found that a subset of the types supported by CCLU RPC, the built in immutable types, are used in Sun XDR (eXternal Data Representation standard) and the Courier data standard. CLU RPC was therefore extended to allow selection of any one of these data representations.

CCLU clients can access existing Xerox and Sun services, UNIX and Xerox XDE (Xerox Development Environment) and Interlisp clients can access CCLU servers and limited support is provided for new multi language distributed applications.

4. Distributed Systems Research on CDCS

4.1 Processor Bank Management and Dynamic Software Configuration

In the original CDCS design each available system configuration was held as a single, fully-linked load module in the file server and was loaded into processor bank machines under the control of the Resource Manager (RM). This is reasonable for the small number of system services originally available but is undesirable as a basis for research into extensible, heterogeneous systems with dynamically loaded utilities and applications. Craft's RM [Craft 83,85] proposes multi-level resources which may consist of several software layers on a variety of hardware and which are configured dynamically when requested. One or more processor bank machines with associated software may be requested, or a session on a shared system such as a Unix system. Automatic preloading of commonly used systems avoids delay to users.

Allocated resources are monitored by an **Aliveness Server** using a dead-man's handle mechanism and interested parties are notified of any events in which they have registered an interest by an **Event Notification Server**.

4.2 A Debugger for Distributed Concurrent Programs [Cooper 87, 88]

A debugger supporting source level debugging of distributed CCLU programs in the target environment under real conditions of use was implemented in CCLU. Research issues include the policies and mechanisms associated with breakpointing processes of a distributed computation, determining the operating system and run-time library support desirable for implementing this kind of debugger, and defining a more appropriate format than flat files in which to store debugging information produced by compilers and linkers.

A small debug agent is included at every CCLU node (within the Mayflower kernel or within the run-time system for CCLU on the Unix emulation of Mayflower) and a small amount of statistical data, for example on the most recent RPC calls, is gathered. The relevant agents are activated from a debugger machine acquired from the processor bank when the program is to be debugged. The policy on breakpoints is that all processes of a computation should be halted "instantly" when any breakpoint occurs.

Special emphasis is given to debugging system services, both before and after installation, and to the fact that a program being debugged will be using shared services. A new service or a new version of an existing service may be installed on a processor bank machine under the control of the debugger. It may be tested, at first with an artificially generated test load, and may subsequently be released to real clients. It is argued that services should be written to compute the elapsed time of their clients excluding the time halted at breakpoints.

4.3 A Distributed Mail System [Brooks 88]

The processor bank model is particularly suited to providing network services which have very uneven resource requirements such as mail. The system load from mail has infrequent peaks so that timesharing systems degrade when mail is being processed and dedicated mail servers remain idle for substantial times. Users' private workstations cannot be trusted to run mail since the software could be modified to allow confidential mail to be read into the workstation or mail to be altered. The approach used in this research is to have a small dedicated server as a permanent mail daemon augmented by processors from the pool at times of high load. A mechanism for dynamically acquiring machines is required for this type of application and, ideally, for releasing some if they are requested by higher priority tasks. A processor bank machine, unlike a workstation, can be loaded with trusted, unmodifiable software which provides the mail program interface.

The distributed mail service uses the CFS interface directly and this has provided useful experience for the design of future network storage services. A read only capability is required for mail objects, for example.

4.4 A Distributed Compilation System [Wei 89]

A distributed compilation system was developed for CCLU in which compilation of separate modules is assigned to individual processors under the direction of a controller server of which there is one per active user. A library server maintains the interface specifications of library clusters and of compilation units which are written by the compiler instances when a unit is compiled. These specifications are read by the compiler instances when external calls are being type checked. The library server must also ensure that the concurrent compilations carried out by several users do not conflict, for example, when the specification for a module is changed as it is being used in the compilation of other modules.

As well as contributing to research in distributed compilation this project provides an example of the requirement for a minimum configuration of three machines but the possibility of dynamically acquiring other free machines for both compilation servers and library servers, and releasing them to higher priority tasks when requested.

4.5 A Distributed File Directory Service [Seaborne 88]

The provision of file naming and directory facilities for heterogeneous operating systems connected by a LAN was investigated. A replicated and distributed directory service was developed in prototype form in CCLU under Mayflower on processor bank machines. The directory service is designed to function as a universal directory service and is located above a low level file storage service such as CFS.

The design is based on a generalised directory structure and a generalised pathname comprising a list of components. New directories may be created and attached to the naming graph. A directory entry is a string, naming an inferior file or directory object together with an access control list and a unique identifier for the object. The directory service returns to the client the identifier of the file or directory named by the full pathname specified in the request.

The service is implemented as a set of servers and a primary site cache management policy is used for maintaining consistency of the directories cached by the service instances.

File servers hold the contents of files and the transfer of the contents only involves the clients and the file servers.

4.6 Project Universe [Leslie 84]

In the Universities Extended Ring Satellite Experiments (Universe) project, a number of CR based LANs running CDCS software were connected by a 1Mbit/s satellite broadcast channel [figure 3].

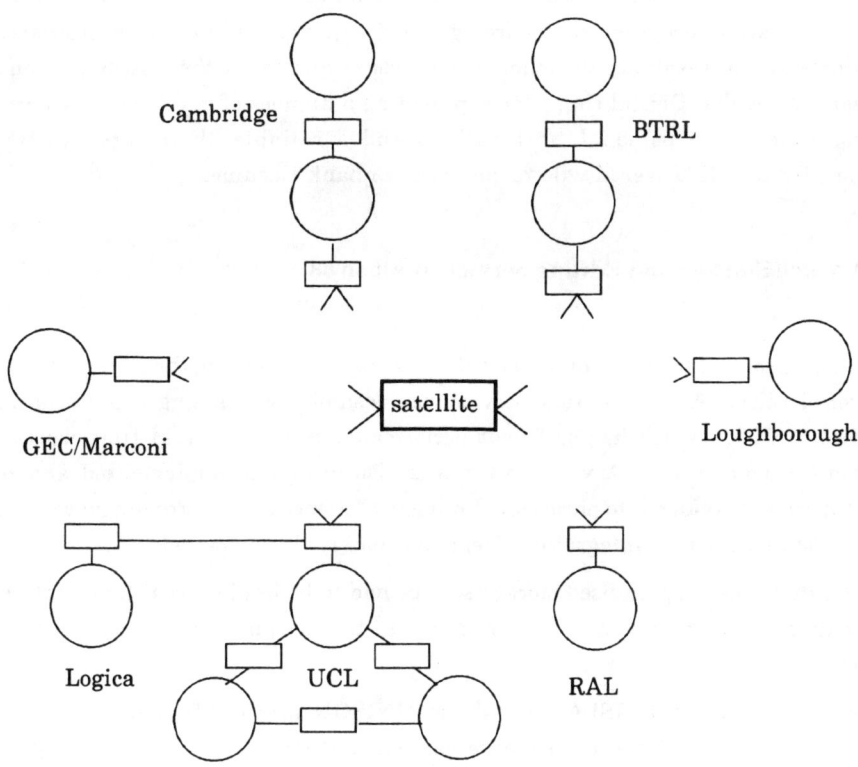

FIGURE 3. The Universe Network

To avoid delay in gateways and therefore to be able to regard the whole network as an efficient distributed system, a single network rather than an internet was constructed. Experiments included remote bootstrapping of trusted system software; use of the Cambridge file servers as a remote storage service for multiple instances of Tripos Filing Machines; and transfer of voice and video.

4.7 A Reliable, Distributed Telephone Exchange [Want 88]

The ISLAND project at the laboratory studied the provision of integrated services on a local area network. Transporting data, voice and video in the same network has the practical advantage of minimising wiring and also allows applications to integrate these media. The intended network medium for this work was the CFR but prototype systems were developed on CDCS.

The control and management of a network telephone is in the domain of distributed computing in such a system. The voice connections between telephones are virtual circuits. Control and data information can be freely mixed with voice at a network interface. The new problems that result are the management issues relating to the distributed control of the real time media. Digital ring phones providing a number of novel services were built and controlled from personal workstations and a reliable, distributed PABX was implemented in CCLU over Mayflower on processor bank machines.

4.8 A Voice Storage and Editing Service [Calnan 88]

CCLU was also used for work under the ISLAND project concerning the storage and editing of encoded voice. A voice storage service was designed, comprising a protocol and an interface to CFS, which has sufficient performance to support real time working for telephone conversations. A voice editor was also designed, implemented and tested. Encoded voice is divided into phrases, delimited by "silences" (background noise) and each phrase is stored as a file. Integration of text and voice is also supported.

The fact that a new, specialised storage service had to be used for real time performance rather than existing file services is relevant to the design of future network storage services.

Following experience in ISLAND and the UNISON project [Tennenhouse 87], the Laboratory is about to carry out further research in multimedia systems, including video as well as voice, based on the CFR.

5. Current Work, Summary and Conclusions

A major advantage of the processor bank approach is that new systems may be made available to users as technology evolves without any change in the underlying system. Also, the model of independently managed subsystems sharing common services is widely applicable. Some ten years of experience with CDCS have shown that the two major functions provided above the basic communications infrastructure, processor bank management and support for service invocation by heterogeneous, independently managed subsystems, form a good basis for distributed system design.

Although single user, diskless systems were originally envisaged in the processor bank, a range of configurations may be accommodated. Special purpose hardware may be included, several systems may be acquired to run a parallel application and a range of operating systems may be made available to users. A new processor bank would now include the DEC Firefly shared memory multiprocessors, currently used as research systems. A system model under investigation proposes a high quality graphics terminal per user, rather than a conventional terminal or workstation, supported by processing resources available across the network [Dixon 88].

CDCS had started out with heterogeneity as a central design aim. The Mayflower project produced a single language subsystem within CDCS; CCLU over the Mayflower supervisor on 68000's. Subsequent work allowed a number of transport protocols and data formats to be selected. Current distributed systems research is making use of CCLU but a new lightweight kernel, capable of running on VAX architectures, including multiprocessors, as well as M68000's is being developed.

After some years of experience with CCLU RPC we feel that non-transparent syntax best reflects the realities of an environment comprising distributed programs. Finer control over timeout and retry strategies than those provided may be desirable. A fully type checked high level language facility is highly desirable. Extension of CCLU to experiment with object mechanisms such as inheritance and dynamic linking is in progress [Hailes 88].

A number of research projects have used CCLU on CDCS and have illustrated that the processor bank approach to distributed computing, supported by system and language level mechanisms, provides a good basis for distributed computing. The processor bank provided a testbed for research into distributed implementations of services and into the possibility of acquiring extra machines dynamically in response to load on a particular service.

A new processor bank comprising Ethernet-based Microvaxes is now used. Various software systems are offered including Ultrix, VMS and Amoeba and a new lightweight kernel is being developed. Distributed Systems simulation experiments are currently being programmed in CCLU on the new processor bank [Dickman 88]. Other research projects which follow directly from the experience gained in CDCS include the design of network storage services [Thomson 87, Wilson 87], naming services [Ma 88] and monitoring services [Lam 88]. For current large scale systems each service must be designed as a set of servers and again, processor bank machines are being used to prototype distributed service implementations.

Acknowledgements

This paper presents work of the Systems Group at the Computer Laboratory over many years. Some individuals' work is referenced above and many others have contributed.

References

[Bacon 87]   Bacon J M and Hamilton K G, "Distributed Computing with RPC: The Cambridge Approach", Proc IFIPS conference on Distributed Processing, eds. Barton M et al. 355-369, North Holland 1988

[Birrell 80]   Birrell A D and Needham R M, "A Universal File Server" IEEE Trans SE, SE-6 (5), 450-453, Sept 80

[Birrell 84]   Birrell A D and Nelson B J, "Implementing Remote Procedure Call" ACM Transactions on Computer Systems 2(1), 39-59, Feb 84

[Brooks 88]   Brooks P M, "Distribution of Functions in Computer Networks" University of Cambridge submitted PhD thesis, 1988

[Burrows 88]   Burrows M, "Efficient Data Sharing" University of Cambridge PhD thesis and TR 153, 1988

[Calnan 88]   Calnan R, "The Integration of Voice within a Digital Network" University of Cambridge submitted PhD thesis, 1989

[Cheriton 84] Cheriton D R, "The V Kernel: A Software Base for Distributed Systems" IEEE Software, 1(2), April 84

[Cooper 85]   Cooper R C B and Hamilton K G "Preserving Abstraction in Concurrent Programming" IEEE Trans SE, SE14(2), 258-262, Feb 88, and University of Cambridge Computer Laboratory TR 76, August 1985

[Cooper 87]   Cooper R C B, "Pilgrim: A Debugger for Distributed Systems" Proc IEEE 7th ICDCS, Berlin 1987

[Craft 83]   Craft D H, "Resource Management in a Decentralised System" ACM SOSP9, Operating Systems Review 17(5), 11-19, Oct 1983

[Craft 85]   Craft D H, "Resource Management in a Decentralised System" PhD thesis, University of Cambridge 1985, TR 73

[Dickman 88]   Dickman P J, Thesis proposal 1988

[Dion 80]   Dion J, "The Cambridge File Server" ACM Operating Systems Review, 14(4), 26-35, Oct 80

[Dion 81]   Dion J, "Reliable Storage in a Local network" University of Cambridge, PhD thesis, 1981

[Dixon 88]   Dixon J, Thesis proposal 1988

[Hailes 88]   Hailes S M V, Thesis proposal 1988

[Hamilton 84] Hamilton K G, "A Remote Procedure Call System" University of Cambridge PhD thesis, TR 70, 1984

[Hopper 88]   Hopper A and Needham R M "The Cambridge Fast Ring Networking System". IEEE Trans on Computers Sept 88

[Lam 88]   Lam K Y, Thesis proposal 1988

[Leslie 84]   Leslie I M et al, "The Architecture of the Universe Network", Proc ACM Sigcomm 84, CCR 14(2), 2-9, June 84

[Liskov 81]   Liskov B et al , "CLU Reference Manual" Springer Verlag, LNCS 114, 1981

[Ma 88]   Ma C, Thesis proposal 1988

[Mullender86]   Mullender S J and Tanenbaum A S, "The Design of a Capability Based Distributed Operating System" Computer Journal, 29(4), 289-300, March 86

[Needham 82]   Needham R M and Herbert A H , "The Cambridge Distributed Computing System" Addison Wesley 1982.

[Richards 79]   Richards M et al, "Tripos - A Portable, Real -time Operating System" Software, Practice and Experience, 9, 513-526, 1979

[Richardson 83] Richardson M F and Needham R M, "The Tripos Filing Machine" ACM Operating Systems review, 17(5), 120-128, 1983

[Richardson 84] Richardson M F, "Filing System Services for Distributed Computer Systems", University of Cambridge PhD thesis, 1984

[Seaborne 87]   Seaborne A F, "Filing in a Heterogeneous Network" University of Cambridge PhD thesis , 1988

[Shrivastava 82] Shrivastava S and Panzieri F, "The Design of a Remote Procedure Call Mechanism", IEEE Trans Computers, 31(7), July 82

[Tanenbaum 85] Tanenbaum A S and van-Renesse R, "Distributed Operating Systems" ACM Computing Surveys 17(4), 419-470, Dec 85

[Tennenhouse 87] Tennenhouse D L et al, "Exploiting Wideband ISDN's: The Unison Exchange", Proc IEEE Infocom 87, 1018 - 1026, 1987

[Thomson 87]   Thomson S, Thesis proposal 1987

[Want 88]   Want R, " Reliable Management of Voice in a Distributed System" University of Cambridge PhD thesis, and TR 141, 1988

[Wei 87]   Wei M, "Distributed Compilation" University of Cambridge PhD thesis in preparation, 1988

[Wilkes 79]   Wilkes M V and Wheeler D J, "The Cambridge Digital Communication Ring" Local Area Communications Network Symposium (sponsors MITRE corp. & NBS), Boston, Mass. May 1979.

[Wilson 87]   Wilson T D, Thesis proposal 1987

MANDIS: Management of Distributed Systems

David Holden & Alwyn Langsford

Harwell Laboratory, UK

ABSTRACT

This paper gives an overview of the MANDIS programme of COST 11 ter. It presents the architectural approach taken and how this influenced, and was influenced by, work on monitoring. The paper discusses some of the work on control and on a language with which to exercise distributed systems management which is now the focus of current work.

1. Introduction

MANDIS is a pilot study and implementation in the MANagement of DIstributed Systems. Its primary aim has been to explore management issues where both local and wide area network have to co-operate. But it is more than a study of network management, which tends to concern itself with the communications environment alone. MANDIS recognized that to consider management of the communications network in isolation is to consider but part of the requirement. The approach has been to consider the management of communications, processing and information storage as a coherent whole.

Many earlier experiments in managing the distributed processing environment have been within the context of a local area network (LAN) or within a single organisation[1][2][3]. Whereas ISO, in considering Open Systems Interconnection (OSI) have considered the wide area networking (WAN) environment, it has only recently begun to develop recognisable standards for management. Even these are essentially concerned with communications.

In MANDIS we wanted to bring the concerns of distributed processing, its management and wide area open systems together into one activity. At the outset, the project set itself five demanding objectives:

- to define an architecture for distributed systems management and the necessary set of management functions which are required to enable distributed information systems to interwork in an effective, application independent manner across local and wide area networks;

- Authors' current address: Building 7-12, Harwell Laboratory, Didcot, Oxon., OX11 0RA, England.

- to develop communications protocols in support of distributed systems management;
- to specify and build tools (as appropriate) which are needed by managers of distributed systems to assist them in their management task;
- to study the options for the location of management functions in distributed processing systems and to establish guidelines for implementation;
- to set up a pilot implementation to provide a focus for the project and a framework for specification, design and implementation.

A discussion of the implementation is described elsewhere within this volume[4]. We concentrate here on the architectural issues, the studies carried out on monitoring and, more recently, on control. We comment on the new work which has followed from the decision to under take this project; work which could not readily have been anticipated at the start.

MANDIS is a collaborative research project carried out within the scope of COST 11 ter. It has its roots in a series of studies undertaken during the earlier COST 11 bis programme. Contributions came from 13 organisations in 8 countries. As well as organising technical meetings between its experts, the project has also sponsored the interchange of workers between organisations and given presentations and demonstrations of its achievements. A number of related MANDIS publications are given in the references[5][6][7][8][9].

2. A Management Architecture

2.1 Management Requirements

The MANDIS approach to analysing and constructing a management activity consists of five main stages:

i. capture of information (theories)

ii. architecture, structure of management information

iii. choice of computational model and environment

iv. design

v. implementation

This approach is described more fully by Holden et al[7].

The consensus among distributed systems researchers is for a basic request/response communications paradigm. This serves well when the concern is simple operations which have no real time or concurrent processing actions. In those research approaches, the implementation (real or conceptual) has been carried out in terms of a "light weight" kernel. This provides the basic services of communication, processing support and (where appropriate) security. Other processes, even those carrying out system related functions, have operated in a manner similar to any application program in the environment, though they may have had special privileges conferred upon them to manipulate system resources.

Our early thinking was guided by the work of the Free University of Amsterdam whose Amoeba LAN operating system formed the basis of subsequent implementation. However, in considering management in a regime of interworking WANs and LANs we had to take account of the fact that management had to operate both within and between different processing domains. In each, managers would wish to retain independence and the freedom to establish their own policy. Each must be able to carry out its handling of faults, its monitoring of performance, its approach to accounting and security and handle its configuration mechanisms in its own way. This has a profound effect upon the design of a distributed processing system which spans several organisations. Whenever systems offer distributed processing services spanning several domains, the management of those services has to be shared across those domains.

In the local case, services are often freely available to users (subject to accountancy and security constraints). However the accounting or security policies for example may be strikingly different across domains. This completely changes the way protection must be handled within a system and changes the way accounting must be done.

We found it preferable to take an object model paradigm for distributed processing, providing each system object not only with its usual information processing interface, but adding a management interface also. A distributed system designed in accordance with this approach must be able to provide support for operations upon objects. To do this in a WAN environment requires all objects to be named in a consistent manner, for binding to be provided between object names and the current location of the object and for a communications service to transport invocation requests to remote objects. Objects must be protected against unauthorised access by suitable protection mechanisms. These must ensure that it is the appropriate requester which seek to carry out that specific operation on the selected object instances. And the kernel and associated communications mechanisms must be sufficiently secure and reliable so as not to compromise that protection.

2.2 The MANDIS Kernel

The heart of the kernel is a secure message passing mechanism. Security is handled by associating a capability with every object and operation. When a client wishes to invoke a service from an object which provides it, the client must issue a request to the kernel with a capability for the object and operation. The MANDIS kernel uses the capability to find the server managing the object and, having located the server, guarantees that the object receives the request. Responses are handled in the same manner.

This mechanism of the kernel achieves two important goals of distributed systems management. It provides information hiding and access control. Moreover it does it in such a manner that the user accessing the object does so in such a way that it is immaterial whether the object is local or remote. Indeed the only difference the user is likely to see on present day networks between accessing a object on an attached LAN and the same access across a WAN is one of response time. With the trend towards faster WANs (e.g. Broadband ISDN) even that may not be apparent for simple transaction. However, we must expect the LAN to remain always one or two orders of magnitude faster than a WAN for economic networking. Complex interactions will therefore always be subject to greater delay over the WAN.

2.3 Adding Management to the Kernel

The MANDIS Kernel only becomes useful to its clients when the distributed system becomes populated with servers. A number of management services have been implemented. The directory service provides a mapping between names and capabilities. It enables names (useful to people) to be translated into capabilities (useful for systems). The bank server enables accounting to be performed. We implemented a number of monitoring services. These are discussed in greater detail later in the paper. We also implemented a gateway server. Although invisible to a normal client, this server provides for management control at the interface between management domains.

Management information transfers we find are basically very simple, though the amount of data to be transferred can be considerable. The primitives of the management communication interface are:-

a. from a managing object to a managed object:

GET	a directive to return the value of a specified management attribute;
SET	a directive to change the value of a specified attribute;
ACTION	a directive to initiate an identified procedure;
CREATE	a directive to provide a new instance of an object or to specify a new type of object;
DELETE	a directive to remove an instance of an object.

b. from a managed object to a managing object:

RESPONSE	a value returned in response to an associated operation (eg. GET) or an acknowledgement (eg. to a SET);
REPORT	a notification that a specified event has been received.

These primitives can be readily mapped onto the OSI application layer communication service provided by the Common Management Information Service primitives and carried between systems by the Common Management Information Protocol. Not only are they sufficient to handle simple interchanges, they can also support the interchanges between systems when the components of the management algorithm are distributed over a number of systems.

However, these primitives are insufficient as a prescription of an action which is to be carried out remotely. We find that management has to deal with the unexpected just as often as it deals with those situations which can be anticipated. An example of the latter would be the decision to gather traffic statistics to monitor performance. But if the performance were found to fall below an acceptable value, there could be a multiplicity of reasons to be investigated. Not all could be guessed beforehand.

In these situations managers need more powerful diagnostic tools. Where it is desirable to place the locus of management control in a remote system, the manager needs to be able to instruct the remote system on the diagnostic procedures to be carried out. These will use the interface primitives listed above and may also include additional instructions to control the sequencing of such instructions. Thus we find that we need to add to our basic set of management primitives constructs which are found in programming languages. These can be communicated as "scripts" between systems.

Scripts extend the repertoire of operations which can be performed on managed objects. By giving names to these operations and having them retained in a remote system, the manager may subsequently invoke them through a ACTION primitive. In the later sections of this paper we give examples of such operations and their invocation.

2.4 A Framework for Management

As well as taking an operational view of management we also took an architectural view. This arose from our studies of monitoring. As it evolved, complementary approaches being undertaken in the ANSA project[10] were brought to our notice. We were able to demonstrate that the approaches were essentially the same. ANSA identify a four layer hierarchy of management activity in which policy decisions, made at the top of the hierarchy, are effected first through administrative procedure and then through management activities to be realised in terms of the primitive operations discussed in section 2.3. Matching this downward flow of control is a corresponding upward flow of monitoring information. We have further elaborated this to model the feed-back paths which can take place in the intermediate layers. These offer mechanisms both to limit the upward flow of information (and so prevent a potential overload of the management system such as could occur whenever a fault is detected) and to delegate limited responsibility for control. Our model for monitoring covers the lower three layers.

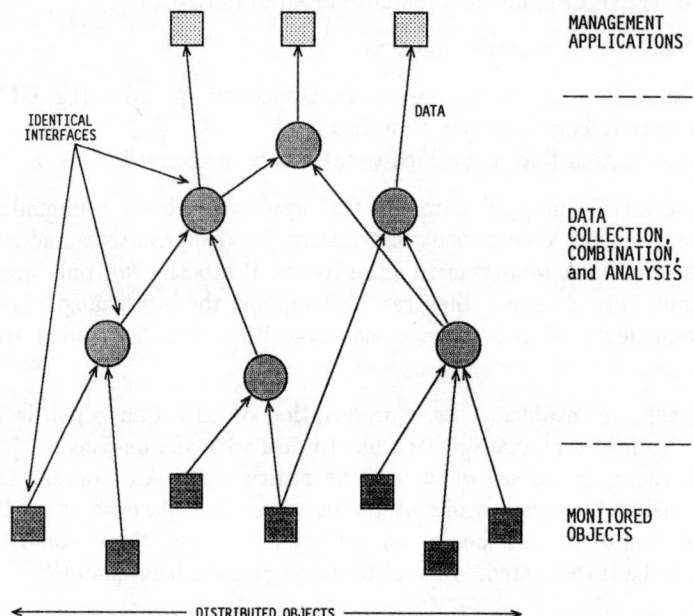

Figure 1. Architectural Model of Monitoring

The architectural model for monitoring activities in a distributed system is shown in figure 1. Activities are regarded as objects existing somewhere within the distributed system, which internally perform monitoring activities, accessed through a defined monitoring interface. They are termed the **monitored objects**. The data collected from these objects are combined and analysed in one or more co-operating **combination objects**. Finally, the analysed data are passed to the ultimate clients, the **management applications**.

The need for a structure for monitoring information can be illustrated by considering how a system appears to a programmer and a business administrator. The programmer sees hardware consisting of processors, memory, disks, networks, etc; software for compiling, communicating, writing, drawing, calculating, etc; activities composed from interacting and independent processes. The business administrator sees a collection of computers and peripherals networked together, providing a uniform service to a large staff for the performance of cost accounting, stock control, factory automation, word processing, etc. Both see the same system, but at different levels of abstraction. The MANDIS structure of monitoring information essentially allows the system to be described (in terms of its observable behaviour) at corresponding levels of abstraction. A description of a monitoring activity can then be clarified by stating the abstraction level at which it is being described.

The MANDIS structure of monitoring information defines three abstraction levels, and describes them in terms of three types of data:

Behaviour Indicators: the highest abstraction level of monitoring information defined by MANDIS, giving a generalised description of part or all of the (distributed) computing system. Typical *behaviour indicators* might be *"system 80% efficient"*, *"system load factor = 0.57"*, *"database service degrading because disk Y is full"*. Behaviour indicators will typically be used by business administrators and distributed systems managers.

Object Set States: form an intermediate level description of the monitoring data, typically at the level of *services* (which map to objects in the MANDIS architecture). Examples of object set states are *"service has 83% availability"*, *"service has 47% resource utilisation"*, *"service is down"*. Object set states are used by the service managers (administrators).

Basic Monitoring Data: the lowest abstraction level defined by MANDIS, describing the real events and states measured within the system. These are highly dependent on how the item being monitored has been implemented. Examples of these might include system error messages such as *"E$NODIR"*, software reports like *"disk access failed"*, or hardware measurements such as *"+4 volts"*,

3. Realising Management

3.1 Methodology

Management is the interaction between a manager (be it a human, a committee, or a piece of software), and the entity being managed (here, a distributed information system). This interaction has two elements: **monitoring**, from which the manager gains information so that decisions can be taken about changes to the system; and **control**, through which these changes can be made. Although these two elements are very much dependent on each other when performing an integrated management activity, they can be studied in isolation. Having developed theories for the structuring of monitoring activities in a distributed system environment, we produced a pilot implementation from these theories. More recent and on-going work focuses on the control aspects. By building a monitoring system we have been able to prove the validity of our approach. We are now using that early experience to construct an improved version of a management system.

3.2 Implementation

Our implementation of monitoring followed the architectural model shown in figure 1, and contains three layers:

- Analysis layer
- Combination layer
- Detection and Retrieval layer.

These layers correspond to the three levels in the architectural model, and also to the types in the structure of monitoring information.

3.2.1 Analysis Layer and Management Applications

The top level in the monitoring layer model is the analysis layer, which analyses high-level monitoring information, and processes it in management applications. The analysers provide the *behaviour indicators* defined by the structure of monitoring information, while the management applications use the behaviour indicators for various purposes:

- as feedback from some controlling actions made upon the distributed system;
- for detecting behaviour in the system which requires some action to be taken;
- for high-level measurement of system performance;
- for routine recording of system activities (eg. accounting, audit trails).

3.2.2 Combination Layer

The purpose of the combination layer is to collect monitoring information from one or more sources, and correlate the data in order to gain views of the behaviour of the system at higher abstraction levels. The combination layer provides the *object set states* defined by the structure of monitoring information. The data are combined according to a set of rules specified to the layer by the manager. These rules describe the system at a particular abstraction level, and the rules and data used at one abstraction level are available for use by higher abstraction levels. The MANDIS project has devised a language for specifying these rules (SESL), and has built a parser for it.

3.2.3 Detection and Retrieval Layer

The detection and retrieval layer is the lowest layer, and implements the *basic monitoring data* class defined by the structure of monitoring information. Its purpose is to generate the low level events and states to indicate the behaviour of the system at this level. It provides the interface between the management system and the system itself.

3.3 Management languages

We identify 2 key reasons why a language is a useful medium for expressing management requirements:

- it bridges the information requirements gap between managers and programmers
- it provides a powerful tool through which to specify management algorithms and issue control commands

3.3.1 The Manager-Programmer Gap

On most distributed information processing systems, the person(s) responsible for managing the system will not be involved with those writing the software to run on it. Indeed, the manager is probably responsible for maintaining a working system containing hundreds of programs, with very little idea about the details of how each is implemented. Therefore there is a problem of being able to manage many different programs with many different management interfaces. Conversely, those who program that software will have little idea about how it is going to be managed, or for what purposes. Thus the programmers cannot provide a suitable interface for *every* manager. For the same reason, it is not possible to decide on a standard management interface, except at a very basic level (such as those defined for communications management in ISO CMIS[11]). These do not go far enough to solve the problem for the manager.

This "gap" between the programmer and the manager can be bridged by dividing it into a series of small steps. These steps are achieved by describing the system at different abstraction levels, and making simple mappings between adjacent levels. Not only does this bridge the gap, but it can also lead to new insights into the system's behaviour. A language is a suitable medium for expressing abstraction levels (and the mappings between them), since it is easy to learn and use, and provides the same operations for mappings at all layers. The language should be dynamic, to reflect the dynamic environment of a distributed system, and extensible to provide the same look and feel whatever level of abstraction is being programmed.

3.3.2 Management Algorithms

Distributed systems are very complex entities (and becoming even more so), and their management is equally complex. In order to manage them at all, **management algorithms** must be derived which specify how to relate observations of the behaviour of the system, and what actions should be taken. Some management algorithms will be defined in management standards; others will be set by the system manager according to local requirements. Management languages are an appropriate way of expressing and implementing management algorithms.

Filtering is a commonly needed management algorithm. It is needed both for monitoring and control to limit the profusion of data generated in a large system. It is important that

i. the manager gets the right information, it is clear, and he is not swamped by a mass of insignificant data;

ii. the manager has a "filtered" set of instructions for carrying out the right commands at any particular level of abstraction.

A language provides a simple way of providing automated filtering, since the filtering mechanisms know from language statements exactly what data are required; everything else may be safely filtered out.

A significant proportion of the management task can be done by predictive methods, ie. most of the events that occur will be known, and most of the commands used will be foreseeable. This lends itself to automation. Management by prediction has the advantages that it is simple to implement, efficient in terms of impact on the system being monitored, and simple to understand due to the fact that the events are already known and explained. It is also easy to make decisions about any necessary actions, as these can be made when the events are defined, and not when they are detected. A language is a very effective way to describe automated activities. However, a language is a powerful tool which, if properly supported, enables the manager to specify alternative management procedures quickly, whenever the unexpected happens.

3.4 SESL: a language for monitoring

One of the aims of the MANDIS project was to investigate the use of monitoring in distributed systems[7]. This resulted in a method being proposed for the processing (filtering) of monitored events and states, and a language was developed for expressing these processing activities. It was named the **State and Event Specification Language (SESL)**. This section briefly describes the processing method (SESL architecture) and gives an example of its use. (An alternative implementation of SESL is described by Drenth and Wilcke[12]).

The SESL approach starts from a model in which a system consists of a number of active objects (represented by processes), and passive objects (representing data). Monitored active objects present a management interface which allows three types of operation:

i. Commands (stop, halt, change configuration, etc.);
ii. Requests (for internal information);
iii. Unsolicited messages (events) generated by the object.

Monitoring is concerned with processing events, and requesting state information. When a SESL specification is made, the object implementing the language (the SESL Parser) will set up tables to record the processing it must perform, enable the generation of event messages from the layer below, request state information when necessary, and generate its own event messages. SESL also has some commands for its own internal management.

SESL statements fall into three categories: declarative statements, which define relationships and allow various things to be computed; procedural statements, which define a series of actions to be taken at some indeterminate time; and imperative statements, which require an action to be taken immediately.

The following is an example of a SESL specification for monitoring the file cache of a file server. The size of the cache is the result of the tradeoff between use of memory resource (for the cache) and delay in retrieving a file from disk because it is not in the cache. The goal is to match the size of the cache to the current demand for files so that the trade-off is kept near an optimum value. The measurement used is the ratio of cache hits (request for a file currently in the cache) to cache misses. A good value for this may be around 70%.

```
hit   when event("cache hit")
miss  when event("cache miss")
set age_factor 20
on miss set hit_miss_ratio ( ... aging algorithm ... )
on hit  set hit_miss_ratio ( ... aging algorithm ... )
hmr_too_high when $hit_miss_ratio > 90
hmr_too_low  when $hit_miss_ratio < 50
await hmr_too_high, hmr_too_low
enable hit, miss
```

When the low level events "cache hit" and "cache miss" occur, the hit/miss ratio is calculated using an aging algorithm with aging factor of 20. This algorithm uses a weighted sum of all events, with the nth *previous* event receiving a weighting of $(20/21)^n$ to produce a smooth but up-to-date measurement which is not subject to random fluctuations. The important high level events are *hmr_too_high* and *hmr_too_low*, and are triggered by the hit/miss ratio going outside the 50% to 90% range. The **await** command instructs SESL to send an event message when these events happen, so that actions may be taken to increase or decrease the size of the file server's cache (or alternative actions which the manager has specified).

3.5 FORTH: a language for controlling

We are currently evaluating Forth as a control language for distributed systems. It has the important features of being dynamically extensible, and ability to express both imperatives and procedures. Forth is programmed by defining procedures, called **words**, made from combinations of words in a dictionary. The new word is compiled and added to the dictionary, making it available for use in new definitions, thus extending the language. Words can be used for building procedures, or used interactively as imperative commands.

An example manager has been written in Forth to manage the file server described above. The extensible nature of Forth is exploited to hide low level details from the manager. A typical manager's session might look like:

```
FSH>  LOAD FS.F
           # load the file server's management program
FSH>  COMMAND CMD "hmr_too_low" INCREASE_CACHE
           # specify that the command INCREASE_CACHE is to be
           # executed when the event hmr_too_high is received
FSH>  COMMAND CMD "hmr_too_high" REDUCE_CACHE
           # the commands INCREASE_CACHE and DECREASE_CACHE
           # are defined in FS.F
```

```
FSH> SERVER
```

This last command starts a loop which waits for incoming events, and executes the defined procedure when each specified event arrives. The manager may break in to loop to issue a direct command:

```
FSH> INCREASE_SERVICE
          # another defined command: increase the size of the
          # service by creating another copy
```

Through these SESL and Forth statements we are able to realise the GET, SET, RESPONSE and REPORT primitives identified in section 2.3.

4. Conclusions

The MANDIS project has met all the demanding objectives we set at the outset. It has also brought a number of benefits which we had not anticipated. At the technical level, we could not have foreseen the development of SESL and its more recent extension to deal with management control. At the organisational level it demonstrated that laboratories with a common interest can not only work together collaboratively in performing studies, they can collaborate to provide demonstrable and tangible results by implementing the concepts developed in the studies. This is all the more remarkable when one considers that the financial support provided through the COST 11 ter initiative is limited to the support of travel and related costs. Finally, but by no means least, MANDIS has successfully promoted the exchange of staff between participating organisations. This has assisted in developing people professionally and helped generate friendly relationships, both of which must be of significance for the growing integration of European interests.

What of the future? MANDIS still has some unfinished business to extend our common understanding of both monitoring and control. Even so, this work will still only provide us with the material for a basic management tool kit. The next steps could be to use this basic set of tools to explore distributed systems management further. We need to identify management objects and establish management algorithms which are common to many systems and so furnish a library of distributed systems management objects and operations. We need to investigate the requirements for management interactions between management domains and see to what extent managers are prepared to trust external systems to have a management interface to the systems under their control.

Some of these questions are technical. They concern the extent to which distributed management functionality is sufficient to convert a set of independent autonomous systems into a distributed processing system in cases where the basis of the local system is other than the light weight kernel as used in MANDIS.

Other questions concern the interactions between cooperating business enterprises. These are of an institutional nature. Although possibly of less concern to the computer scientist, they are never the less very real. Unless they too can be resolved, distributed system of the type we have been investigating may remain interesting demonstrations. MANDIS has given us tools; we must now make use of them.

References

1. Bacon, J. M., and Hamilton, K. G. Distributed Computing with RPC: the Cambridge Approach. Proc. IFIP Conf. on Distributed Processing, Oct. 1987. eds. Barton et al, North-Holland 1988

2. Leach, P. J., et al. The Architecture of an Integrated Local Network. IEEE Journal on selected areas of communications 1(5), Nov 1983.

3. Mullender, S. J., and Tanenbaum, A. S. The Design of a Capability Based Distributed Operating System. Computer Journal, 29(4), 289-300, March 1986

4. van Renesse, R. and Tanenbaum, A. S. MANDIS & Amoeba: Progress in Distributed Operating Systems and Distributed Systems Management. This volume.

5. Langsford, A. MANDIS: An Experiment in Distributed Processing. Proc. European Teleinformatics Conf., 787-794, North-Holland, 1988.

6. Bacon, J. M., et al. MANDIS: Architectural Basis for Management. Proc. European Teleinformatics Conf., 795-809, North-Holland, 1988.

7. Holden, D. B., et al. An Approach to Monitoring in Distributed Systems. Proc. European Teleinformatics Conf., 811-822, North-Holland, 1988.

8. van Renesse, R., et al. MANDIS/Amoeba: A Widely Dispersed Object-Oriented Operating System. Proc. European Teleinformatics Conf., 823-831, North-Holland, 1988.

9. Holden, D. B. Predictive Languages for Management. Proc. 1st Int. Sym. on Integrated Network Management, Boston 1989. To be published.

10. Advanced Networked Systems Architecture Group, Cambridge, UK. ANSA Reference Manual, release 00.03, June 1987.

11. IS 9595 Common Management Information Service Definition.

12. Drenth, G. D., Wilcke, M., van Renesse, R., and van Staveren, H. Monitoring in Distributed Client-Server Environments. Free University of Amsterdam report no. IR-155, June 1988.

OAI - Concepts for Open Systems Cooperation

V. TSCHAMMER, K.-P. ECKERT, J. HALL, G. SCHÜRMANN, L. STRICK
GMD FOKUS BERLIN
HARDENBERGPLATZ 2
D-1000 BERLIN 12
TEL. 49-30-25499-200, FAX: 49-30-25499-202

The advent of wide-spread optical fibre networks using broadband communication techniques together with the extension of ISO activities to Open Distributed Processing will generate and support innovative applications based on broadband-ISDN and wide-area networks. In such open systems distribution will be the consequence of the geographical and organisational situation rather than the result of a dedicated design decision, and the system will be assembled from existing entities rather than being built from scratch. Enterprise networks, inter-organisational networks and very large distributed systems are examples of such systems where cooperation between autonomous and heterogeneous components must be achieved.

OAI (Open Application and Interaction Systems), the main research project of GMD FOKUS Berlin, is developing concepts for such cooperating open systems, including adequate modelling techniques and design principles. This paper first describes the abstractions of the environment from which dedicated concepts and structures are derived. These concepts and structures are then elaborated in a first approach towards a general OAI architecture. Finally, it is demonstrated how this architecture together with related principles is being adopted in some short- to medium-term projects which are aiming at more detailed concepts and prototype implementations.

1 Introduction

We are currently observing the development of a wide-spread optical fibre infrastructure combined with broadband transmission, switching and access techniques. Further developments are concerned with future communication systems and multifunctional end systems. This promotes a new communication technology based on interconnected subnets and backbones which will provide very high transmission rates and enhanced dependability in local as well as in wide area networks, and which will integrate different protocol architectures and management concepts. Advanced end systems with extended processing and storage capacities as well as innovative user interfaces will complement this new communication technology.

One of the major developments in this area is the introduction of broadband-ISDN and related switching and interfacing techniques where efforts are being made to design and develop a B-ISDN global network which includes an adequate transport system combined with new communication services and applications. An example is the BERKOM pilot project which is developing a global reference model to coordinate the development of new, multifunctional data structures and concepts for their handling in an open cooperative environment ([BERK-REF],[POPESCU88]).

2 The Open Cooperative Environment

Future communication technology will promote distributed applications based on cooperating open systems such as are found in enterprise networks, inter-organisational networks (IONs), and very large distributed systems. One driving force behind this development is the fact that performance and dependability characteristics of future LANs and WANs will be quite similar. This will make long distance communication as fast, reliable and secure as local communication, so that LAN application structures and communication techniques may also be used in wide area networks.

However, large distributed systems will have no closed user group, and no homogeneous management and administration environment, as typical LANs have. Instead, there will be a vast number of potential resources and services, an open, heterogeneous community of service providers and service users, and a variety of adjoining or overlapping organisational structures.

In this environment distribution is usually not a dedicated design principle, applied to meet specific performance or dependability constraints, for example. Instead, distribution is the consequence of the geographical and organisational situation to which the system must adapt: the user community and the work are distributed and, therefore, the end systems and the application entities are distributed, too. Consequently, such systems are less likely to be built from scratch but rather assembled from existing entities which have developed separately and independently at different locations and under different organisational and operational conditions. Systems of this type are characterised by the term 'open', as they usually have no restrictions on the number, type and behaviour of components and as they are basically ready to admit any customers, clients, and users. The local conditions, however, may require that the components stay under local control and that their characteristics remain more or less unchanged within the open environment.

This may be in direct contrast to the requirements imposed by global objectives and the need to undertake tasks jointly. Therefore, design concepts for cooperating open systems must harmonise the requirements for diversity Band local autonomy which result from the organisational and operational environment with the requirements for uniformity and co-ordinated interactions which are imposed by cooperative ventures and joint activities.

Aspects of the environment which are relevant to the modelling work introduced in section 3 are discussed below.

2.1 Openness

From our point of view, 'open' is a synonym for unlimited, accessible, heterogeneous, autonomous, and decentralised.

These terms are further elaborated in order to give an introduction to the factors determining the open cooperative environment.

Unlimited, free from restrictions: The components of open systems may belong to different organisations and may be distributed across large geographical areas. In principle, there are no restrictions on the number and the geographical location of components. Organisations may organise their own components as they wish and may create dedicated operational conditions and arbitrary load situations. Therefore, the set of system components is subject to continuous change: existing components may be altered, new components added, and old ones removed.

This is in direct contrast to the well-known 'closed world' assumption which postulates a global and comprehensive view of the entire system, embracing all its properties, events, and activities. In such a closed world, everything that exists or happens is observed and becomes common knowledge. In open systems, however, such assumptions cannot be made. Instead, it is totally uncertain how many entities exist at a given time, which attributes they have, and which interactions and interdependencies they are involved in.

Accessible, free to be entered, used, shared, etc.: Generally, open systems are ready to admit all kinds of clients and users. In principle, nobody is restrained from occupying system resources and from using system services. Consequently, open systems have an unlimited, continuously changing user community with varying requirements and varying interactions with the system. Free access for everyone, however, is only a theoretical approach. For practical purposes there will be a complex network of regulations and mutual agreements which will regulate the access rights of individual users and user groups.

In an open user community it is inevitable that certain users will use their system knowledge and access rights to corrupt the entire system or some of its components through obvious or concealed attacks, intrusions or other malicious actions which produce obvious or hidden errors, faults, or exceptions.

Heterogeneous, characterised by diversity: Each organisation has the freedom to install and use its subsystems according to its own internal needs. It may plan, design, implement, operate, and develop each component so that it optimally meets its specific tasks. This results in a mixture of general purpose and special purpose entities which are introduced by different enterprise policies, design strategies, management concepts and operational conditions, and which must continuously adapt to the characteristics and requirements of their local environment. The consequence is heterogeneity at all system levels.

We must allow for two different aspects of heterogeneity, syntactic and semantic. Syntactic heterogeneity typically results in different hardware and software characteristics such as data representations, system software interfaces, file structures, and interaction protocols. Semantic heterogeneity often results in different views and interpretations of the information, the significance of facts, the consequences of events, and the meanings of rules and agreements.

Autonomous, independent and self-determined: Components of open systems have developed independently at different locations and operate under the influence of different authorities. Consequently, each component has its own local environment, which it can monitor and influence, and which it is familiar with. Within this local environment, the component determines its behaviour by itself or according to some local rules or in response to some local commands. From a general point of view, it is self-determining and independent of outside concepts and regulations. Thus, in principle, an outside observer has no means of learning about the internals of a component or of influencing its state or behaviour.

Under these circumstances, the assumptions about system properties and global behaviour must be kept minimal: a priori, there exists no global information or knowledge, no commonly accessible objects, and no globally co-ordinated behaviour. The only assumption that can be made is the common ability to communicate, because otherwise the entities would be completely isolated from each other and there would be no way of setting or configuring them in a global system.

Decentralised, not conducted, not organised, not regulated: In principle, all components of open systems are considered equal. There is no entity which has the authority to supervise or organise others or to enforce uniform concepts, rules or principles. Consequently, there is also no possibility of achieving a comprehensive system design which would allow the planned configuration of resources and the controlled assignment of functions and activities. Instead, all capabilities and capacities are randomly distributed amongst the components, just as they have developed within the local environment.

Moreover, no entity is able to get a complete and up-to-date view of the total system as the designer of a closed system would have. Consequently, open systems must be considered from a component's view rather than from the system's view, i.e. each observation - and also each attempt to influence others - is only partial and must be made by means of system-inherent mechanisms. The latter influences the behaviour both of the observing component and of the observed component. The more accurate an observation needs to be, the more effort and system capacity must be involved, and the more falsifying influence is exercised on the behaviour of the components. Thus, components of open systems can never observe other components with absolute correctness and, therefore, a consistent and up-to-date system state can never be achieved.

The latter is one of the typical properties of distributed systems. In open systems, however, the situation is even more complex because the general assumptions about global concepts and objects must be kept to a minimum, while local autonomy is the predominant principle. Strictly speaking, in open systems, there is no global state, no global object, and no co-ordinated action towards a common goal or result.

2.2 Cooperation

The minimal requirement which must be satisfied by components of cooperating open systems is the ability to communicate, i.e. to give or exchange information. By means of communication, components can gather information about activities and events outside their local environment, and inform others about local observations, experiences and results. In this way, they may achieve some form of common knowledge about the system state and other data.

Communication requires physical connections and logical agreements about the data exchange procedures and about the interpretation of the exchanged information. In open systems, a tight coupling by means of global objects such as a global memory cannot be assumed. Therefore, the information exchange can only be achieved by message passing, which requires network hardware and network protocols to overcome geographical distribution and syntactic heterogeneity and to define information exchange and control procedures. This is regulated by the ISO/OSI-standards, whereas interpretation of the information in a uniform manner must be achieved by specific mutual agreements.

Communication is the basis for joint activities and co-ordinated actions, but cooperation needs further agreements and extended regularisation. The ISO has recognised this need and has extended its standardisation activities from OSI (Open Systems Interconnection) to ODP (Open Distributed Processing).

Within a cooperative environment the following concepts are of particular relevance.

Roles and Services: Cooperation within a system requires the planning and co-ordination of the components' activities so that they can achieve a common result or fulfill a common task. Each component is assigned a specific part within the overall task, which implies dedicated rights and duties and requires particular interactions with other components. In accordance with other approaches to the modelling of cooperating open systems, OAI uses the term 'role' to designate a component's part in the overall activity. Roles also allow the establishment of direct relationships between system components and human users, the latter can be the original source of activity within the system.

Combined with roles are dedicated functions which a component has to perform. From the designer's point of view, it is obvious that these functions are not self-contained but have specific interrelationships with the functions of other components in the course of the overall activity. From the point of view of a component - from which the global context is hidden - the interesting question concerns the assistance that can be expected from others or the actions that can be requested. OAI uses the term 'service' as an abstract notation for a component's view of a function which another component has made available for external use.

Abstractions, roles and services allow the structuring of complex systems and activities by providing basic building blocks for which only the interface to the outside world must be schematised while the internals need no regularisation and may be constructed according to local requirements.

According to the scope and the context of related global agreements, application and system specific services can be distinguished. *Application specific* agreements regulate the cooperation of components within particular application scenarios. Such agreements have local as well as temporal limits and global regulations are needed only in so far as they must inhibit undesirable interdependencies with entities outside the particular scenarios. *System specific* agreements, in contrast, have a global and long-term significance as they are intended to provide a global platform of system services on which distributed applications can be built. They must be introduced via global design or global standards.

Negotiations. The most elementary interactions in cooperating open systems are of the client-server type. Due to local autonomy, however, servers need not necessarily service a request at a given rate with the required quality. Instead, they may offer a different quality or rate, reject the call or just be silent. A requesting entity must therefore ensure beforehand that a particular server is willing to accept and service the call as required.

Usually, these negotiations will need the support of particular activities as in open systems it is generally not guaranteed that entities always have enough information and trust others sufficiently to initiate and maintain direct relationships and connections. Such supporting activities may be fulfilled by particular system specific roles such as those of a 'broker' acting as an agent or intermediary in negotiations, or a 'supervisor' monitoring or controlling quality arrangements.

Service qualities. A further means of supporting the 'market' is a global strategy for defining, evaluating and handling the quality of service offers which will be formulated at various locations within open systems and which occasionally may differ only in some detail. In this case, service qualities enable service providers and users to express requirements and offers unambiguously, to balance offers against requests, and to include performance and dependability characteristics in agreements, guarantees, and accounting procedures.

The problem is to define a limited but sufficient set of quality parameters and to reach a global agreement on the syntax and semantics. A further problem is to agree on rules which regulate the processing of quality information and which define the local actions and mutual interactions necessary to establish service qualities and to react to changes in quality.

Many of those agreements will be specific to particular application scenarios. They will be negotiated between the application and communication entities concerned, and these entities will also be responsible for maintaining the service qualities which have been negotiated and guaranteed. In order to support negotiations and to guarantee and supervise quality related agreements, however, system specific services may be provided which could be requested to simplify general procedures of the 'quality-oriented market', such as the monitoring and management of quality-related information.

Domains. The aspects of free access, heterogeneity, and freedom from restrictions lead to problems of complexity and scale in open systems. Therefore, some means of structuring very large open systems is required which reflect the different organisational boundaries, operational domains, and the cooperation agreements between individuals, groups, and organisations. These means must support the definition of domains, their establishment and demarcation, and the definition of various static and dynamic relationships between domains. This enables system components to be grouped according to common tasks, common agreements, mutual trust, or various other aspects.

Domain-oriented structuring simplifies many procedures within cooperating open systems, including the administration of system specific services, the design of applications, and the management of global information. We may assume that within domains all regulations and agreements have a more local character because of the availability of more detailed information and greater trust between components. Consequently, domains provide means for defining 'closed areas' within the open environment, where - at least in some respects - the well-known closed view of distributed systems may be applied, and where many aspects of scale and complexity and some problems of autonomy, heterogeneity and decentralisation can be relaxed.

3 OAI - Concepts in Open Cooperative Environments

Cooperating open systems consist of a loosely-coupled federation of autonomous components which have made common agreements and global arrangements which enable or support their joint activities. OAI (Open Application and Interaction Systems) is an overall approach which places a set of concepts and methods at a designer's disposal to develop an architecture for the support of distributed applications. The design principles involved will take into consideration these common agreements, arrangements, and installations. The first step towards this goal consists of developing appropriate abstractions for the operational and organisational environment (openness) and of specifying the basic requirements of the joint activities and co-ordinated interactions (cooperation).

3.1 Viewpoints and Architectural Framework

One purpose of an architecture for open systems cooperation is to define concepts and methods for open system design and development which allow the use of common concepts. Because of the complexity of distributed systems it seems to be necessary to consider the system from different *viewpoints* with each viewpoint representing a different set of abstractions of the distributed system. Informally, a viewpoint leads to a representation of the system with emphasis on a specific concern. More formally, the resulting representation is a set of abstractions of the system, where the abstraction is a description that recognises relevant or ignores irrelevant objectives.

In the standardisation group for ODP (open distributed processing) [ISO-ODP] five viewpoints have been identified as focuses of concern which represent a pragmatic approach. Each viewpoint allows modelling and reasoning about an ODP system that is oriented to a particular area of concern. A viewpoint that addresses a given concern is responsible for doing so completely.

Two matters - *consistency* among the viewpoints and *completeness* of coverage - do not fit within a single viewpoint. This common ground between the viewpoints must be treated consistently.

In the real world there exists some information system which is a technical system to be described in the world of models. There are two viewpoints that tie the model to the *real world*.

The **enterprise viewpoint** describes the distributed processing system in terms of what it is required to do for the enterprise concerned. The model from this viewpoint captures business requirements that justify and influence the design of the distributed system - it is a description of a technical system in the context of the enterprise that it serves. The enterprise units that support and participate in the distributed processing system are explicitly identified and described (domains, resources, people involved).

The **technology viewpoint** concentrates on the technical artifacts (realised components) from which the distributed system is built. It must model the hardware and software involved (local operating system, I/O devices, storage, points of access to communication etc.).

These two viewpoints delimit the design space given to the distributed application designer: **what it is for** (enterprise viewpoint) and **with what** (technology viewpoint). The remaining three viewpoints are necessarily about the **structure** and **behaviour** of the distributed system itself.

The **information viewpoint** concentrates on information and information processing aspects of distributed processing systems. Information structures and information flows are modelled and the rules and constraints that govern the manipulation of the information are identified.

The **computational viewpoint** describes the operation and computational characteristics of the distributed processing system and the processes which change the

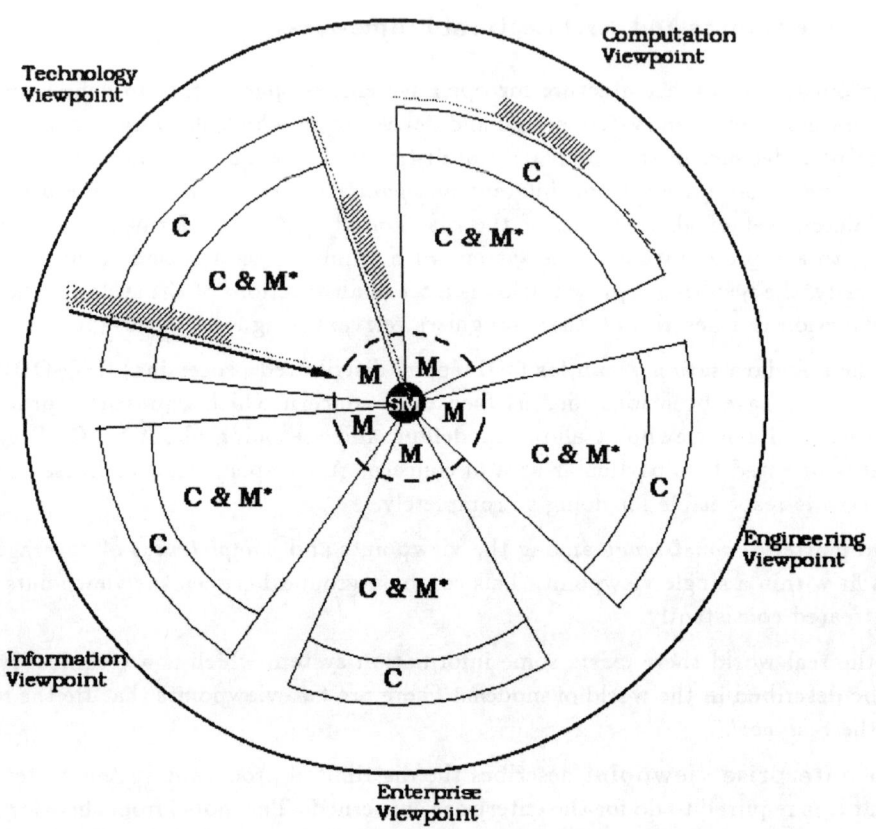

C   Constraints

C &M*   Concepts and Methods

M   Models

SM   System-Model

Figure 1 : Framework for ODP

information. It concerns the structuring of applications so that they are independent of the computer system and network on which they run. It yields a computational model (design) of the information representations and manipulations identified in the information viewpoint.

The **engineering viewpoint** describes the distributed processing system in terms of the engineering necessary to support the distributed nature of the processing. It is concerned with the provision and guarantee of desired characteristics such as performance, dependability and distribution transparency. It could be considered a model of how to support the distributed application design identified in the computational viewpoint. It should allow the definition of interfaces to families of system components and show how to organise them in order to achieve the desired characteristics.

The five viewpoints described are not to be treated as a model for a multi-layer implementation of open distributed systems. Neither are they to be interpreted as equivalent to phases in the design process for there is no implied sequence in the viewpoints. These viewpoints should be used to help focus work on particular concerns at a given time rather than be rigidly bound to specific portions of work.

3.2 Concepts and Methods

The main problem in the above outlined architectural approach is to develop consistent and complete system models integrating the different approaches in the different viewpoints. Four basic concepts for modelling the OAI-architecture have been identified:

- Object-Oriented Approach

    The Object-Oriented Approach allows the behaviour and the operations provided by specific objects to be described by abstracting from their internal implementation.

- Information Model

    The information model is used to structure the information and to define rules for the information flow and for logical data structures.

- Activity Model

    The *activity model* ([AAM]) allows cooperating components to be described by defining the roles, rules and relations between them.

- Formal Description Techniques (FDT)

    FDTs are required to formalise the behaviour of objects so that it can be verified.

This paper describes the first concept only.

3.2.1 Object-Oriented Approach

The object-oriented approach is considered as one basic concept for at least the informational, computational and engineering views. The enterprise and technical views may also be modelled using object-oriented techniques and so it is conceptually possible to define a consistent system model.

A *distributed system* can be seen as a set (or pool) of *components*. The combination of components defines a *distributed application* or more precisely: a distributed application consists of a set of loosely coupled, cooperating components. With regard to the enterprise viewpoint a distributed application has a special *functionality*: it provides one or more *services* to its users. From the engineering viewpoint two questions arise:

– What is the internal structure of the components?
– How can components cooperate?

The object-oriented approach gives answers to these questions. But what does object-oriented mean?

The idea of describing objects by defining their *external interface* uses the paradigms of encapsulation, information-hiding and abstraction, and serves to abstract from details of their internal realisation. The object interface itself consists of a set of basic *operations*. Semantically related operations, together with these relations, define a *service* provided by the object. An object is able to provide more than one service.

An *object-oriented* system consists of a set of interacting objects. Interaction means the request and provision of operations between the objects. The internal structure of an object is hidden from its users but it has, of course, to be specified by the *designer* of the object. The implementation of an object, i.e. the implementations of all operations offered by the object, can be regarded as a 'local' (hidden) object-oriented system where all 'local' objects are known only to their master-object.

Let us translate these definitions to the world of cooperating systems. The components of a distributed application can be mapped on to objects. A component offers services to its environment, every service can be divided into basic operations. The internal structure (implementation) of a component can be regarded as a distributed application. In the other direction, a distributed application can be regarded as a *composed component* and as a component it also offers services to its environment.

In the enterprise viewpoint there exists a well-defined *communication relation* between components. Information has to be transferred between components or they have to share the information. Object-oriented systems exchange information using *message-passing* mechanisms. Message passing can be defined as a unidirectional non-blocking form of information flow or as a bidirectional blocking form of information exchange. It has the property that every message arrives error-free at its destination. In a distributed system, especially from the engineering viewpoint, this definition is insufficient. In a distributed system a safe and error-free message passing mechanism cannot be assumed and there exist types of communication (broadcast, multicast, bulk data transfer) which are different from message passing. Therefore the communication between components has to be modelled explicitly. In order to establish a *consistent model*, the communication also has to be described using object-oriented techniques. This is done by defining so-called *correlation objects* (see [DAF79]). Correlation objects offer a set of *communication services*, with each service having its own semantics and characteristics. The two-party communication seen from the enterprise view has changed into a three-party communication in the engineering and computational views.

A *correlation* defines relations between two objects. But what can occur between objects? The basic events are the sending and receiving of messages. The reaction of an object on receiving a message can be one of the following:

- to change its internal state
- to send new messages to other objects
- to create or destroy other objects

The two events *sending* and *receiving* a message define a *basic interaction* between objects and a *correlation* can be formally defined as a set of basic interactions. Using these definitions, the *behaviour* of a distributed application or the *interaction* between the participating components can be described by both the correlations and the specific reactions of the components receiving messages. The entire interaction can be represented as a directed graph or, using the activation order between the basic events, as a binary tree.

The notations of objects and interfaces capture the idea of encapsulation and abstraction of well-defined behaviour and serve to abstract from irrelevant details of internal realisation. An object is a behavioural component capable of some or all of the following. Each component can, but need not, be considered from all aspects:

- processing
- storage
- management
- communication
- information

The **processing aspect** is concerned with the methods for processing and decision making within each component, as defined by the internal behaviour of objects.

The **storage aspect** is concerned with the storage and retrieval of data/information.

The **information aspect** is concerned with data structures for representing information.

The necessary support for the interaction between components is **communication**. Interaction is possible between objects which have cooperative relationships (correlations) [DAF 79]. The **communication aspect** is concerned with the distribution of components and information with allows the objects to be connected.

The task of controlling and monitoring the components in order to reach a defined state within a distributed application is the task of the **management aspects**. Management aspects cover the capability of objects in the distributed system to maintain the defined and expected behaviour of distributed application components. This includes acting on and monitoring aspects of the "real" world.

3.3 Supporting environment

To support the development of distributed applications it is essential to develop a component infrastructure supporting all aspects of open systems cooperation (see also [DAF83] and the [ECMA ODP-SE] approach). As a first pragmatic step to support distributed applications it is necessary to develop the supporting environment which encompasses all aspects of open system cooperation. According to the viewpoints the computational and engineering viewpoints should be considered first.

The supporting environment represents a service pool with generally useful services. These services are defined as basic building-blocks which can be tailored for the use of individual applications, with each application building its own service platform. Defining a service in the supporting environment is a matter of perspective. This is because a distributed application (i.e. its components) may provide basic support for another and thus, from the latter perspective, forms part of the supporting environment [DAF 83].

Before defining some individual services in the supporting environment it is necessary to state some general requirements:

- naming

  Naming provides the means of identifying local or remote objects within an open distributed system.

- binding

  A binding is a relationship that exists between two interacting objects (see also correlation). A binding is a contract to engage in interactions within a specific context (use of the same alphabet).

- information retrieval

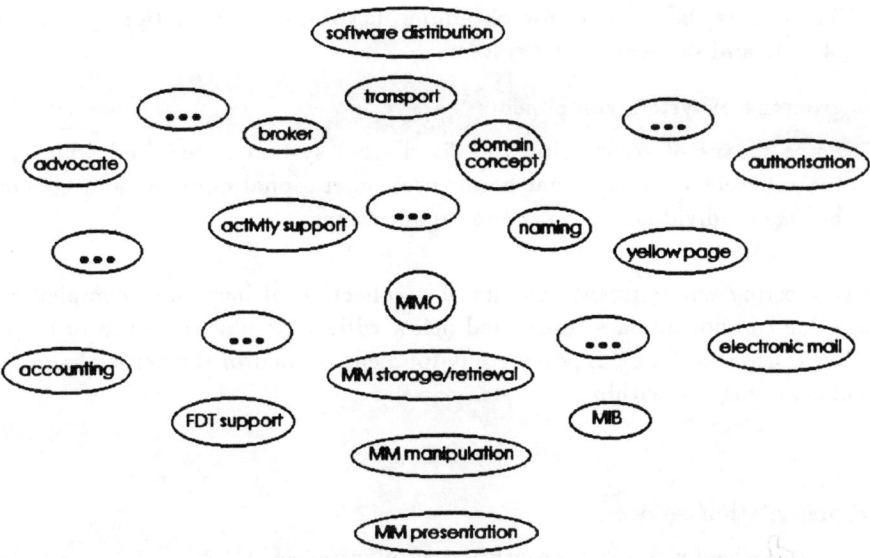

Figure 2 : Supporting Environment (Component Infrastructure)

There must be support for obtaining distributed information about existing objects and services in the system.

- grouping of system components

    Some means of structuring the distributed system is required which reflects the different organisational boundaries, operational domains and cooperation between individuals, groups and organisations.

The supporting environment consists of a collection of basic and complex components. The components are considered below with particular reference to the above-mentioned aspects. The supporting environment is open in the sense that the components can migrate within the system.

- presentation service

    is concerned with the presentation of information

- storage and retrieval service

    allows database access, storage etc. considering storage and retrieval aspects.

- control service, monitoring service and domain service

    allows monitoring and control in the global system

- transport service

    considers different communication requirements [(asynchronous/synchronous) (broadcast/multicast)]

- name service

    offers information about services in the sense of white pages and administration of the name space under the information aspect

- yellow page service

    offers information about existing services in terms of some of their properties

- activity support

    definition of roles, rules and activities for asynchronous group-communication

An example of a complex component is the 'broker'. Its role is to act as an agent between cooperating components, for whom it obtains information about services and to mediate in negotiations between these autonomous components. The broker has to be used by applications which do not have knowledge of their partners or which do not want to control their interactions with other partners within a common task. Various tasks of the broker can be identified:

- finding a partner and serving as an information-office. It is the functionality offered by the directory or yellow-page service.

- selection of an appropriate service provided by those objects which have already exported their interfaces. Selection is based on some kind of interface-matching.

- The broker needs intelligence so that it can make decisions about selecting a service if there is more than one service fulfilling the requirements of service provision.

4 FOKUS Projects within the OAI Framework

FOKUS is involved in several national and international projects that are being carried out within the OAI framework. Some are being carried out in conjunction with BERKOM [1], which is a pilot project promoting the planning and development of new and extended telecommunication services and future end systems for Broadband-ISDN which is being funded by the German PTT and the Senate of Berlin (West)/ Germany. The BERKOM project incorporates designs for the architecture of a global system based on a broadband integrated service data network. As well as the development of a testbed for STM and ATM, technologies a generalised telecommunication model will be developed in order to guarantee the consistent specification of cooperating components within the global system.

The main task of the *Multi-Media Document Handling* project is to explore the information aspects of open cooperating systems. In particular, the problems of multi-media document handling and the relation of multi-media information objects to the processing (interpreting) and communication objects are being studied. The basic information types are text, graphics, audio, raster image and moving pictures (video). But also *application dependent* information types such as modelling data supporting the wide domain of product modules in the motor industry, shipbuilding, aircraft engineering, etc. and trading data are included. The project is also concentrating on the *activity support* concepts which include roles, rules and functions and the development of a generalised telecommunication model.

The general target of the BERCIM project is to develop innovative concepts for structuring distributed, fault-tolerant CIM-applications. This is based on concepts for the realisation of fault-tolerant systems and the demonstration of future communication techniques in open application and intercommunication systems such as the integration of information flow within a factory. A fundamental aspect of the project is the definition of a suitable communication architecture which encompasses the integration of the information flow between the different technical and administrative departments of one enterprise or between sub-enterprises. The project is aiming

---

[1] BERliner KOMmunikationssystem

to implement the very first OAI-approach and so gain experience in developing a generalised telecommunication model.

Management aspects are very important for OAI. Management aspects encompass the capability of objects in the OAI system to maintain the defined and expected behaviour of distributed applications' components. In order to avoid the separate development of management methods and objects for every distributed application, the project 'Management for Distributed Applications in BERKOM' (BERMAN) is developing common concepts and methods for all objects. In particular, a management model based on OSI concepts as well as on the general concepts of OAI supporting all distributed applications will be developed. Furthermore, basic management components (X.500 Directory, important management objects (MO) and management services and protocols (CMIS/CMIP)) will be prototyped.

5 Conclusion

The increasing availability of high-speed wide area networks has prompted widespread discussion of how they can best be used to support distributed systems. In order to develop very large open systems, modelling concepts are required that are general enough to provide a stable platform not only for applications that are currently being designed but also for future applications. The BERKOM architecture that is being developed will provide through its terminology and concepts such an approach that can be adopted by all the FOKUS projects as well as by other applications that are being developed in conjunction with the BERKOM project. In this way an open architecture will be provided, the prerequisite for open systems cooperation.

6 References

AAM   T. Danielson, U. Pankoke-Babatz, The AMIGO Activity Model, Research into Networks and Distributed Computing, ed. R. Speth, pp. 227-241. North-Holland, Amsterdam, 1988. Proceedings European Teleinformatics Conference EUTECO 88, Vienna, April 20-22, 1988

BERK-REF   BERKOM Referenzmodell, Version 1, 4.6.87 Berkom-Dokument 0075/06/87

POPESCU88   R. Popescu-Zeletin, B. Butscher, P. Egloff, and J. Kanzow, A Global Architecture for Broadband Communication Systems: The BERKOM Approach, Proceedings Workshop on the Future Trends of Distributed Computing Systems, September 14-16, 1988, pp. 366-373

DAF83   Support Framework for Distributed Applications (DAF): Working Document on Component Infrastructure, 1989

DAF79   Support Framework for Distributed Applications (DAF): Working Document on Modelling and Design Methodology, 1988

ISO-ODP   ISO JTC1/SC21/WG7 N3194, Report on Viewpoints under Task 1 of Topic 2.3 - Framework of Abstractions, December 1988

ECMA ODP-SE ISO JTC1/SC21/WG7 N052, Open Distributed Processing Support Environment (ODP-SE), Technical Report, July 1988

Annex

Position Papers

Robbert van Renesse
Vrije Universiteit
Amsterdam

Position paper for the workshop

"Progress in Distributed Operating Systems
and Distributed Systems Management"

- A European Update -

At present we have an explosion in the number of computers in the world. There are large mainframes in computer centers, minicomputers for departmental use, and personal computers used by a single individual. Many people use more than one computer, for example, a personal computer for writing papers and documents, a mainframe for heavy computing, and remote computers for accessing specialized databases. Although there exist networks connecting many machines, they are extremely primitive, inconsistent, and user-unfriendly. In my view, the key research issue for the next decade is finding a way to allow users to access all this computing power in a simple, efficient and consistent way.

Current research is focused on network protocols, such as X.25 and ISO OSI. While necessary, this research really misses the point. What these protocols do, is allow users to move messages from one computer to another without error, but they do not address the much deeper issue of how to hide all the complexity of networking and multiple machines from the user. What is really needed is a way to tie together multiple computers in such a way as to make the whole collection look like a single integrated computer, in effect, one giant time-sharing system with unlimited computing power and none of the technical details of where files are kept or jobs are run visible to the user. The user should be able to type a command on the terminal or personal computer, and have the system automatically determine where it should be run, collect the necessary input files, and run it, without the user even being aware of all the machines involved. Such a view may seem like utopia to today's computer users, but I believe that such a situation is achievable within 10 years if we can only solve some of the key research problems.

Probably the key item missing is the lack of a conceptual framework for dealing with all the myriad of problems present in the current chaotic situation. We need a uniform way to deal with naming, access, protection, and accounting of objects; we need support for distributed and parallel applications, reliability and consistency of objects, efficiency and real-time constraints, and ways of dealing with hierarchically structured systems.

Many small scale laboratory distributed systems have been built. One of the hardest problems now is scaling these ideas to an integrated, consistent, large-scale version. Scaling up can take two forms. In one form, we have a very large number of computers located in a single room, and the goal is to harness them together to make a very fast parallel system, faster than current mainframes (which are increasingly limited by speed of light and energy dissipation problems). In another form, we want to connect up many computers spread over a large geographic area, and have them act like a single system.

An important aspect of the latter goal is try to understand how one could build a distributed computing system that spans the world. There are several potential features that can emerge from such a system. First, the amount of data in such a system is virtually unlimited, and can be shared among users in different countries, enhancing international cooperation in many areas. Second, the computing resources can be indefinitely increased by adding computers to the system (incremental growth). Third, the system can be potentially very reliable, since if 10 percent of the computers are unavailable for some reason, 90 percent are still available and people should be able to continue working, although at slightly lower speed. Finally, the personal computers can be connected to this system providing a customized user interface to the system.

However, there is more work to be done than just connecting the computers. Each of the goals above brings with it serious research problems that have not yet been entirely solved. Sharing data world-wide requires replicating large amounts of data at many sites, both for efficiency and availability reasons. How to name, locate, manage, and safeguard all this information, and how to keep all the copies identical, raises many unsolved issues, especially when large amounts of information are being stored at many sites.

Having many computers and being able to incrementally add new ones is fine, but brings up the problem of scheduling. How does one assign jobs to computers in an efficient way. Should one move the data to the program or the program to the data? Should a big job wait for a fast computer with a long line of jobs waiting for it, or is it better off on a slower computer that is available right now? Some work has been done on scheduling, but much remains, especially in very large systems.

Achieving high reliability is also hard. Clearly parts of the hardware, software, and data must be replicated, but how much and where? If too little is replicated the system will not be reliable. If too much is replicated, it will be overly expensive. Finding good choices is hard.

Position Paper

Sape J. Mullender
Guido van Rossum

The Amoeba Project, CWI, Amsterdam

In the past decade, distributed systems have become a prominent subject of computer systems research. It is obvious why this is so: People have come to rely on computer systems and traditional systems are prone to failures. Distributed systems have the potential of being much more reliable. A distributed system has enough redundancy that, when one component fails, others can take over. Increasingly, people interact through their computers by using electronic mail, file sharing, remote databases, electronic banking, and so forth. Distributed systems can bring structure and unity into the interactions between computers. People require so much computer power for some applications that a single processor cannot provide enough. Distributed systems provide an infrastructure for parallel applications.

A decade or more of distributed-systems research has yielded many techniques for solving the problems posed by distributed computing. Some of these techniques have been in daily use for some time, others are still in an experimental phase. Many research groups have built distributed operating systems, but few have become popular. This impopularity is only partly due to computer users' infamiliarity with distributed systems. It is a fact that many distributed systems that have been built to date are disappointingly slow, much slower than a traditional time-sharing system of comparable power.

The Amoeba project is a distributed systems research project that concentrates on performance aspects of distributed computing. In the project it is felt that if the system doesn't perform better than other systems in every aspect, something has been done wrong. Today, the Amoeba distributed operating system may well be the fastest of its kind.

Amoeba is a joint project of the Vrije Universiteit and the Centre for Mathematics and Computer Science in Amsterdam and the Computer Laboratory of Cambridge University. Currently, the Amoeba group is working on the first release of the Amoeba system to academic and industrial research groups by the end of 1989. Meanwhile, work continues to make Amoeba live up to its reputation of a high-performance distributed system. Research themes currently are the investigation of distributed computing over wide-area networks and in multi-organizational environments, designing user interfaces for distributed systems, developing a multiprocessor version of the Amoeba kernel, and issues of scale.

Keep things as simple as possible

Wolfgang Schröder-Preikschat

It is a well-known software engineering guideline to keep things as simple as possible. This implies high modularization, i.e. each modul encapsulates simple things and design decisions are going to be postponed. If the design is strongly modularized, the resulting system becomes manageable and, potentially, high performance will be the pleasant side effect. Moreover, if the actual system structure is strongly modularized, the opportunity for large scale configuration as well as application is given. Unfortunately, several operating systems today suffer from a monolithic and rigid organization.

Both aspects, conceptual as well as actual modularization, are especially important for design and development of operating systems, for the layering between application systems and hardware systems. An operating system has to be open to both ends, not to say that *open system* is a natural attribut. Therefore, in order to build up a totally well performing computer system, it is one of the most important responsibilities of operating system designers to influence work at the adjacent levels. However, if we cannot refer to a simple and modular system structure, this knowledge transfer will end up in a nightmare of incomprehensible statements. Thus, operating system development never is an end in itself.

To strive for openness is especially important for future hardware design. Requirements on hardware support become clearer, for the concentration on substantial facts. Considering state-of-the-art technologies, there is a chance for dedicated firmware/hardware implementations, i.e. downward migration of operating system functionalities. In order to improve communication performance of future distributed systems, it is much more interesting to state realistic requirements on network hardware interface capabilities, rather than spending all the manpower to improve throughput on the communication wire. In spite of all the efforts in distributed operating systems design, the interface is still the bottleneck and not the wire.

Similar statements can be made concerning the upper interface of operating systems, i.e. in case of design and development of distributed applications. Moreover, we need a system organization that gives the application programmer the opportunity to configure its own special purpose operating system. This especially implies the free decision about what functionality to remove from and add to the operating system, even at runtime. Progress in distributed operating systems design means not to stop with the virtual idealization of distributed hardware architectures for application programs, but to influence hardware design in order to keep the gap between application level and hardware level really low.

RESEARCH DIRECTIONS FOR DISTRIBUTED OPERATING SYSTEMS

Tim King
Perihelion Software Limited

The following three research topics are of particular interest.

Load balancing

An operating system is responsible for distributing resources among its users in a fair and equitable fashion. When multiple processors are available, the system has to manage the initial processor allocation and the dynamic movement of processes from one processor to another. Even monitoring the load on a network of processors is quite complex as CPU usage, link usage and latency of message passing must all be taken into account.

Dynamic topology changes

In a MIMD system the inter-processor communication channels are often seen as the potential bottleneck. Hardware inter-processor connections commonly include the option of electronic reconfiguration, which is used to set the network topology before running a program that requires a fixed hardware interconnection.

Using a distributed operating system, it should be possible to dynamically reconfigure the network of processors to maintain optimum performance. This could be done whenever a new job is loaded into the network, or whenever a processor becomes busier than its neighbours. It could also be possible to configure the network so that a direct route between two processors is created whenever a message is sent between those two processors. Other issues involve the behaviour of the rest of the system when a link is altered and a message traversing that link is lost.

Heterogenous networks

Although much commercial work on distributed systems centres around networks of identical processors, more attention has been paid to networks of mixed processors by academic research groups. A distributed operating system should be capable of running on a network of different types of processors, where each processor has certain useful attributes. For example, a network might contain floating point processors, fast integer processors, DSP processors, vector processors and graphic processors.

In this environment it should be possible to describe a multiple process job in a way that allows the operating system to map certain parts of the job to suitable processors. As these processors would have different binary instruction sets, programs would have to be kept in an intermediate form which could be code-generated for a particular processor as the job is loaded.

Position Paper for Panel Discussion

Chris Horn
Distributed Systems Group,
Department of Computer Science
Trinity College Dublin,
IRL - Dublin 2.

This is a position paper for the international workshop in distributed operating systems and distributed systems management, in Berlin April 1989, sponsored by the CEC Cost11ter action and the Gesellschaft für Informatik.

Designing, building and operating applications is a difficult task. Attempting to re-use designs and code so as to improve productivity is even harder. Designing, building an operating applications which must operate in distributed environments is extremely difficult.

Any approach and methodology which we can take to make this task easier and produce more reliable software is attractive, to both academics and industrialists.

As an observation, building systems which execute extremely efficiently does not necessarily make them easier to program and operate. That is, programming support is just as, if not more, important as execution speed.

What is also important is the predictability of the system. That is, as the system is scaled up, or as it degrades, there are not too many unexpected surprises. Predictable performance is an ingredient of this.

Our observations so far in the Comandos project are that object orientation, as a philosophy, certainly helps some issues and yet does not seem to get in the way of others: it is beneficial for some items, and not damaging for others.

The key issues which we perceive are: good coupling with a distributed persistent store; the ability to scale up with communication systems of vastly varying latency; the ability to survive faults; and supporting flexibility through re-useable system and application components.

Key Research Directions in Distributed Operating Systems
Position Statement
Hermann Schmutz
IBM European Networking Center Heidelberg

Knowledge of and experience with distributed systems of interconnected autonomous computers and subnetworks has made considerable progress over the past few years and the use of such systems in a real production environment is rapidly growing. From this and from technology developments we can expect the following major trends:
- an increasing number of distributed applications,
- an increasing number of users and uses, and
- the opportunity for novel types of applications.

These trends are associated with open research problems which are subsequently briefly described.

Support for Development of Distributed Applications
Today, the advanced support for the application developer is provided at the system level, i.e. at a low level. With the growing importance of truly distributed applications, the demand for more comfortable support will become strong. It is therefore necessary to define concepts and interfaces for distributed processing at the programming language level, i.e. at a higher level. Consider Object Oriented Programming as an example of a promising concept, understood as Abstract Data Types (ADT) plus Inheritance. The notion of ADTs and its value for distributed processing is recognized, however, inheritance - although well accepted as a high level concept - needs still some clarification of its role even in a local environment. **The overall goal is a high level SW engineering environment for distributed applications**, an immediate challenge is to understand the role of inheritance in a system of cooperating heterogeneous and autonomous subsystems.

Distributed Systems Management
With an increasing number of "real world" users and uses, the management of distributed systems will become of top priority. The expected areas of concern to users and owners of systems are those of security, performance, failures and accounting. **Management services are needed to keep operations under control, to ensure a fair distribution of resources and to allow for capacity planning and cost control.** Major topics for research are a Distributed Systems Architecture which includes management services and mechanisms which implement strategies for the different areas of concern. In particular, very little is known in the area of performance management of large distributed systems consisting of autonomous computers.

System Support for Distributed Multimedia Applications
Technological developments offer the opportunity for novel types of distributed applications. We see already now a growing interest in vendor supplied multimedia workstations and it is only a question of time when these workstations will be interconnected via public broadband networks which are capable of transmitting audio and video traffic. Multimedia applications combine data, audio and video and place thus a number of specific requirements on the system support. For example, real resources (sources and sinks of media traffic, network bandwidth) and new types of synchronization (between data, audio and video streams) must be offered. **The system support for distributed multimedia applications represents not only an important, but also a very interesting area for research.**

Hermann Härtig
GMD Birlinghoven

Position Statement for the Panel Discussion

As key area for distributed systems research I see the problem of building "real" distributed applications at reasonable costs and within reasonable time. By "real" I mean an application, that is not just yet another fileserver and is used and trusted by many people, not just the developers. To this and a number of key problems have been addressed.

Scalability, especially in the presence of new high speed multi purpose widearea networks will be a major problem. Experience with large university seems to show, that reliable and secure administration of such systems is the key issue.

Another key problem is to obtain a number of tools that allow building a variety of application programs at reasonable costs. Among these are operating systems, data bases, transaction managers, ..., that can be used in a general way. The problems of maintaining existing programs in such an environment through compatibility to older systems will remain important.

In the presence of growing scepticism about the use of computers and the recent misuses of networks, much higher demands will have to be placed on availability and protection of distributed systems. A generally accepted protection paradigm which is understandable for users is a key precondition for the acceptance of read distributed applications. It will have to incorporate somehow such contradictory requests as such for anonymity of users in some cases and the reliable identification of users in other cases.

J. Nehmer

Position Statements
on
"Distributed Operating Systems"

---

1. Research on operating systems is presently influenced too heavily by attempts to stay compatible with UNIX (e.g. defining downward compatible extensions, extending the semantics of UNIX OS-functions to work in the network environment, etc.). Substantial progress in future operating system technology requires to experiment more intensive with new ideas and concepts beyond the UNIX philosophy.

2. The organization of <u>adaptive services</u> in large scale distributed systems is considered the most challenging research problem for the future generation of distributed operating systems (adaptability with respect to server selection, server placement and migration, server creation and delection, load balancing, degree of fault tolerance of services, etc.).

3. Future distributed operating systems will have an increasing fraction of the overall system power devoted to the support of highly flexible and comfortable user interfaces.

4. To make unused computing power in distributed systems better available to applications it seems useful to clearly separate the functions of user interfacing (e.g. window management) from computation service usually combined in present day workstations. This will naturally lead to the concept of computation servers which carry out program executions in behalf of user requests.

5. Efficient implementations of advanced distributed operating system concepts will heavily rely on an appropriate hardware support missing in today's microcomputer and communication hardware components. Examples are
   - multi-microprocessors for separation of computation / communication / test
   - doubled working storage for stable storage implementations
   - network interfaces supporting security policies.

Some Unsolved Problems of Distributed System Management,
as seen from Project Athena

J. H. Saltzer

1. Making firewalls understandable to users. When one of 35 file
servers goes down temporarily, we can say that "server 18 will be off
the air until 1300 hours," but that doesn't tell users what they can
and can't do. Arranging so that the firewalls correspond to
user-visible entities is not at all systematic.

2. Assuring integrity of the operating system of a networked desktop
computer. How can a user be assured that the operating system of his
or her workstation hasn't been tampered with, or simply reconfigured
slightly to someone else's taste? Theoretical analyses of this
problem haven't been reduced to practice because they involve
management-expensive activities such as visiting every workstation in
order to do a system update.

3. Avoiding terrorism in shared data. Using a shared program (or in
some systems, even reading a shared file) exposes one to the
possibility of a virus attack. What is needed is a padded cell in
which to run shared or imported programs, which limits the range of
things they can touch and out of which they cannot escape.

4. Coordination of management between one site that has several
thousand users and hundreds of other similar sites. The problem is
one of dealing with large numbers, for example in providing for
authentication and forwarding of credentials.

5. Housecleaning, discarding, deallocating. When a system has
several thousand users receiving mail and storing files in dozens of
on-line servers that provide for information sharing, it is extremely
difficult to decide what data is valuable and what should be
discarded. When a user departs, some of that user's files may be in
(occasional) use by an unknown community of other sharers. And unless
the administration is infallible, it will eventually happen that a
user will not be deleted upon departure; as systems grow in size and
span larger spaces and administrations, the traditional approach of
occasionally scanning a list of users doesn't work.

Extending Distributed Operating Systems to Manageable Large Scale Distributed Processing Environments

Position Paper on Future Research Issues
Jean Bacon
University of Cambridge Computer Laboratory

Distributed Systems research has moved on from kernels for LANs yet we still need kernels and a good deal of software infrastructure as a basis for current research. A consensus drawn from past research is valuable and this is part of the function of projects such as ANSA. We should all like to be able to buy a kernel in the same way that we now buy a compiler.

PhD research often has to be narrowly focussed because of the time and effort available. A design may be tried out in a fairly small scale experiment. For example, an initial aim may be to design a distributed and replicated service whereas experimental work may be restricted to a small number or a single service instance. Discussion on generalisation of the design to multiple instances is no substitute for a large scale experiment. The results are valuable but further work is needed.

There is still scope for clarification of basic architectural issues such as naming, protection and location in the context of large scale distributed systems. It should be assumed that all services are distributed and replicated for availability and reliability. How such services may manage their distributed databases could also benefit from further work on appropriate algorithms and the choices and tradeoffs involved, for example between the consistency of data and its availability, and how client requirements can be made manifest.

The above argues for consolidation and establishing a consensus but changes in technology can totally change the best way of doing something. Memory sizes and speeds; network and processor speeds will increase far in excess of disc speeds. Large client caches will affect the design of network storage services so that they may become log structured, write-mostly servers, with background consolidation to read-mostly servers. It will be feasible to support real time voice and video in multimedia systems and we will learn how to do this. Cross-network paging and processing will be feasible.

It is not sufficient to measure the load from and requirements of existing clients and build future systems on this basis. We must build in the minimum of mechanism to avoid constraining future clients but also attempt to provide general and flexible facilities.

These remarks are based on personal research experience. I have not attempted to address the many other current research areas.

Future Collaborative Research in Europe

Alwyn Langsford

Harwell Laboratory, UK

The author's association with the COST 11 ter MANDIS project on distributed systems management and more recent interaction with the CEC in their ESPRIT II 1989 and FRAMEWORK programmes has shown that there is considerable scope for collaborative R & D between European laboratories. This note provides a brief summary of the author's suggestions for such programmes.

1. Basic Communications

It is becoming accepted that, although OSI provides an excellent reference against which to develop families of communication protocols, the protocols which have emerged are very much products of early 1980 communication technology. They are essentially over-elaborate and not well matched to the demands of the distribution of processing capability around the office. Also OSI suffered from focusing upon the communications environment to the exclusion of the demands of the information processing environment. This was true even of such notable research projects as the European Informatics Network, (the first COST 11 project)[1].

There is a growing use of the object oriented paradigm in computing. Its effect on communications could be to encourage the light weight protocols which are conspicuously absent from OSI. One interesting concept, worthy of investigation, is to move the network location, routing and other management functions behind the communications socket on the wall (cf. modern telephone wiring). We are then left with a simple applications interface plus a simple data link between the computer and the communications environment. Given suitable R & D, this application interface could be realised through standard library routines supporting the common programming languages.

2. Further research in Distributed Systems Management

Elsewhere, I have commented that MANDIS has shown the way and provided the tools for further R & D in distributed systems management[2]. This basic set of tools can be used to explore distributed systems management further by identifying management objects and management algorithms. Those which are common to many systems can be further refined to furnish a library of distributed systems management objects and operations. Another area calling for more work is the investigation of management interactions between management domains. This will investigate an area of management protocol little explored either by research or considered in terms of management standards. It will also allow us to investigate the extent to which managers are prepared to trust external systems to have a management interface to the systems under their control.

3. A Systems Approach to Open Systems Management

We at Harwell are beginning an R & D programme which will take the existing elements of OSI Management, the language approach typified by SESL[2] and our experience of OSI communications in an attempt to validate three propositions:

1. that the present, object oriented approach being taken by OSI Management has the potential for extension to provide for all aspects of open systems management;

2. that this approach, coupled with a suitable management control language, will prove effective in the support of distributed processing;

3. that these elements together with the facilities of the local operating system are all that is required to satisfy the needs of the distributed operating system.

Because management is just a specific example of a distributed processing system needing to process transactions in real time, we are interested in the prospect that this approach will meet, not just the requirements for distributed systems management, but will provide a more general basis to computing in the networked processing environment of the future.

References

1. Barber, D. L. A. The European Informatics Network — Achievements and Prospects. Proc ICCC 76 Conference, Toronto 1976.

2. Holden, D. B. and Langsford, A. MANDIS: Management of Distributed Systems. This volume.

Progress in Distributed Operating Systems and Distributed Systems Management

Panel Discussion on:
Future Research Issues in Extending Distributed Operating Systems to Manageable Large Scale Distributed Processing Environments

Position Paper

V. TSCHAMMER
GMD FOKUS BERLIN

The computer communications world is evolving towards very high-bandwidth capabilities in wide-spread optical fiber networks. This will have a major impact on future distributed processing. New applications and new processing environments will develop on the basis of interconnected LANs and WANs and the integration of high-speed data and telecommunication services in broadband-ISDN.

In our opinion, the following topics will be of prime interest within the various research and development issues which must to be tackled in order to build a manageable large scale distributed processing environment:

Cooperation across organisational domains: Very large distributed systems may span various organisational domains. The processing environment will include interorganisational, intraorganisational, and special purpose ("closed") subsystems with different requirements and operating conditions. The structuring and administration concept must provide for divisions into public and private objects. Autonomy (incl. heterogeneity), cooperation, and interdependency are key issues.

Qualities in communication and application services: Various services will develop in very large distributed systems. Some may differ only in detail. New applications, especially those based on multi-media information, will require particular processing and communication capabilities. A global strategy of defining, evaluating, and handling service qualities will allow users to express requirements unambiguously and to include performance, security and dependability attributes in agreements, interactions, administration, etc.

General architecture for open distributed processing: The general architecture must integrate different networking techniques (LANs, gateways, WANs) and endsystem software and hardware. New system architectures (gateways, end systems) are required to match the quality requirements. With respect to the overall architecture, manageability becomes the prime concern, including configuration and control of the various services available in order to satisfy the quality requirements in a mesh of organisational structures.

All activities must be accompanied by an adequate theory which provides the appropriate semantics and the basis for a comprehensive set of tools for the modelling, testing, verification, and realisation of very large distributed systems.